Foucault

Key Contemporary Thinkers

Published

Peter Burke, *The French Historical Revolution: The Annales School 1929–1989*
Simon Evnine, *Donald Davidson*
Phillip Hansen, *Hannah Arendt: Politics, History and Citizenship*
Christopher Hookway, *Quine: Language, Experience and Reality*
Douglas Kellner, *Jean Baudrillard: From Marxism to Postmodernism and Beyond*
Chandran Kukathas and Philip Pettit, *Rawls: A Theory of Justice and its Critics*
Lois McNay, *Foucault: A Critical Introduction*
Philip Manning, *Erving Goffman and Modern Sociology*
Michael Moriarty, *Roland Barthes*
Georgia Warnke, *Gadamer: Hermeneutics, Tradition and Reason*
Jonathan Wolff, *Robert Nozick: Property, Justice and the Minimal State*

Forthcoming

Jeremy Ahearne, *Michel de Certeau*
Alison Ainley, *Irigaray*
Michael Best, *Galbraith*
Michael Caesar, *Umberto Eco*
James Carey, *Innis and McLuhan*
Colin Davis, *Levinas*
Eric Dunning, *Norbert Elias*
Jocelyn Dunphy, *Paul Ricoeur*
Judith Feher-Gurewich, *Lacan*
Kate and Edward Fullbrook, *Simone de Beauvoir*
Andrew Gamble, *Hayek and the Market Order*
Graeme Gilloch, *Walter Benjamin*
Adrian Hayes, *Talcott Parsons and the Theory of Action*
Christina Howells, *Derrida*
Simon Jarvis, *Adorno*
Paul Kelly, *Ronald Dworkin*
William Outhwaite, *Habermas*
Susan Sellers, *Helene Cixous*
Geoff Stokes, *Popper: Politics, Epistemology and Method*
Ian Whitehouse, *Rorty*
James Williams, *Lyotard*

FOUCAULT

A Critical Introduction

Lois McNay

Polity Press

First published in 1994 by Polity Press
in association with Blackwell Publishers.

Editorial office:
Polity Press
65 Bridge Street
Cambridge CB2 1UR, UK

Marketing and production:
Blackwell Publishers
108 Cowley Road
Oxford OX4 1JF, UK

ISBN 0 7456 0990 2
ISBN 0 7456 0991 0 (pbk)

British Library Cataloguing-in-Publication Data
A CIP catalogue record for this book is available from the British Library.

Typeset in 10½ on 12 pt Palatino by Pure Tech Corporation, Pondicherry, India
Printed in Great Britain by Hartnolls Ltd, Bodmin, Cornwall

This book is printed on acid-free paper.

Contents

Acknowledgements

I would like to thank John Thompson for suggesting this project to me and for his comments on a late draft of the text. I am grateful to Desmond King and Ben Cairns for reading sections of the manuscript and to Andrew Coleman and Andy Davies for their encouragement and support. I am also grateful to St John's College, Oxford, for financial assistance in the form of a Research Fellowship.

Lois McNay

Introduction

The scope and sophistication of the thought of Michel Foucault is imposing. His work straddles the disciplines of philosophy, history, sociology and literary theory. He has written detailed histories of the development of psychology, of clinical medicine, of the birth of the asylum, of the modern penal system, and of Ancient Greek and Roman morals. He has also written extensively on modern literature and has produced a structural analysis of the development of Western thought since the Renaissance. These literary and historical studies are, in turn, informed by philosophical reflection on the nature of rationality, truth and power, and on what it means to be an individual in modern society.

The breadth and complexity of Foucault's work defies easy categorization and this has often led to certain difficulties in its critical reception. Historians have rejected Foucault's work for being too philosophical, philosophers for its lack of formal rigour and sociologists for its literary or poetic quality. It is this breadth and complexity that has resulted in what Maurice Blanchot has called both the 'difficult' and 'privileged' position of Foucault's work in relation to twentieth-century thought: 'do we know who he is, since he doesn't call himself . . . either a sociologist or a historian or a structuralist or a thinker or a metaphysician?'[1] Foucault himself underlines the impossibility of such a task by claiming, in a well-known passage, that he writes not in order to disclose the self but to escape it: 'I am no doubt not the only one who writes in order to have no face. Do not ask who I am and do not ask me to remain the same.'[2] Despite its impossibility, the desire to know who Foucault the thinker is has generated an enormous amount of secondary literature. With regard to the aims of this book, there already exist many excellent introductions to Foucault's work. The justification for yet another critical overview is that most of the existing introductions do not include a sustained consideration of Foucault's final work on the themes of government and the self. My objective is to fill this gap.

The ideas of government and the self encapsulate Foucault's final thought on two major themes that run throughout his work, those of power and the subject. Indeed, it is probably these two themes that are the most well-known aspects of Foucault's thought in so far as it is linked to the proclamation of the death of the subject and to the idea that all knowledge is ineluctably embedded in power relations: 'power-knowledge'. It is the development of these two themes – of the addition of the idea of government to the theory of power and of the move from a problematization of the subject to the idea of an 'ethics of the self' – that forms the guiding thread of this introduction to Foucault's work.

Throughout his work, the development and reformulation of a concept of power remains a constant preoccupation of Foucault's. Partly in explicit counterposition to a Marxist perspective, Foucault's interest was not directed at the expression of power in its most central and institutionalized forms such as state apparatuses or class relations. Rather, he was concerned to examine how power relations of inequality and oppression are created and maintained in more subtle and diffuse ways through ostensibly humane and freely adopted social practices. In short, Foucault questions the rationality of post-Enlightenment society by focusing on the ways in which many of the enlightened practices of modernity progressively delimit rather than increase the freedom of individuals and, thereby, perpetuate social relations of inequality and oppression.

While the concern with uncovering the dark side of modernity remains the undiminished force informing Foucault's entire output, the conceptualization of power and its realization in social relations varied with the development of his thought. In his early work on madness, Foucault demonstrated how the apparently therapeutic practices of psychology, psychiatry and psychoanalysis were instrumental in depriving mad individuals of a voice by construing their disorders in the univocally negative language of mental illness. The mad are not listened to and hence are alienated from themselves because modern clinical practice effaces the specificity of each individual case through the imposition of archaizing and alien concepts. The model of power relations that Foucault worked with at this stage is, on his own account, an essentially negative one in which power is always expressed in strategies of repression and exclusion. No differentiation is made between forms of thought and institutional practices which become indistinguishable in the uniformity of their repressive effects on the social realm. This leads to a rather bleak view of the total bankruptcy of the Enlightenment legacy both in terms of the philosophical rationality and the processes of societal rationalization it unleashed.

Foucault subsequently attempted to reformulate this negative conception of power as repression to account for the conflictual, unstable and empowering elements inherent in any set of social relations. In the 'archaeological' phase of his work where Foucault sought to uncover the deepseated rules of formation that determine thought, the issue of power is not addressed directly. However, the transcendence of the previous monolithic view of power is implied in Foucault's treatment of discourse as a relatively autonomous phenomenon which cannot be encompassed by a monotonous and reductive logic of social control. It is in Foucault's work from the mid-1970s onwards, however, that the issue of power is addressed in the most sustained fashion, resulting in the well-known reformulation of power as an essentially *positive* phenomenon. On this view, power underlies all social relations from the institutional to the intersubjective and is a fundamentally enabling force. To understand power, therefore, it is necessary to analyse it in its most diverse and specific manifestations rather than focusing on its most centralized forms such as its concentration in the hands of a coercive elite or a ruling class. This focus on the underside or everyday aspect of power relations Foucault calls a *microphysics* rather than a macrophysics of power.

However, despite this reformulation of power as a positive and heterogeneous force, a central dilemma runs through Foucault's work: it contains a tendency to fall back into a negative view of power as a unidirectionally imposed monolithic force. This prevents Foucault explaining, among other things, the possibility of social change and the dynamic and relatively autonomous nature of social action. Such difficulties have been noted by many commentators and I will outline in chapter 3 a few of the central aporia that arise from this tension between the positive and negative moments of Foucault's theory of power. However, I will also show that Foucault's subsequent work on government – which has received comparatively little critical attention – is significant because it redefines certain aspects of the theory of power in such a way as to render the original insight of power as a positive phenomenon sustainable. This reformulation of the concept of power has two key elements. First, the idea of governmentality broadens the category of power by distinguishing more clearly between violence, domination and the types of power that characterize relations between individuals. Second, power is defined both as an objectivizing and a subjectivizing force. Power constrains individuals but it also constitutes the condition of possibility of their freedom. In short, the work on government is important because it indicates Foucault's ability to think beyond the limitations of his previous work and to push his thought in challenging and often surprising new directions.

The second theme that lies at the centre of Foucault's work is that of the subject, or rather a critique of the various notions of the rational subject that have governed Western thought since the Enlightenment. Foucault's whole oeuvre is oriented to breaking down the domination of a fully self-reflexive, unified and rational subject at the centre of thought in order to clear a space for radically 'other' ways of thinking and being. With the development of Foucault's work, the critique of the rational subject takes several forms. In his earliest work on madness, Foucault attacks the philosophical subject of Enlightenment thought by revealing its implication in certain social practices which, since the end of the seventeenth century, have led to the marginalization and silencing of mad individuals. Thus the effects of Descartes' dismissal of the mad as beyond the realms of the rational cogito are not confined to the realm of speculative philosophy, but are directly linked to the development of certain institutional practices which have deprived the mad of their own voices through their categorization as inhuman. The claims of Enlightenment thought to universal legitimacy in virtue of its accurate reflection of transcendental structures of rationality are undermined by revealing its dependence on oppressive and brutal practices which derogate and exclude that with which it cannot cope: 'the other'.

In the subsequent archaeological enquiry into the conditions of possibility of thought, the attack on the rational subject takes a more general form. Here Foucault shows that the idea of the subject as the sole origin of meaning is in fact an illusion generated by deep-level rules of formation that govern all thought and speech. Far from being the source of meaning, the subject is in fact a secondary effect or byproduct of discursive formations. By laying bare these deep-seated rules that constitute the condition of possibility of thought, Foucault undermines not only the notion of an originative subject but also associated notions of truth and progress. The development of Western thought can no longer be characterized as a shift from superstition and magic to objective, scientific knowledge, but is seen rather as a series of abrupt and arbitrary paradigm shifts or epistemic breaks. The effect of this demystificatory strategy is to dislocate the rigid identity logic that orders modern thought and thereby to create a space in which it is possible to think difference or otherness.

With the move during the mid-1970s to a more explicit concern with power, Foucault resumes and develops the line of attack initiated in the work on madness. In an analysis of the modern penal system and of contemporary notions of sexuality, Foucault shows how the assumption that individuals have a deep interiority and innermost truth – expressed in concepts such as the soul, psyche and subjectivity – is a coercive illusion. The idea of an inner and essential depth is in fact an effect of material processes of subjection. To be a subject, in Foucault's view, is necessarily to be subjected. Even when individuals think that they are most free, they are in fact in the grip of an insidious power which operates not through direct forms of repression but through less visible strategies of 'normalization'. In this respect Foucault's work resembles the critique initiated by Weber and continued in the work of Lukács, Adorno and others, which emphasizes the ways in which an Enlightenment notion of universal rationality has degenerated into a pervasive instrumental logic that homogenizes the social world, emptying it of meaning and purpose.

Foucault's critique of Enlightenment rationality and of the rational subject of thought is mounted on several fronts and is devastating in its conclusions. It has had a profound influence on many other areas of thought. It has resonated, in particular, with feminist and postcolonial critiques of Enlightenment thought as a highly gendered and ethnocentric construct that implicitly naturalizes a white, masculine perspective and correspondingly denigrates anything directly or analogously associated with a feminine or non-European position. Yet despite the extent to which Foucault's critique of the rational subject of Enlightenment thought has been drawn on in other areas, it is also not without certain theoretical limitations connected to the failure to rethink subjectivity in terms of the excluded 'other' of thought. In short, Foucault's attack on the subject is so total that it forecloses any alternative theoretical space in which to conceive non-hegemonic forms of subjectivity. Throughout this book, it will be shown that the difficulty in thinking through alternative or oppositional subject positions forms a persistent dilemma in Foucault's work. Although very different in many respects, *Madness and Civilization* shares with the works of the archaeological period – *The Order of Things* and *The Archaeology of Knowledge* – a problematic conception of the other in terms of an 'epistemic' or absolute break. The tendency to present the domination of Enlightenment rationality as absolute means that the other can only be conceived as external to this identity logic and, therefore, only expressible in terms of a complete rupture with the dominant system.

The problem with such an antinomic conception of the relation between the dominant and its others is that it is unclear, given the absence of any interconnection or dialectical relation between the two moments, how the transition from a history of the same to an acceptance of difference is to be effected. This antinomic formulation also results in a rather Romantic presentation of the other as a liminal and eschatological figure that hinders a recognition of the social and historical forces that routinely and persistently construct difference as otherness, femininity as irrationality, skin colour as inferiority, and so forth. In short, the other is not always a marginal figure; rather its construction as such is always central, in a mundane way, to the maintenance of any hegemonic system of norms. The failure of Foucault to conceive of the other in such a way is intensified in *The Archaeology of Knowledge*, where the category of the subject is completely rejected and so too any theoretical framework in which to conceive of alternative positions which are at once within and also marginal to the dominant epistemic order.

With the shift to the 'genealogical' method and a more explicit concern with the theory of power, Foucault's conception of the other is significantly altered. The other is no longer conceived as a shadowy, contestatory force on the margins of society, but as an effect of the power relations that permeate the social realm. The points at which power relations are exerted most forcefully are the points at which resistance to a dominatory force arises. Domination and resistance are no longer conceived of as ontologically different but as opposing effects of the same power relations. Thus the labelling of certain groups of individuals as 'deviant' provides those groups with a coherent identity from which resistant counter-identities may be formulated – for instance, the idea of 'queer' politics. The problem that arises in connection with this phase of Foucault's work is that, by dispensing with the category of the subject and replacing it with that of the body, the idea of resistance is severely undermined because there remains no category around which a notion of active agency may be formulated.

Again, just as the notion of government represents an important advance in Foucault's understanding of power, so the introduction of the category of the self overcomes some of the problems in the conceptualization of individuals as active agents. Derived from the notion of government, the idea of 'technologies of the self' enables Foucault to conceive of individuals as active agents with the capacity to autonomously fashion their own existences. This notion transcends the limitations of the etiolated view of individuals as docile bodies that characterizes the middle phase of Foucault's work. It also overcomes the difficulties arising from an understanding of the other in terms of a complete break or rupture. The idea of technologies of the self enables Foucault to elaborate a theory of resistance – an *'ethics of the self'* – which is situated in the interstices of power relations, at the level of individuals' daily practices. In a characteristically indirect fashion, this idea of an ethics of the self is most fully explored by Foucault in his study of Ancient Greek and Roman moral practices in the second and third volumes of *The History of Sexuality*. In other essays, Foucault also pondered the problem, raised by Kant, of the nature of critique. This preoccupation is reflected in Foucault's work, where the negative or critical moment in his attack on the subject is complemented with a positive moment – essential to critique – in which a theoretical framework to explain the construction of counter-hegemonic forms of identity is allowed.

The shift from criticism to critique also signals a modification in the way in which Foucault viewed the relation between his work and the tradition of Enlightenment thought. The idea of an 'ethics of the self' relies on a cluster of terms drawn explicitly from the Enlightenment tradition, including the notions of reflexivity, critique and autonomy. The rapprochement with Enlightenment thought should not be interpreted as a refutation, on Foucault's part, of his previous critique of the rational subject of thought. Rather it should be seen as a retrospective attempt to situate his oeuvre more clearly with regard to such a tradition. As many commentators have noted, even at its most hostile, Foucault's work is more indebted to Enlightenment thought than is explicitly acknowledged. In common with writers such as Max Weber, Theodor Adorno and Georges Bataille, the emphasis that Foucault places on the dark side of the Enlightenment legacy derives much of its force from an implicit reliance on certain other Enlightenment categories such as dignity, reciprocity and self-determination. The failure to acknowledge this indebtedness to or covert reliance on a tradition of thought that is explicitly denounced results in what Jürgen Habermas has called the 'cryptonormativism' of Foucault's earlier work. However, in his final work, notably, the important essay 'What is Enlightenment?', Foucault acknowledges more explicitly his ambivalent relation to Enlightenment thought. His aim is to reread the philosophy of the Enlightenment in such a way as to salvage a critical ethos that may be relevant to the contemporary era: 'the thread that may connect us with the Enlightenment is not faithfulness to doctrinal elements, but rather the permanent reactivation of an attitude – that is, of a philosophical ethos that could be described as a permanent critique of our historical era.'[3]

It perhaps goes without saying that Foucault's interpretation of Enlightenment thought is far from straightforward. It cannot be dissociated, in part, from his derivation of a notion of the ethical subject from classical morality. It is also achieved by reading the philosophical moment of the Enlightenment through a stream of thought on aesthetic modernity. Foucault identifies Kant as the founder of two critical traditions between which modern philosophy has divided. On the one hand, there is the tradition of philosophy that is concerned with uncovering the transcendental foundations of true knowledge – an 'analytics of truth'. On the other hand, there is a stream of thought concerned with formulating an 'ontology of the present', that is to say, a critical analysis of the present moment, of the 'present field of possible experiences'. It is this second tradition, associated with the Kantian notion of the mature use of reason, that Foucault places at the heart of his ethics of the self. Foucault attempts to jettison its foundations in an ahistorical categorical imperative, associated with the first tradition, by reading Kant through the Baudelairean figure of the dandy.

The reading of philosophy through aesthetics in order to separate the critical moment of Enlightenment thought from its foundations in transcendental notions of rationality and human nature concurs with a more general critical vigilance that characterizes Foucault's oeuvre, namely the attempt to eradicate a certain essentializing tendency associated with notions of depth or interiority. In Foucault's view, it is the idea that all experience has an essential core or hidden truth that enables normalizing and, in the final analysis, oppressive systems of thought and behaviour to function. To borrow a phrase from Maurice Blanchot, it is this 'distaste' for depth that underlies Foucault's attacks on systems of thought which attempt to define and impose notions of the normal, the natural and the inevitable through reference to a fixed and essential human nature. Perhaps Foucault's best known attack on the idea of depth is associated with the work on power and the body. A radically anti-essentialist view of the body is proposed in the argument that sexuality is not an innate or natural quality of the body but is, in fact, a historically specific effect of the operations of different regimes of power on the body. By emphasizing the socially determined and hence arbitrary nature of what are usually taken to be immutable and natural characteristics, Foucault aims to radicalize the realm of sexual behaviour by pushing it away from heterosexual norms and towards a more imaginative exploration of 'bodies and pleasures'.

The idea of ethics of the self continues this anti-essentialist project through the emphasis on an aesthetic self-fashioning or the re-creation of daily life as a 'work of art'. By reading Kant through a Baudelairean notion of stylization, ethics of the self is oriented not towards the recovery of an essential inner identity but towards an exploration of a myriad of potential identities and ways of existing in the world. It is based on a principle of self-critique that is experimental, endless and gives up any hope of attaining a 'complete and definitive knowledge of what may constitute our historical limits'.[4]

While a certain notion of the aesthetic enables Foucault to retrieve a moment of critique from its metaphysical foundations, it is also a source of considerable theoretical difficulty in his work. By relying too heavily on an unexamined notion of the aesthetic – associated with a specific tradition of avant-garde and surrealist art and literature – Foucault reintroduces an essentialist moment into his thought. By neglecting to situate the notion of aesthetics within an analysis of historical and social relations – that is to say, by failing to perform the type of genealogical analysis that he so rigorously performs on other categories – Foucault finishes by assuming rather than demonstrating the inherently contestatory nature of the idea of an aesthetics of existence. I will show that this tendency is not confined to the final work but recurs throughout Foucault's thought. It can be seen in the tendency to romanticize the contestatory force of madness and in the assumption of the inherently revolutionary status of certain avant-garde art forms. In his final work on the self, Foucault imputes a self-evident or apodictic radicality to the idea of an aesthetics of existence in the absence of a more sustained consideration of the social and political implications of his theory of ethics.

This book is intended as a critical introduction to Foucault's work. The emphasis placed on some of the problematic aspects of his thought is however not meant in a dismissive spirit. Indeed, it is apparent that Foucault is often his own most trenchant critic, ceaselessly overcoming the limitations of his thought by pushing it in original and challenging new directions. However, I concur with the judgement of Edward Said that Foucault was a brilliant thinker whose work was simultaneously marked by pronounced blindspots. Given the productive convergence there has been between his work and feminist and postcolonial theory, Foucault's apparent indifference to some of the issues raised by gender and identity politics in general is striking. Foucault's silence on such issues may be interpreted, to some extent, as a tactical withdrawal in the sense of a legitimate refusal to legislate for other autonomous movements. Nevertheless, there are points in his work where silence on these issues raises considerable difficulties and, indeed, these lacunae have provoked widespread accusations of gender blindness and ethnocentrism from cultural and feminist theorists. It is some of these issues, particularly those arising from recent feminist work on identity, that compose the implicit backdrop of the critical consideration of Foucault's work in this book. It is only by engaging with these weak points to see how they may be overcome that the continued relevance of Foucault's work for a range of academic research may be sustained, renewed and pushed into new areas of debate.

The book is divided into four chapters that roughly correspond with what are perceived as the main stages of Foucault's work. The first chapter considers Foucault's early work on the cultural construction of madness and the devastating critique of Enlightenment rationality that arises from this critique. The varying critical responses to this work will be examined and also Foucault's own retrospective critique that the impoverished conception of power with which he worked at the time led to an overstatement of the case against rationality. The status of 'madness itself', a problem raised most forcefully in Jacques Derrida's critique of *Madness and Civilization*, will also be examined. It will be shown that an unresolved tension permeates Foucault's work, expressed in a vacillation between a conception of madness as a cultural construct or empty space on to which society projects its discontents, and a conception in which madness is ascribed some essential contestatory core with the potential to overthrow the edifice of Western reason. The subsequent work on transgression overcomes, to a certain extent, this theoretical ambivalence, but at the cost of replacing an awareness of the cultural and historical specificity of the experience of madness with a romantic and aestheticized view of the phenomenon.

The second chapter examines the work of Foucault's 'archaeological' phase and its critique of the constitutive subject of thought. It is this period of Foucault's work that has led him to be associated, along with thinkers such as Roland Barthes, with the proclamation of the 'end of man' and the 'death of the subject'. Foucault argues that there does not exist any prediscursive subject that can be located as the origin of meaning, but rather that the notion of a unified subject is an illusion generated through structural rules that govern discursive formations. The technique of archaeology – the disclosure of these latent, deep-level structures that constitute the condition of possibility of all thought and speech – represents a powerful attack on the subjectivism of phenomenological and biographical approaches to intellectual history, but it will be shown that it is excessively antinomic in its formulation. An absolute separation is maintained between discursive formations and their social and cultural context. Issues raised by a consideration of the necessary social embeddedness of discourse – in particular the issue of how individuals come to occupy certain discursively constructed subject positions – problematizes the validity of Foucault's complete rejection of any notion of the subject. Indeed, it will be shown that power relations and struggles are ineluctably provoked in a consideration of the social context of discourse; and they do in fact creep into Foucault's archaeological analysis on a covert level, creating several theoretical aporia.

It is Foucault's celebrated reformulation of his theory of power from an essentially negative to a positive conception that will be considered in the third chapter. While, on an abstract level, the notion of power as an enabling and constitutive force rather than as a repressive one is theoretically innovative, there is in fact an inability, on Foucault's part, to sustain this claim and a resultant tendency to view power simply as unmitigated domination. This slippage generates a series of contradictions in Foucault's thought. These are partially overcome with the concept of a governmentality elaborated in his final work. First, the idea of governmentality broadens the category of power by distinguishing more clearly between violence, domination and the type of power relations that characterize relations between individuals. Second, power is defined both as an objectivizing and a subjectivizing force. This is to say that power is no longer understood to operate in a unidirectional fashion through the imposition of various effects from above but is conceptualized as an agonistic struggle that takes place between free individuals. This strategy enables Foucault to explain systems of social regulation in less one- dimensional terms than as 'an endless play of dominations'.

In the final chapter, the notion of the self that is derived from the understanding of government as a subjectivizing force is considered. The shift that this implies in Foucault's relation to Enlightenment thought is analysed through the idea of an ethics of the self obtained from a rereading of Kant and Baudelaire. On the one hand, the idea of ethics of the self overcomes many of what have been regarded as the nihilistic implications of Foucault's previous critique of modernity. However, on the other hand, the centrality accorded in this notion of ethics to a rather problematic notion of aesthetics raises difficulties in respect of some of the social and political implications of the Foucauldian theory of ethics.

1

From Repression to Transgression

Introduction

Edward Said has said that at the heart of Michel Foucault's work lies the variously formulated idea that always conveys the 'sentiment of otherness'. This concern with the other manifests itself in a fascination with 'deviation and deviants' and with 'everything excessive, all those things that stand over and above ideas, description, initiation, or precedent'.[1] It is in Foucault's early work on madness that this sentiment or concern for the other receives its most passionate expression. At face value, Foucault's work in *Mental Illness and Psychology* and *Madness and Civilization* constitutes a study of the cultural constructions of madness in Western society from the Renaissance to the late nineteenth century. However, the implications of Foucault's argument extend far beyond this narrow remit, resulting in an impassioned denunciation of the modern attitude towards madness which, in Foucault's view, is profoundly dehumanizing. Foucault's arguments are addressed here at modern psychiatric practices which construct a negative and, therefore, alienating view of madness as mental illness. However, on the most general level, Foucault's argument constitutes an attack on Enlightenment thought and the notion of rationality with which it is underpinned. Foucault shows how Enlightenment thought is predicated on various strategies, expressed at both a philosophical and social level, that exclude and derogate forms of experience that cannot be readily assimilated into the notion of a pure, self-sustaining rationality.

Like much of Foucault's subsequent work, *Madness and Civilization* has provoked controversy, particularly with regard to the bleak assessment of the Enlightenment legacy. Foucault's negative view of rationality as a univocally oppressive system arises in part from the rather underdeveloped theory of power with which he worked at the time. The spatial model of confinement and exclusion is extended to a theory of power as always negative and repressive in its effects. In retrospect, Foucault recognized the limitations of such a formulation. The nihilistic implications of Foucault's critique are also connected to ambiguities in the conceptualization of 'madness itself', a problem addressed most forcefully by Jacques Derrida. An unresolved tension permeates Foucault's work between a culturally relative view of madness as a blank category on to which society projects its discontents and a view where madness is accorded an essential contestatory status with the potential to overthrow the edifice of Western reason. The subsequent work on transgression attempts to overcome this theoretical ambivalence by generalizing the moment of contestation from a specific, marginal experience to a potential inherent in language and, therefore, in all experience. However, the work on transgression does not have the powerful political implications of the critique in *Madness and Civilization* because it replaces an awareness of madness as a specific historical construct with a diffuse and aestheticized view of the phenomenon.

Mental Illness and Psychology

Foucault's earliest work, *Mental Illness and Psychology*, is of interest because it prefigures some of the methods and central arguments of *Madness and Civilization*.[2] The premise of *Mental Illness and Psychology* is that the modern understanding of madness is fundamentally misguided on two counts. First, modern psychiatric practice has profoundly alienating effects in its negative understanding of madness as mental illness. Second, the specificity of each individual case of madness is effaced through the imposition of artificially unifying analytical categories on what are, in fact, different forms of pathological behaviour. Foucault argues that mental illness can only be understood in a framework which emphasizes the historical, cultural and existential specificity of each disorder rather than in one which obscures differences under the syncretic terms of a 'metapathology'.

The origin of the modern conception of mental illness is traced back to classical medicine, where both mental and organic illnesses were regarded as autonomous and unified botanical species which existed independently of the individual bodies in which they emerged. However, with the development of medicine during the late eighteenth century, this conception of mental and organic illnesses as autonomous and self-sustaining phenomena was gradually rejected in favour of a synthetic view of the illness and its connection with the 'psychosomatic totality' of the sick individual. The new understanding of illness linked organic and mental illness around an idea of the psychological and physiological *totality* of the individual and his or her pathological reactions to the surrounding environment: 'The personality thus becomes the element in which the illness develops and the criterion by which it can be judged; it is both the reality and the measure of the illness.'[3]

The linking of mental and organic illness through a conception of the human totality is, in Foucault's view, equally as erroneous as the classical view of illness as a pathological essence in so far as it allows the same meaning to be attributed to illnesses of the body and of the mind: 'a unitary pathology using the same methods and concepts in the psychological and physiological domains is now purely mythical.'[4] Against such unifying abstractions, Foucault argues that, to be properly understood, mental pathology requires methods of analysis that are fundamentally different from those of organic pathology. Orthodox pathology obscures the 'specificity of mental illness' under the archetypal and syncretic categories it employs.

Foucault goes on to propose a series of analytical approaches through which it is possible to recover a more differentiated and, therefore, accurate understanding of mental illness. On the one hand, a cluster of analytical approaches are suggested which focus on the various existential and psychological dimensions of mental illness. First, it is necessary to acquire a detailed understanding of mental illness in relation to an evolutionary structure. Mental illness is usually conceived in the negative and simplified terms of the failure or suppression of normal psychological functions. However, in Foucault's view, the essence of mental illness cannot be defined in such a negative way, but must be understood instead as a complex synthesis of positive and negative behaviours, of suppressed and accentuated functions: 'the essence of mental illness lies not only in the void that it hollows out, but also in the positive plenitude of the activities of replacement that fill that void.'[5] An evolutionary notion of human development provides a framework in which to analyse this web of complex behaviours. If mental illness commonly produces both positive and negative behaviours, these can be traced back to an earlier phase in the development of the sick individual which has eliminated recently acquired forms of behaviour. Such an analysis yields a more accurate view of mental illness. It goes beyond the idea of 'difference of essence between illnesses' to a notion of the 'degree of depth of the deterioration' in which 'the meaning of an illness might be defined by the level at which the process of regression is stabilized.'[6]

At this stage of his thought, Foucault's hostility to psychoanalysis has not yet developed and he notes that the work of Freud and other psychoanalysts provides a thorough account of the evolutionary forms of various neuroses. He remarks, however, that psychoanalysis is still 'situated in the frontiers of myth' and tends to subsume the specificity of the individual case into a typology of archaic personalities and instinctual drives. To guard against this mythicizing tendency, the first stage of evolutive analysis must be complemented by a second stage which examines the history of the mentally ill individual. If the past is invoked by the mentally ill person as a substitute for the present situation, an attempt must be made to grasp the significance of this dilemma between the actual and the anterior for the individual: 'The psychology of evolution which describes symptom as archaic behaviour must be complemented, therefore, by a psychology of genesis that describes, in a given history, the present meaning of these regressions.'[7]

The final dimension of mental illness that must be taken into account is an understanding of the sick consciousness and a reconstitution of its 'pathological world'. It is an erroneous assumption that mad individuals are unaware of themselves and their illness. Mentally ill patients do recognize their anomalous position and it is essential, therefore, to examine the dimensions of this consciousness: the ways in which individuals may accept, reject and interpret aspects of their illness. The morbid consciousness is never entirely closed in on itself; rather it is deployed within a 'double reference' to the normal and pathological worlds. The paradoxical forms that this split consciousness takes may be analysed through the individual's understanding and experience of time, space, the body and intersubjective relations.

Analysis of the various psychological dimensions of the morbid consciousness does not constitute a comprehensive approach to mental illness on its own. A second cluster of approaches are suggested which attempt to contextualize the individual experience of mental illness in respect of broader cultural understandings of madness. For example, the modern notion according to which, by and large, the mad are regarded as deviants and are excluded from mainstream society forms part of a 'cultural illusion' in which 'our society does not wish to recognise itself in the ill individual whom it rejects or locks up'.[8] While in any culture madness involves a deviation from certain norms, the relative recentness of such an understanding of madness emerges in comparison with more primitive societies, for example, where the mad often occupy a central place in religious and other social activities. Such a comparative, historical approach highlights both that madness has no presocial essence and also that there is nothing natural or inevitable about the strategies through which, in modern society, the mad are confined and socially excluded. Indeed, a historical perspective underscores the extent to which, in a short period of time since the Renaissance, Western attitudes towards madness have been radically transformed. As Foucault puts it: 'Madness is much more *historical* than is usually believed, and much *younger* too.'[9] It is this argument that is to form the basis of *Madness and Civilization*.

Finally, the diachronic analysis of the varying cultural constructions of madness must be supplemented by a synchronic analysis of how, in a given culture, the theoretical organization of mental illness is bound up with a diverse system of institutional and social practices: 'the organization of the medical network, the system of detection and prophylaxis, the type of assistance, the distribution of treatment, the criteria of cure, the definition of the patient's civil incapacity and of his penal irresponsibility';[10] in sum, a whole set of diverse practices that defines the concrete life of the madman in a given society.

Emphasis on the culturally specific nature of the treatment of the mad serves to counteract the mythical and essentialist explanations of mental illness that arise from a focus on the individual in isolation from the cultural context. From such a perspective, the tendency of mentally ill people to retreat to infantile forms of behaviour should not be interpreted as some kind of archetypal behaviour – the 'essence of mental pathology' – but must be related to the way in which the relation between childhood and adulthood is constructed in contemporary culture. If infantile behaviour is a refuge for the patient, it is partly because childhood is violently separated from adulthood through processes of idealization and archaism resulting in past experience often being radically unrecuperable in the present.[11] In sum, the paradoxical nature of much mental illness indicates as much about the contradictions and constraints of the actual social conditions of existence as it does about the nature of the morbid consciousness: 'The contemporary world makes schizophrenia possible ... because our culture reads the world in such a way that man himself cannot recognize himself in it. Only the real conflict of the conditions of existence may serve as a structural model for the paradoxes of the schizophrenic world.'[12]

Madness and Civilization

Mental Illness and Psychology prefigures, in important respects, the arguments of *Madness and Civilization* and indeed some of the general theoretical concerns of Foucault's subsequent thought. Of most significance is the argument that madness is not a self-evident behavioural or biological fact but is the product of various sociocultural practices. Madness has no presocial essence but acquires its density of being in relation to the needs and demands of a given culture. This idea is developed in *Madness and Civilization* not so much in relation to the psychological and existential dimensions of the individual experience of madness but, at a more general level, through a historical study of the varying constructions of madness in Europe from the Renaissance to the late nineteenth century.[13] Foucault claims that during the Middle Ages it was leprosy, not madness, that was perceived as representing the greatest threat to the social order. Lepers bore the corporeal marks of punishment by God for their sins, physical reminders of God's omnipotence and the Christian duty of charity. The threat presented by lepers was contained through confinement in a network of leper houses that stretched throughout Europe, located on the edge of major cities.

With the advent of the Renaissance, however, the figure of the leper abruptly disappears and is replaced by a new image of social unease: the ship of fools. Madmen and vagabonds come to assume the symbolic significance that had once been attached to the leper.

The mad, in particular, come to acquire an ambiguous status where, on the one hand, the menace they are seen to embody renders them figures of a widespread denunciation expressed in their ritual exclusion in the Ship of Fools. On the other hand, they are held to epitomize a certain truth about the nature of post-Lapsarian humanity. Seen to embody the dark necessity of the world and the fate of humanity in its weakness, dreams and illusions, there is a widespread fascination with the image of madness – illustrated in the literature of Shakespeare and Cervantes. The mad person is both a liminal figure and also a central one in so far as he or she gives access to a moral universe beyond the reach of humanity in its everyday existence.

With the advent of the classical period, however, a fundamental change occurs in the perception of the mad. Madness ceases to be imbued with moral significance or an eschatological force and comes to be seen simply in terms of deviance and disruption. As Foucault remarks: 'By a strange act of force, the classical age was to reduce to silence the madness whose voices the Renaissance had just liberated, but whose violence it had already tamed.'[14] These changes during the classical period are reflected in the symbolic representations of madness as a disturbing and violent force in the paintings of Bosch and others.

Coterminous with these transformations in the symbolic representation of insanity is a fundamental change in the social treatment of the mad. Mad individuals are no longer set afloat in a ship of fools, rather they are 'detained and maintained' in houses of confinement and hospitals. This shift in the treatment of madness from the act of embarkation to practices of confinement took the form of a rupture or a sudden transformation which was, in part, a response to the economic crisis affecting Western Europe during the seventeenth century. By detaining troublesome elements of the population, confinement provided both a source of cheap labour and ensured some measure of social protection against uprisings and agitations. It was not simply the mad, therefore, that were confined but all those who could not or would not work: the unemployed, criminals, the sick, aged, etc. Indeed, Foucault cites the remarkable figure that, at a certain point during the seventeenth century, one in every hundred inhabitants in Paris found themselves detained in houses of confinement for a certain period. Confinement was what Foucault calls a 'police matter' – a concept that assumes greater significance in the later work on government – in so far as it was an authoritarian attempt to manipulate the population on a large scale to ensure social order.[15]

The significance of the houses of confinement exceeded their functional role as a form of repressive state apparatus. The practice of confinement also served to organize a new sensibility or 'ethical consciousness' with regard to the moral worth of labour. Replacing leprosy in the 'landscape of the moral universe', sloth became the absolute form of rebellion and those idlers who were confined were 'forced to work, in the endless leisure of a labour without utility or profit'. Madness became implicated in this new sensibility concerning the moral worth of labour. The mad no longer represented the dreadful fall of humanity from Grace as they had in the Renaissance, but came to be seen simply as those who fail to assimilate into the bourgeois order and its ethic of work. The mad are torn from the 'imaginary freedom' they assumed in the Renaissance and, instead, are bound to the rule of reason and judged according to a bourgeois morality: 'in less than a half-century, it [madness] had been sequestered and, in the fortress of confinement, bound to Reason, to the rules of morality and to their monotonous nights.'[16]

It is this symbolic and moral perception of madness generated by the houses of confinement that, in the final analysis, is of greater significance than the economic function they performed. The process in which madness ceases to lose any significance in itself but rather is incorporated as the 'other' within the alien realm of bourgeois morality and rationality constitutes the basis for the formation of the modern perception of madness. In the rest of *Madness and Civilization*, Foucault traces the processes through which the construction of madness as the deviant or morally 'other' was consolidated and confined until the end of the nineteenth century and the advent of psychoanalysis. Within confinement, the status of the mad underwent several modifications inasmuch as they acquired a more paradoxical status than the other categories of detainees. In so far as madness was regarded as a specific manifestation of unreason, it was a shameful phenomenon to be concealed because of the threat it presented to rationality through the production of contagious examples of transgression and immorality. However, unlike other forms of unreason, the mad provided a spectacle which could be exploited in so far as it served as a warning to individuals of the levels of depravity that fallen humanity could reach. In this regard, the animal, frenzied aspect of madness was constructed as an anti-natural phenomenon whose negativity threatened order and endangered the positive wisdom of nature: 'the madman, tracing the course of human degradation to the frenzied nadir of animality, disclosed the underlying realm of unreason which threatens man and envelops – at a tremendous distance – all forms of his natural existence.'[17]

It was only possible to master the animality of the mad through discipline and brutality. Madness ceases to be the sign of another world and becomes the paradoxical manifestation of non-being. Madness is the other of reason, and as such to be suppressed and distrusted as error. The Cartesian formula of doubt typifies this distrust or 'great exorcism of madness'.[18] In Descartes's meditation on doubt, Foucault discerns a fundamental imbalance in the treatment of doubt that derives from sensory deception and from imagination and dreams, on the one hand, and in the treatment of doubt that arises from madness on the other hand: 'Descartes n'évite pas le peril de la folie comme il contourne l'éventualité du rêve ou de l'erreur.'[19] A parallelism exists between Descartes' treatment of sensory doubt and doubts deriving from the imagination and dreams. With regard to sensory doubt, Descartes argues that the senses may sometimes deceive us with regard to things that are hardly perceptible or that are very far away, but, on the whole, there are many things that cannot be reasonably doubted. For example, the fact that I am here, seated by the fire, clad in a dressing gown – 'que je suis ici, au coin du feu, vêtu d'une robe de chambre'. Although one's senses may deceive one occasionally, there is always a bedrock of truth – 'un résidu de vérité' – that cannot be doubted. Similarly, although one may dream of incredible things ('des sirènes ou des satyres par des figures bizarres et extraordinaires'), the very elements that make up these fantastic compositions cannot be doubted in so far as they constitute the basic ('plus simples et plus universelles') building blocks of physical nature, 'la nature corporelle en general et son étendue'.

When Descartes comes to consider doubt initiated by madness, however, it is no longer possible to discern the inevitable mark of an ineradicable truth at the centre of such doubt. This is because madness is excluded at the outset from the paradigm of truth, falsehood and doubt. For Descartes, the very fact that he is thinking is enough to prove that he cannot be mad. To illustrate this, Descartes asks himself whether his belief that he has a natural body is not a more solid truth than someone who believes that their body is made of glass? His circular response is that of course his belief is more truthful because, if he were to believe otherwise, his beliefs would be as extravagant as those of the mad: 'ce sont des fous, et je ne serais pas moins extravagant si je me reglais sur leur example.' Unlike doubt that derives from the senses or the imagination, no residue of truth resides in madness. It is, therefore, impossible for the thinking subject to be mad because madness itself is the condition of the impossibility of thought. This exclusion of madness from philosophical consideration – an impossible manoeuvre for a Renaissance thinker such as Montaigne – signals the ascendancy of the *ratio* or the rational subject of thought. In the realm of philosophy, Descartes's exclusion of madness parallels the social practices of the confinement and exclusion of the insane: 'Le doute de Descartes dénoue les charmes des sens, traverse les paysages du rêves, guidé toujours par la lumière des choses vraies; mais il bannit la folie au nom de celui qui doute, et qui ne peut pas plus déraisonner que ne pas penser et ne pas être.'[20]

The exclusion of madness from the philosophical realm of the cogito is paralleled by understandings of madness as a physical disorder manifesting itself in the forms of hysteria, hypochondria, mania, melancholia. Arising from this notion of madness as a type of physiological disorder, is a tendency towards the *medicalization* of the various treatments of madness. Although madness came to be treated as a bodily disorder, the physiological cures that were applied were in fact overlaid by what Foucault calls a 'moral therapeutics' of the body. An ethical understanding of madness overdetermined the medical perception of the body and the physiological treatments that were applied. For example, immersion in water was a common treatment for the mad, combining the physiological theme of a cleansing impregnation with a religious theme of ablution from sins.[21] The organization and imbrication of a corporeal space around a moral sensibility becomes increasingly important in the treatment of madness during the nineteenth century.

The mad not only had a more ambivalent status than other categories of confined individuals, but also, because of their assumed disruptive influence on other detainees, they were increasingly isolated. Eventually, as poverty came to be construed as an economic problem rather than in the morally laden terms of an innate laziness, the poor were released back into society. By the end of the eighteenth century, the mad alone were confined: a process that gave birth to the asylum at the beginning of the nineteenth century.

The creation of asylums is generally regarded as a significant advance in medical practice, a 'great philanthropical gesture' heralding the advent of more humane attitudes towards the treatment of the mad. In a move which is to become characteristic of his later work, Foucault argues that this notion of progressive enlightenment is a myth. The asylum in fact institutes more insidious forms of control over the mad, it is more brutal and dehumanizing in its effects than previous treatments of madness. In Foucault's view, the most oppressive aspect of the asylums was the extent to which control over the mad was achieved through the deployment of a judgemental and moralizing ethos. At the beginning of the classical age, the mad were regarded as blind to the truth and, as such, were held to be unredeemable and trapped in a 'solitary exaltation'. During the nineteenth century, however, madness comes to be regarded as the psychological effect of a morally enfeebled nature. Error and sin became the dominant terms in which madness was assessed and judged. Madness is withdrawn from the world and from truth and by that very fact is imprisoned in evil. The aim of those who treated the mad was to restore them to an initial state of moral purity and thereby reintegrate them into the world. The most significant consequence of this increasing moralization of the problematics of madness is the creation of the notion of the mad as morally *responsible* for their own shortcomings. The mad are deemed responsible for their illness and must expect punishment for their failings. Thus a consciousness was organized for the mad through the therapeutic intervention of doctors and other medical personages into their existence: 'The madman as madman . . . must feel morally responsible for everything within him that may disturb morality and society and must hold no one but himself responsible for the punishment he receives.'[22] The truth and cure of madness becomes located exclusively in the moral space of a psychological inwardness.

The introduction of a notion of responsibility into the treatment of madness led to a subtle change in the techniques of treatment from overt repression to a more covert form of authority which manifests itself through continuous surveillance and judgement. A thematics of the family is recreated in the asylum as the most humane 'milieu' possible in which to combat madness. In fact the theme of the family serves to situate the asylum more firmly within bourgeois morality, reinforcing an atmosphere of permanent moral scrutiny and increasing the burden of shame of the mad. As Foucault puts it: 'The asylum is a religious domain without religion, a domain of pure morality, of ethical uniformity.

Everything that might retain the signs of the old differences was eliminated . . . The asylum sets itself the task of the homogeneous rule of morality, its rigorous extension to all those who tend to escape from it'.[23]

The version of the family that comes to organize relations within the asylum leads to an elevation or 'apotheosis' of the paternal role of the doctor and other medical personages in the treatment of madness. The doctor plays a dominant role in the asylum in so far as he converts it into a medical space, but also, more significantly, because he represents the figure of the father and therefore a figure of authority and law. His intervention is legitimated not by virtue of the medical skill or expertise he may possess but because he has the status of 'a wise man', of 'a juridical and moral guarantee'.[24] Madness is judged perpetually by an 'invisible' tribunal of doctors in permanent session. The asylum became a juridical instance which recognized no other authority; it judged immediately and without appeal and made use of the instruments of punishment as it thought fit. Foucault observes that it is not until Freud that the brutality of many of these moralizing and judgemental practices is exposed. Despite this, Freud still exploited the structure which elevates the doctor into a thaumaturgical figure, 'a Judge who punishes and rewards in a judgement that does not even condescend to language'. The doctor as an alienating figure, Foucault claims, remains the key to psychoanalytic practices.

Far from being liberated, the mad are reduced, in the asylum, to a state of silence and shame and trapped under a perpetual, objectifying gaze that does not listen to madness in its own being, but obscures it beneath a condemnatory morality. It is only possible occasionally to glimpse madness in a state resembling the 'solitary exaltation' of its existence in the Renaissance and in the literature of certain writers: 'Since the end of the eighteenth century, the life of unreason no longer manifests itself except in the lightning flash of works such as those of Hölderlin, of Nerval, of Nietzche, or of Artaud.'[25]

$\Rightarrow 26$

Historical method

Madness and Civilization has generated significant critical controversy that has clustered around three issues: the issue of his-

torical accuracy; the validity of Foucault's critique of Enlightenment rationality; and the status of 'madness itself'. With regard to
the first issue, perhaps the most cogent critique has been made
by Erik Midelfort, who, while sympathetic to Foucault's general
philosophical aims, is critical of his historical method.[26] Midelfort's critique consists of a problematization of the historical
schema set up by Foucault in which the mad are held to progress
from an 'easy wandering life' in the Renaissance, to confinement
during the classical period, to a state of total abjection and silence
in the asylums. Midelfort questions the assumption that the mad
did have an open existence in the Renaissance by demonstrating
that practices of confinement were in fact widespread in Europe
before the seventeenth century. The idea that the mad had a tragic
significance captured in the phenomenon of the ship of fools –
which epitomized the link of liminality between water and madness – is shown by Midelfort to have no empirical historical basis
but to be a symbolic image.[27] Foucault's literal reading of this
image romanticizes the status of the mad in the Renaissance and
obscures the extent to which they were the objects of widespread
criticism and abuse.

The connection that Foucault establishes between the classical
practice of confinement and the imposition of bourgeois morality
is undermined by showing that confinement has its roots in a long
monastic tradition of dealing with the destitute: 'Lumping such
diverse groups together was not a classical innovation prompted
by bourgeois reverence for work or by a new episteme, but an
echo of a long ecclesiastical tradition of dealing with misery and
dependence.'[28] Similarly, Foucault's assertion that in the nineteenth century the medical treatment of madness was overdetermined by a moral therapeutics is problematized by reference to
historical evidence demonstrating that doctors regard moral ther-
apy as a lay threat to medical monopoly.[29] Midelfort concludes
that many of the arguments of *Madness and Civilization* 'fly in the
face of empirical evidence' and that many of its generalizations
are based on serious oversimplifications.[30]

Colin Gordon has defended Foucault's work against such criticisms by claiming that they only have force with respect to the
abridged English translation of *Histoire de la folie* and not with
regard to the unedited French editions of 1961 and 1972.[31] Gordon
succeeds in countering a few specific criticisms; however, he does
not invalidate the force of Midelfort's arguments, which have
been reinforced by criticism of Foucault's historical method in his

subsequent works. Also Midelfort's argument that the speci-
ficities of the French, English and German experiences of madness
are effaced under the general term of the classical experience
signals later criticisms that were to be made about the ethnocen-
tricity of Foucault's analyses.[32]

A more general problem with Gordon's defence is that by re-
maining on the same theoretical ground as Foucault's critics, that
is by confining the debate to questions of empirical accuracy, some
of the crucial ideological and theoretical issues at stake are ob-
scured. As Dominick LaCapra points out, *Madness and Civilization*
presents a challenge to conventional historiography by showing
how the reconstruction of the past has been too often complicit in
the structures of rationality that have marginalized and excluded
the mad. By accepting Midelfort's definition of history as an
accurate empirical reconstruction of the past, Gordon fails to
address the general problem of 'the interaction between reconstruction of the past and dialogic exchange with it'.[33] In this
respect, Midelfort is more sympathetic than Gordon allows in so
far as he concedes that, despite historical inaccuracies, the tragic,
anti-heroic thrust of Foucault's thought yields significant insights
into the history of madness.

It is such a distinction that may be used in a defence of Foucault,
namely that while his historical method may be problematic, it
does not invalidate his general observation of certain tendencies
in the modern treatment of madness. If there is a problem in
Foucault's work, it arises from the overstatement of these tendencies as fully imposed and monolithic effects. This may be a result,
in part, of the empirical haziness of Foucault's historiography,
which replaces diversity and complexity with an oversimplified
schema. However, it is also a result of certain theoretical ambiguities in Foucault's more general conceptualization of power
relations and the way in which they operate in the social realm. It
is this conception of power underlying Foucault's critique of Enlightenment rationality that will be considered in the next section.

Critique of rationality

Madness and Civilization is a significant work because it initiates
the first in a series of sustained and devastating critiques by
Foucault of the forms of rationality inherited from the Enlighten-

ment and which constitute the foundations of modern Western thought. Coterminous with the development of the strategies through which the mad are increasingly confined and silenced is the birth of Enlightenment thought. Foucault asserts that these two phenomena are linked in a fundamental way. The claims of Enlightenment thought to be based on an equitable and just rationality with universal validity are in fact sustained, at a profound level, by processes which involve the exclusion and repression of forms of thought that are inaccessible to reason, for example madness. As Descartes's meditation on doubt illustrates, reason can only know itself as such if it is sure of what it is not: unreason. However, the implications of this process of derogation and exclusion of madness are not confined to the philosophical realm. In a way that proleptically hints at the later category of 'power/knowledge', Foucault sees all systems of thought as embedded within a network of social relations. Knowledge is not a form of pure speculation belonging to an abstract and disinterested realm of enquiry; rather it is at once a product of power relations and also instrumental in sustaining these relations. The rationalist certainty of the classical age is predicated on 'the prior constitution of an ethical experience of unreason', which in turn rests on the social practices of the confinement and marginalization of the mad.[34] By revealing this underside of institutional brutality, the claims of Enlightenment rationality to respect the integrity of all individuals are challenged.

Once the fundamental notion of 'enlightenment' is undermined – this is to say the idea that scientific and rational thought progressively acquires a greater proximity to the truth, thereby attaining a greater humanity – then a whole series of social practices can be viewed in a new light. The modern treatment of madness through processes of 'normalization' and 'medicalization' are insidiously dehumanizing in that the mad are deprived of the fundamental liberty that lies at the heart of what Foucault calls their 'solitary exaltation'. Modern psychiatry alienates the insane from themselves by imposing on them moral categories under the guise of an ostensibly objective medical knowledge. The experience of madness is internalized as shame or sin. It is this critique which led to *Madness and Civilization*'s association with the antipsychiatry movement. Foucault's observation that in the modern asylum the mad are, in some senses, denied their own voice accords with the insistence of the antipsychiatrists that madness can only be understood within the context of wider social relations, rather than within the hierarchical and hermetically enclosed structure of the mental institution.[35]

The implications of Foucault's argument extend beyond a critique of the institutional practices of psychiatry. The processes of normalization that are brought to bear on the mad are indicative of a wider cultural movement involving an introspective turn in the perception of the self. Here Foucault employs a methodological strategy that is to typify much of his subsequent work, where apparently marginal cultural phenomena are interpreted as paradigmatic examples of widespread social tendencies. The 'truth' of individuals is no longer linked to the position they occupy in the universal order of things, as it is in traditional and hierarchical societies, but is constructed around a normalizing notion of inner responsibility requiring an endless and thorough examination of the depths of their own souls: 'The purely moral space which is then defined gives the exact measurements of that psychological inwardness where modern man seeks both his depth and truth.'[36] It is this modern preoccupation with uncovering one's 'true' self, the association of truth with inwardness, that is to become the prime focus of attack throughout all Foucault's subsequent work, most notably the first volume of *The History of Sexuality*.

Foucault's claims about the bankruptcy of the moral foundations of Enlightenment rationality have provoked much critical outcry. The general counterclaim is that the emphasis that Foucault places on the dark side of Enlightenment thought is so overstated that it obscures the genuine freedoms and rights that have been attained in modern society. While Foucault is correct to draw attention to its normalizing effects, advances in psychiatric medicine have also led to a greater understanding and more compassionate attitudes towards the experience of madness. Thus, against such a one-sided view, defenders of modernity argue for a dialectical understanding of the rationality that pervades modern society as the means through which substantive freedoms are both established and jeopardized.[37]

Again, Colin Gordon has defended *Madness and Civilization* against the criticism that it presents a nihilistic vision of Enlightenment rationality both as a system of thought and a form of social organization. Reference to the original French version of *Folie et déraison* undermines the interpretation of Foucault's work as a polemic against the whole of Western reason in which the internment of the mad is posited as a direct effect of the Cartesian formulation of the cogito. Rather a reading is yielded where Foucault is understood to problematize the way in which 'different conceptual formations operative in different regions of social practice' coincided sufficiently to formulate the problem of madness as a moral issue.[38] Gordon's defence of Foucault is supported by Robert Castel, who argues that the historical reception of *Folie et déraison* has in fact skewed many of its subsequent interpretations. Although published in 1961, *Folie et déraison* did not gain prominence until 1968, when its arguments resonated with the political activism and anti-repressive sensibility of the time. As a result, what was intended as a specific study of madness was interpreted as a paradigmatic study of deviancy in general and read as a denouncement of all forms of institutional activity as violent, repressive and arbitrary. As Castel puts it: 'at the price of often outrageous simplifications, Michel Foucault's work would appear to have served as a cover for institutional struggles inspired by an ideology of spontaneity, and this slide into activism may well have skewed the rigour of the theoretical analyses.'[39]

While the historical circumstances of its reception may have distorted subsequent readings of *Folie et déraison*, there are none the less certain problems immanent in Foucault's analysis of Enlightenment rationality which can be related to the reductionist way in which the relations between knowledge and power are formulated. In his later work, Foucault comes to encapsulate this series of coextensive effects in the realm of knowledge and power as the discursive 'apparatus' (*dispositif*). By apparatus Foucault means a system of relations that is established between heterogeneous elements in such a way as to realize a 'dominant strategic function'. For example, the 'apparatus' of madness in the nineteenth century would refer to the relations that existed between 'institutions, architectural forms, regulatory decisions, laws, administrative measures, scientific statements, philosophical, moral and philanthropic propositions', etc., which led to the constitution of the mad person as an individual with moral responsibility for his or her own behaviour. Any oversimplified understanding of the apparatus as a consciously articulated strategy of repression is avoided by stressing that although there is an ultimate moment of 'functional overdetermination', the effects generated by the heterogeneous elements are discontinuous, often unintentional and contradictory.[40]

In *Madness and Civilization*, however, the relation between the philosophical space of classical reason and the social practices of confinement is not elaborated in such a complex fashion and there is a resultant tendency to posit a monocausal sequence between the birth of the Cartesian ratio and the exclusion of the mad. In a subsequent interview, Foucault acknowledges that he simplified the complexity of relations between the epistemological domain of knowledge and the institutions of repression, leading to a history of the birth of reason which is indistinguishable from one of domination.[41] He regards the concept of power with which he worked at the time as a theoretically underdeveloped notion of power, in its 'juridical' form, as a repressive force operating only through a range of negative strategies, such as exclusion, rejection, denial, obstruction, occultation, etc.:

> When I wrote *Madness and Civilization*, I made at least an implicit use of this notion of repression. I think indeed that I was positing the existence of a sort of living, voluble and anxious madness which the mechanisms of power and psychiatry were supposed to have come to repress and reduce to silence. But it seems to me now that the notion of repression is quite inadequate for capturing what is precisely the productive aspect of power.[42]

A consideration of, for example, the way in which a notion of madness is deployed in dominant constructions of feminine identity would problematize this categorically impoverished model of a form of power that invariably operates through strategies of exclusion and repression. As in much of his later work, there is a gap in Foucault's study of madness in that it fails to consider how the processes of social control he describes may be internally differentiated with regard to gender.[43] In the study of madness this omission is surprising given that in the historical period Foucault surveys, mental disorder was increasingly associated with women who by the mid-nineteenth century composed the vast majority of patients in lunatic asylums.[44] The perception of madness as a peculiar 'female malady' goes beyond that of statistical evidence to include a fundamental imbrication of the categories of femininity and madness. As many feminist thinkers have pointed out, femininity occupies a position structurally analagous to other derogated terms in the mind/body dualisms that shape Western thought. Thus femininity is inextricably linked with the embodied condition, emotionality, irrationality and madness. Normalizing constructions of femininity are implicated in a profound manner within dominant images of mental disorder, and vice versa. As Elaine Showalter writes: 'the gender asymmetry of the representational tradition remains constant. Thus madness, even when experienced by men, is metaphorically and symbolically represented as feminine: a female malady.'[45]

This fundamental imbrication of femininity and madness results in the symbolic and social practices of the derogation and marginalization of women but in a way that cannot be explained in the absolute terms of repression and silencing. While femininity is undoubtedly a subordinate category, it is nevertheless both included and set apart in dominant constructions of identity. Similarly, while women have a secondary social status, they are not invariably situated on the margins of society. The implication of madness within a more general notion of female irrationality also suggests that the social significance of madness exceeds a monotonous logic of exclusion and silence. As Foucault himself observes, liminal social phenomena always have a status in excess of their marginal position. In retrospect, Foucault outlined a more complex view of the relations between power and madness in which madness, as both a symbolic term and a social fact, is deployed, in both a positive and negative fashion, in the production of sexuality during the nineteenth century:

> The technology of madness changed from *negative to positive*, from being binary to being complex and multiform. There came into being a vast technology of the psyche, which became a characteristic feature of the nineteenth and twentieth centuries; it at once turned sex into the reality hidden behind rational consciousness and the sense to be decoded from madness, their common content, and hence that which made it possible to adopt the same modalities for dealing with both.[46]

This more complex understanding of the relation between power and madness is undeveloped, however, and in *Madness and Civilization* analysis remains ostensibly within the monolithic and univocally negative framework of domination and subordination.

Madness Itself: the debate with Derrida

Running counter to the explicit reliance on a unidirectional and dominatory account of power and rationality is a submerged narrative that relates to the status Foucault imputes to the experience of madness itself. The other side to the story of the unchecked ascendancy of a dominatory rationality is a history of silence and powerlessness. By attempting to write the history of madness or 'the archaeology of that silence', Foucault appears to envisage the possibility of recuperating some essentially liberated experience of madness from the oppressive structures of conventional rationality. In Foucault's words: 'We must try to return . . . to that zero point in the course of madness at which madness is an undifferentiated experience, a not yet divided experience of division itself.'[47]

Many commentators have noted the problematic implications of such a project. Hubert Dreyfus and Paul Rabinow explain it in terms of the continuing influence on Foucault of hermeneutic and phenomenological forms of analysis which attempt to uncover and articulate a deep meaning behind appearances. Applying Foucault's own subsequent critique of hermeneutics back on to his work on madness, they write: 'Thus Foucault's account of madness as profound otherness comes dangerously close to being "an exegesis which listens, through the prohibitions, the symbols, the concrete images, through the whole apparatus of Revelation, to [madness], ever secret, ever beyond itself".'[48] Similarly, Gary Gutting argues that there are serious methodological flaws in *Madness and Civilization* arising from Foucault's antipathy towards bourgeois morality that leads him to posit a romanticized notion of madness as an infrarational source of fundamental truth.[49] Foucault himself was later to criticize *Madness and Civilization*, which he says he wrote in a 'state of happy semi-consciousness, with a great deal of naïveté and a little innocence'.[50] In *The Order of Things*, he explicitly writes against the 'experiment' of *Madness and Civilization*, which attempted to write the 'history of the referent', to 'reconstitute what madness itself might be, in the form in which it first presented itself to some primitive, fundamental, deaf, scarcely articulated experience, and in the form in which it was later organized . . . by discourses'.[51] However, it is the philosopher Jacques Derrida who has formulated the most well-known critique of Foucault's attempt to write a history of madness with the implicit aim of uncovering an authentic form of unreason.

Derrida begins his critique of *Madness and Civilization* with a set of methodological queries. First, he questions whether it is possible to write a history of madness – an archaeology of silence – from within the language of reason and order. Foucault does not identify his work with the dominant rationality, which from the classical age onwards has subjugated and demonized forms of unreason. However, as Derrida points out, the act of writing itself constitutes a 'juridical imposition' of order and rationality upon the realm of madness. Foucault's history of madness merely repeats, in a different form, the very process of exclusion and objectification of the insane which he attacks. In Derrida's view, the attempt to write the history of madness is the maddest aspect of Foucault's project. Total disengagement from the language of reason would mean to follow the mad person into silence. Madness is necessarily what cannot be said. In Foucault's own description, it is the 'absence of the work'. To speak of madness is necessarily to enter into language and the imposition of order and reason: 'The misfortune of the mad, the interminable misfortune of their silence, is that their best spokesmen are those who betray them best; which is to say that when one attempts to convey their silence itself, one has already passed over to the side of the enemy, the side of order.'[52]

Derrida does not deny that it is possible to hold a critical perspective on the acts of exclusion and repression which covertly underlie the claims of dominant forms of rationality to universality, but this perspective is immanent in the discourse of reason, it is necessarily implicated in that which it criticizes: 'order is then denounced within order.'[53]

Failure to address fully the methodological issues connected with the task of writing a history of madness results in a latent conflict in Foucault's work. Running counter to the stated project of *Madness and Civilization*, Derrida discerns an implicit project which also has problematic methodological implications: the problem of 'convoking the first dissension of logos against itself'. This refers to the way in which the history of madness is constructed by Foucault in terms of a decisive split, occurring in the classical age, that separates reason from madness. Prior to this split, the history of madness appears to be understood as a 'nocturnal and mute prehistory'. The construction of the mad as 'other' occurs only from the seventeenth century onwards and, in support of this, Foucault argues that the Greek *logos* had no contrary.

Derrida regards this claim as problematic and argues that the Socratic dialectic, for example, would have made no sense without an internal notion of negativity or dissension – 'the marks of a deportation and an exile of logos from itself'.[54] For Derrida, the condition of possibility of all thought necessarily turns around a moment, internal to thought itself, of the repression and exclusion of an other. From this perspective, Foucault's historical schema is undermined, for the structure of exclusion that Foucault regards as specific to the classical era, is, in fact, essential to the whole history of thought and philosophical reflection. By arguing that the other of Reason only appeared in the eighteenth century, Foucault runs the risk of reducing the previous history of philosophy to a happy plenitude: 'The attempt to write the history of the decision, division, difference runs the risk of construing the division as an event or a structure subsequent to the unity of an original presence, thereby confirming metaphysics in its fundamental approach.'[55] If Foucault wishes to evoke the singularity of the classical moment, it would be better, Derrida argues, not to emphasize a structure of exclusion peculiar to the eighteenth century, but rather to explain how this structure of exclusion is historically distinct from others.

Derrida goes on to dispute Foucault's interpretation of Descartes's meditation on doubt as the philosophical equivalent of the social practice of confinement. Derrida's argument is detailed and there is not space to consider it in full here.[56] It is sufficient to note that in Derrida's reading of Descartes, madness does not receive any privileged treatment, nor is it submitted to any uniquely exclusionary logic. If all thought is necessarily based on the internal exile of some form of disorder or negativity, then the Cartesian moment cannot be singled out for criticism. Madness, along with other types of disorder, is never entirely other to thought, but remains a 'zero point which determines the whole history of meaning'.[57]

Some commentators have defended Foucault against Derrida's criticism that it is impossible to write the history of madness from within the discourse of reason without perpetuating the very oppressive strategies that are being questionned. Colin Gordon claims that Derrida's argument is based on a selective reading of *Folie et déraison* which overlooks Foucault's own appreciation of the impossibility of such a project. To support his claim that *Madness and Civilization* is an attempt to write the history of madness itself, Derrida quotes a passage in which Foucault speaks of madness 'in its vivacity, before all capture by knowledge'. Gordon points out, however, that Derrida omits Foucault's subsequent acknowledgement in the preface that such a history is a 'doubly impossible task'.[58]

While Gordon's defence is accurate with regard to a specific moment in Foucault's text, it by no means invalidates the general methodological points raised by Derrida. Furthermore, Gordon's method of defence is somewhat contradictory in that he attempts to defend Foucault by reference to explicit authorial statements in *Madness and Civilization* and yet he disregards Foucault's own explicit retrospective critique of the work in *The Archaeology of Knowledge*. References to a phenomenologically pure form of madness are not confined to the particular passage in question but in fact pervade *Madness and Civilization*. Thus, in the preface to the English translation, Foucault writes: 'In the serene world of mental illness, modern man no longer communicates with the madman . . . As for a common language, there is no such thing; or rather, there is no such thing any longer'.[59] The postulation of such an absolute separation between reason and madness undermines the plausibility of a history of madness that does not reproduce the same processes of objectivization that are under attack. This failure to address his own critical standpoint, to outline the basis from which it is possible to institute a non-objectifying process of communication with the mad, is a central weakness not just of *Madness and Civilization* but also, as we shall see, of much of Foucault's subsequent work.[60]

There are other problems highlighted by Derrida that continue to trouble Foucault's later work. For example, the problem of writing a history of madness in terms of a 'decisive break' prior to which exists an original and untrammelled experience of madness reappears, in a different form, in the first volume of *The History of Sexuality*. Here Foucault verges on reproducing a nostalgic *gemeinschaft–gesellschaft* view of social development when he describes sexual relations, prior to the great medicalizing intervention of the nineteenth century, in terms of 'inconsequential bucolic pleasures' occurring between 'simple-minded adults'.[61] Similarly, in his final work, the derivation of the idea of a contemporary ethics from Ancient Greek practices of self-mastery seems to be based on a selective rereading of the past which, as we shall see, has problematic effects for Foucault's conceptualization of the self.

Foucault's reply

Foucault replied to Derrida's critique in an appendix to *Histoire de la folie* of 1972, and it has been translated as the article 'My body, this paper, this fire'.[62] Foucault claims in a detailed argument – which will not be gone into here – that Derrida's rereading of Descartes's meditation on doubt is erroneous because it relies on an inaccurate French translation of the original Latin text. Foucault presents several compelling close textual readings to support his original interpretation of Descartes. It is, however, at the end of the article that Foucault draws out the political issues at stake in what is ostensibly an esoteric academic dispute. For Foucault, Derrida's concern to read Descartes's text not in terms of a philosophical exclusion of madness, but in terms of a metaphysical moment which establishes the conditions of possibility of all thought is indicative of his failure to understand texts as discursive practices or as 'events' with sociopolitical implications. Foucault's primary interest in reading Descartes is to show how even the most speculative forms of thought are implicated in, and reinforce, the network of sociocultural relations from which they arise. No discourse is innocent of power relations and it is these institutional implications that Foucault wishes to make explicit. In Foucault's view, Descartes's statements have a force similar to active juridical and medical interventions in the treatment of madness. In contrast, Derrida's reading of Descartes's meditation in terms of its latent metaphysical movements reinforces orthodox views of the text as a self-contained work irreducible to the set of power relations in which it is embedded. According to Foucault, Derrida reduces 'discursive practices' to 'textual traces' and thereby affirms 'a historically well-determined little pedagogy. A pedagogy which teaches the pupil that there is nothing outside the text.'[63]

It is this difference, which Edward Said has captured in the distinction between an understanding of the text in terms of its 'internal textuality' and the way it inhabits an 'extra-textual reality' that is pivotal to the dispute between Derrida and Foucault. The strength of the latter's analysis lies in the way in which the interconnection between rationality and forms of social domination is revealed. Philosophical and other texts are stripped of their esoteric and hermetic aura by making explicit their affiliations with the institutional and social context. Following an Heideggerian influence, Foucault views the task of the historian as the construction of a 'counter-memory' for the text by filling in the network of its concealed sociohistorical origins.[64] Against this, Derrida's concern is to deconstruct the text from within by exposing the internal logic that holds it together. In the words of Said: 'Whereas Derrida's theory of textuality brings criticism to bear on a signifier freed from any obligation to a transcendental signified, Foucault's theories move criticism . . . to a description of the signifier's place, a place rarely innocent, dimensionless, or without the affirmative authority of discursive discipline.[65]

The incommensurability of the philosophical aims of each thinker has been frequently noted by commentators.[66] It is possible to concede the force of Derrida's methodological comments and acknowledge Foucault's tendency to overstate the dominatory logic inherent in Enlightenment rationality, on the one hand; at the same time, it is difficult to demur from Foucault's central point that the imposition of a rationality with claims to universal status necessarily involves the institution of hierarchical power relations based on the derogation of an 'other'. The strength of the feminist critique of rationality as a masculinist construct revolves around precisely such an argument. A masculinist cultural hegemony is maintained through a process which involves the constantly practised differentiation of itself from what it believes it is not – the feminine. And, in Said's words, 'this differentiation is frequently performed by setting the valorized culture over the Other.'[67]

The status of the other

To return to the question of whether it is possible to write a history of 'madness itself', Alan Megill argues that Foucault is intentionally ambiguous on this point. At certain times, Foucault speaks of a primal experience of madness, while at others he acknowledges the impossibility of recovering such an experience. In Megill's view, any approach which attempts to resolve the matter definitively either way is necessarily reductive and fails to recognize the deliberately rhetorical and playful nature of Foucault's historiographic style, which is pitted against the 'scleroticized and self-contained' categories of orthodox history.[68] While it is undeniable that Foucault's conception of the status of 'madness itself' is ambiguous, these ambiguities are not adequately dealt with in a notion of rhetorical style, which glosses over too many theoretical problems. The ambivalence in Foucault's theoretical approach to madness is indicative of a more general understanding of the construction and status of the 'other'.

The ambiguity in Foucault's conception of madness is manifest in the vacillation between a polarized model of absolute separation in which madness represents absolute alterity, and the assertion that an essential experience of madness may be to some degree recuperable. Thus, on the one hand, Foucault argues that, since the 'decisive break' installed by reason between itself and madness, madness has been subjected to endless practices of confinement and exclusion that 'reduce it to silence'. The break institutes a 'law which excludes all dialectic and reconciliation – truth or darkness – no in between'. Madness becomes the 'paradoxical manifestation of non-being', the 'absence of work'; it is acknowledged to be 'nothing', a 'moment of silence', to be separated by a 'profound break without conciliation'. Such a conception rests on a social constructionist approach which denies that madness has any ontological essence. It is never possible to know what madness really is because it is an empty category upon which society projects its discontents. Thus, throughout history, madness has been construed as sloth, animality and finally reduced to the silence of non-being. This view accords with Gilles Deleuze's reading of *Madness and Civilization*, in which madness is seen as an empty space, the infinite possibility of non-meaning which by circulating allows for the production of meaning.[69]

Alternatively, the claim that it may be possible to unearth an essential experience of madness from the state of silence to which it has been reduced suggests a dialectical relation between rationality and its other. There must remain the residues of some 'common language' between reason and madness in order for it to be possible to glimpse the 'sovereign enterprise of unreason' in a certain literary canon: 'Since the end of the eighteenth century, the life of unreason no longer manifests itself except in the lightning flash of works such as those of Hölderlin, of Nerval, of Nietzsche, or of Artaud.'[70] Indeed, Foucault's general argument that the exclusion of madness is constitutive of the birth of Enlightenment rationality necessarily assumes a relation between the two terms beyond that of absolute opposition or alterity.

From a psychoanalytic perspective, the apparent contradiction between a model of absolute separation or expulsion and one based on mutual imbrication can be overcome. If the act of exclusion of madness is constitutive of rational identity, then the Other is necessarily internalized under the sign of negation and disgust. Negation and disgust, however, always bear the imprint of desire, and, therefore, far from being expelled, the 'other' may return as an object of nostalgia, longing or fascination.[71] Foucault, however, firmly rejects a psychoanalytic perspective and vacillates between the two models of either absolute separation or interconnection.

The inability to overcome a hermeneutic concern with the recovery of deepseated truths from beneath the appearances of social life in favour of a social constructionist approach marks not only Foucault's work on madness but much of his subsequent thought. It is most apparent in the tendency to essentialize a certain experience of alterity. For example, in the essay 'Nietzsche, genealogy, history' and in some of Foucault's interviews in the 1970s, the contestatory force initially ascribed to the experience of madness is transfered to the elusive category of the 'plebs'. Plebs is defined as the permanent, ever silent target for apparatuses of power; it forms the 'underside and limit' of power. It is not, however, an identifiable sociological entity, a category with an objective existence such as a social class. Rather, plebs is defined as a vitalistic force or 'inverse energy' that circulates throughout the social realm, manifesting itself in individuals, groups and classes. It is a force that prevents individuals from becoming passive objects of power relations by imbuing them with a resistant energy:

> There is plebs in bodies, in souls, in individuals, in the proletariat, in the bourgeoisie, but everywhere in a diversity of forms and extensions, of energies and irreducibilities. This measure of plebs is not so much what stands outside relations of power as their limit, their underside, their counter-stroke, that which responds to every advance of power by a movement of disengagement.[72]

The concept of plebs is invested with the apodictic contestatory force previously attributed to madness. Like madness, plebs is radically other, a force which eludes the grasp of power by virtue of it being simultaneously situated in the social realm – manifesting itself in the bodies of individuals – and beyond the social realm in that it cannot be located at any particular point in the social structure: 'There is no such thing as "the" plebs; rather there is, as it were, a certain plebeian quality or aspect ("de la plèbe").' The unlocatable nature of plebs is intended partly in counterposition to orthodox Marxist theory, which essentializes revolutionary force by rendering it an inherent quality of one particular class – the proletariat. However, its very ineffability and assumed ubiquity renders it an equally essentialist category. By positing plebs as an ontological source of resistance, Foucault's thought comes close to joining, in Poulantzas's phrase, 'the camp of idealism'.[73]

The category of the plebs is not developed in Foucault's work and is eventually replaced with a notion of 'subjugated' or 'disqualified' knowledges which form the basis of resistant counter-discourses.[74] However, here also, rather than analysing the specific routes through which resistance might occur, the contestatory nature of such discourses is assumed in the circular formula of a power that necessarily produces its own resistance. As Habermas notes, there is a tendency to ontologize these disqualified knowledges by investing them with a cognitive privilege over the dominant possessors of the system. To imbue such knowledges with an inherently radical force contradicts Foucault's anti-essentialist assertion that all knowledge is an effect of power. Following this logic, it is impossible to attribute an *a priori* revolutionary force to any form of knowledge.[75] The essentialist moment in Foucault's theory of resistance will be considered throughout the rest of this book.

After *Madness and Civilization*, Foucault abandoned the attempt to recover an authentic experience of madness and acknowledged the philosophical impossibility of such a project. The work on transgression that follows the study of madness indicates a shift in Foucault's conceptualization of the relation between the dominant and its others.[76]

Bataille, transgression and eroticism

Foucault's work on transgression is deeply influenced by Georges Bataille's theory of eroticism as a fundamental cultural experience, in that it embodies an elemental dynamic between discontinuity and continuity.[77] The human condition is essentially a discontinuous state in that individuals are necessarily isolated beings who 'perish in isolation in the midst of an incomprehensible adventure'.[78] Erotic activity expresses an elemental human urge to substitute the sensation of isolation and discontinuity with a feeling of profound continuity. In erotic activity – whether in its emotional, physical or religious forms – the boundaries between individuals are partially and momentarily dissolved. The sense of the self is fleetingly taken over by the realm of the senses and the demands of the body.[79] The ultimate state of continuity is death. Death confirms continuity at the level of both the particular individual and human existence in general. In the final analysis, therefore, death and eroticism have a fundamentally isomorphic character: 'Eroticism, it may be said, is assenting to life up to the point of death'.[80]

Human erotic activity – as distinct from the unfettered sexual behaviour of animals – is mediated through structures of prohibition and taboo. Taboos exist in all societies to combat the innate violence of man and to stabilize social existence. The mainspring of eroticism is a profound complicity between law and the violation of law, taboo and transgression. Throughout history the most fundamental taboos on human behaviour have always been concerned with death and sexual functions. These taboos are not necessarily consciously articulated. It is only when they are violated that their full force is experienced. The relation between taboo and transgression is dialectical. The observance of taboos precludes consciousness of them. It is only in transgressing a taboo that an 'anguish of the mind' is felt which signals the existence of the taboo. Taboo is not possible without transgression, or vice versa. The violation of taboos constitutes the necessary basis of human social life: 'organized transgression and taboo makes social life what it is.'[81]

Relating to the conflicting states of continuity and discontinuity that structure human existence are two fundamental impulses towards excess and work. Corresponding to the notion of discontinuity is the world of work and reason which constitutes the bedrock of human social existence. It is only through the world of work – productive activity and objectifying reason – that human beings become conscious of themselves as such. Running counter to the world of work is a fundamental impulse towards excess, violence and destruction which parallels the urge toward continuity. The impulse to excess is expressed in life every time violence or irrationality triumphs over reason. The forces that impel human beings towards death, squander, extravagance are the 'sovereign' forces of nature and life themselves, the 'blind surge of life'. Erotic activity is the primary expression in human existence of this surge of life.[82] The relation between these two conflicting impulses of work and excess is mediated by the dialectic of taboo and transgression. Taboo serves to protect the world of purposive rational activity from the disruptive consequences of the will to excess. Yet, at the same time, socially organized forms of transgression, the periodic release of the impulse to excess, help overcome some of the alienating effects that arise from the regimented aspects of social existence and thus ultimately reaffirm the social collectivity.[83]

For Bataille, the most complex and intense form of erotic activity occurs in religions that predate Reformation Christianity. Here the erotic experience is intensified through the interplay of sacred and profane religious forms. The experience of transgression resides in other practices – war, crime, physical and emotional eroticism – but in an attenuated and less complex form. Following a Weberian notion of disenchantment, Bataille argues that it is these derivative forms of transgression that come to predominate in an increasingly secularized world. The marginalization of the experience of transgression is indicative of the standardized, passionless and increasingly rational nature of modern experience. The capitalist system rests on an imbalance between the principle of work and of excess, between the forces of taboo and transgression. In capitalism, the work ethic or 'the narrow capitalist principle' predominates, binding humankind to an objective awareness of things at the cost of its 'sexual exuberance' or 'inner truths'. The drive to excess or the will to pleasure is repressed and only manifests itself in deformed or 'accursed' forms such as war, stockpiling of nuclear weapons and criminal behaviour.

Foucault has written that Bataille was one of the few thinkers to realize 'the possibilities of thought and the impossibilities in which thought becomes entangled' with the death of God.[84] In 'Preface to transgression', he presents his own gloss on the key Bataillean themes of transgression and taboo, the dissolution of subjectivity, erotic experience and death. The essay foreshadows a major concern of Foucault's later work, namely a critique of the contemporary understanding of sexuality. In Foucault's view, the belief that modern individuals have attained a greater state of liberation and permissiveness with regard to sexual matters than their predecessors is false. In the first volume of *The History of Sexuality*, Foucault will argue that the contemporary preoccupation with sex is a manifestation of the extent to which individuals are controlled by an insidious disciplinary power that produces confessing and self-policing subjects.

'Preface to transgression' develops this critique along different lines with the claim that modern sexuality is impoverished and 'denatured' in comparison with a previous era in which the expression of sexuality was inextricably linked to forms of religious mysticism and spirituality. The key to this greater 'felicity of expression' in sexual matters is related to a notion of a rapturous and mystical union with a divine presence: sexual experience is regarded as the initial stage in a continuum which ends in a ecstatic fusion with the divine. Religiously inspired sexual experience is necessarily more intense because it gestures beyond itself toward an ultimate experience. In contrast, in the secular, contemporary world, sexuality is 'denatured' in so far as it does not aspire to mystical union or an unknowable limit. Rather it is the sexual act itself that marks its own limits: 'What characterizes modern sexuality ... is ... its having been "denatured" – cast into an empty zone where it achieves whatever meager form is bestowed upon it by the establishment of its limits. Sexuality points to nothing beyond itself, no prolongation, except in a frenzy which disrupts it.'[85]

Nevertheless, despite the erosion of the centrality of the sacred in everyday existence, sexuality or eroticism remains one of the few realms in which the residual possibility of transgression remains: 'at the root of sexuality ... a singular experience is shaped: that of transgression.'[86] Just as sexual experience is impoverished, however, so the transgressive experience is attenuated. Religious forms of transgression are bounded by the unknowable, exteriority represented by God, the 'limit of the limitless'. In the modern experience of transgression, the limit is formed by the conventional boundaries of sexual identity. In this case, the unknown is always potentially knowable in so far as the limits of the self can be endlessly redrawn and redefined. The locus of transgression is internalized in the subject and by becoming an experience which is *'interior and sovereign'*, it is also domesticated and diminished in force. This 'limitless reign of the limit' contrasts with the unknowable 'limit of the limitless':

> By denying the limit of the limitless, the death of God leads to an experience in which nothing may again announce the exteriority of being, and consequently to an experience which is interior and sovereign. But such an experience, for which the death of God is an explosive reality, discloses as its own secret and clarification, its intrinsic finitude, the limitless reign of the Limit, and the emptiness of those excesses in which it spends itself and where it is found wanting.[87]

The relation between taboo and transgression is not one of simple opposition. For Bataille, as we have seen, the relation is fundamentally dialectical: transgression does not deny the taboo but transcends it and completes it.[88] Foucault also proposes a relation of mutual dependence between taboo and transgression. Taboo does not have an absolute identity, rather it is a relational entity that can only be sensed in the act of transgression: 'the limit and transgression depend on each other for whatever density of being they possess: a limit could not exist if it were absolutely uncrossable and, reciprocally, transgression would be pointless if it merely crossed a limit composed of illusions and shadows.'[89] However, unlike Bataille, Foucault does not conceive of the relation between taboo and the limit in terms of dialectics. Dialectics indicate the limits of Enlightenment rationality in that the negative, transgressive moment is always caught up within the positive moment of the reaffirmation of the taboo. The recuperative movement of the dialectic effaces the radical negativity of the transgressive act. Foucault understands transgression as a singular, unrecuperable moment whose negative force is radically other to reason. Thus, although transgression affirms the limit, this should not be conceptualized as a dialectial interaction, but rather as a principle of 'non-positive affirmation' or 'contestation' depicted in the notion of the 'singular moment' and the associated images of a spiral or flash of lightning.[90]

The principle of non-positive affirmation refers to the disruption of the boundaries of conventional identity and the resultant questioning of accepted notions of the normal and natural. This process should not lead, however, to the establishment of new certainties or limits. The desire for certainties is one of the legacies of an Enlightenment rationality that privileges a stable, fully self-reflexive consciousness at the centre of thought. Rather than a process which involves the supercession of old by new truths, non- positive affirmation is a movement of ceaseless contestation: 'Contestation does not imply a generalized negation, but an affirmation that affirms nothing, a radical break of transitivity . . . to contest is to proceed until one reaches the empty core where being achieves its limit and where the limit defines being.'[91]

Modern philosophy, as we have seen, is caught within 'the confused sleep of dialectics' and cannot begin to comprehend the singular and fleeting moment of transgression. Indeed, for Foucault, the act of transgression has not yet been expressed in language. Until language can begin to adequate to the principle of nonpositive affirmation, transgression remains an unspoken potentiality:

> How it is possible to discover . . . that form of thought we carelessly call 'the philosophy of eroticism', but in which it is important to recognize an essential experience for our culture . . . the experience of finitude and being, of limit and transgression? . . . Undoubtedly, no form of reflection yet developed, no established discourse, can supply its model, its foundation or even the riches of its vocabulary.[92]

However, even though philosophical language is hampered by dialectical logic, it is possible to discern the glimmering of a transgressive experience at the points where language breaks down. The dissolution of philosophical language brings humanity closer to the possibility of a non-dialectical style of thought and language: 'Next to himself, he [the philosopher] discovers the existence of another language that also speaks and that he is unable to dominate, one that strives, fails and falls silent and that he cannot manipulate.'[93] The disintegration of philosophical language manifests itself in the dissolution of the putative rational consciousness at the centre of philosophical thought. In an argument that parallels Bataille's idea of the dissolution of the personality in the intensity of the erotic experience, Foucault regards the dissolution of the philosophical subject not as the end of philosophy, but rather as its liberation from the domination of a certain notion of rationality.

Transgression becomes an experience located primarily in language: 'it [philosophy] experiences itself and its limits in language and in this transgression of language which carries it . . . to the faltering of the speaking subject.'[94] The implosion of rational discourse is exemplified in certain types of literature, beginning with the work of De Sade which marks the birth of modern literature where language is both 'excessive' and 'deficient'.[95] Excessive, because words are accumulated in a potentially infinite number of permutations in an attempt to describe 'the living body of desire'.[96] Deficient, because the ineffability of desire escapes representation in language, thus shattering the illusion of language as a transparent form of communication. 'It [language] sheds . . . all ontological weight; it is at this point excessive and of so little density that it is fated to extend itself to infinity without ever acquiring the weight that might immobilize it.'[97] Language gestures beyond itself to a transgressive moment glimpsed at the points where it fails: 'in the movement where it says what cannot be said.'[98]

From the politics to the poetics of transgression

The work on transgression marks a significant shift from the conceptualization of the other in *Madness and Civilization*. The contestatory experience of the other is no longer regarded as inherent to the existence of a repressed and marginal social group.

It is no longer a question of trying to penetrate the layers of repression and silence in order to recover an authentic voice of madness or alterity. Rather, otherness is defined as a negative or destabilizing moment immanent in the breakdown of language and the disruption of normal patterns of thought. With the faltering of language, the outline of a form of thought that is no longer governed by a putative rational subjectivity may be discerned. Transgression is redefined in an anti-essentialist manner as signifying nothing in itself except the need permanently to push experience to its limits to discover new ways of being.

The redefinition of transgression as an endless task or permanent process of contestation and experimentation signals the end of the phenomenological quest for an essential experience that characterizes *Madness and Civilization*. The mad are no longer romantically celebrated as the bearers of an ineffable source of otherness. The locus of transgression is moved from a buried experience at the margins of the social realm to a potential experience immanent in the universal medium of language. Yet, while the concept of transgression is broadened in this respect, it is simultaneously rarefied through an aestheticization of the transgressive moment. Foucault's move from madness to transgression is marked by a corresponding shift from a politics to a poetics of transgression.[99] While the experience of transgression is generalized as a potential immanent in language, Foucault goes on to claim that in fact 'the language in which transgression will find its space and the illumination of its being lies almost entirely in the future.' The only place in which Foucault identifies the language of transgression is in a certain literary canon, typified by writers such as Nietzsche, Artaud, Blanchot, Hölderlin where the exploration of the limits of identity is deemed to reach the very borders of madness: 'But a discourse (similar to Blanchot's) . . . that joins madness *and* an artistic work, a discourse which investigates this indivisible unity and which concerns itself with the space created when these two are joined, is necessarily an interrogation of the Limit, understood as the line where madness becomes, in a precise sense, a perpetual rupture.'[100]

Madness in itself is no longer the esoteric source of an experience of transgression. Rather, transgressive experience is located in a literary canon which appropriates the 'exotic costume' of madness in order to play out the disorders of its own identity. Thus the transgressive force that is attributed to this canon is undercut from a perspective that views the exploration of identity through madness as a frequently repeated manoeuvre in a tradition of Romantic and high modernist literature. As Charles Taylor has argued, the dissolution of identity as a characteristic theme of much modernist art has its roots in a Romantic search for a retrieval of experience which privileges the artistic sensibility: 'Decentring is not the alternative to inwardness; it is its complement.'[101]

In a similar fashion, Stallybrass and White have argued that the theme of transgression, as it has been developed in the work of recent French thinkers including Foucault, represents a Romantic and aestheticized form of politics centering on a process where 'bourgeois writing smashes the rigidities of its own identity by projecting itself into the forbidden territories of precisely those excluded in its own political formation.'[102] These authors note that Foucault's assertion that the language of transgression lies in the future amounts to a celebration of bourgeois art and obscures the transgressive element in place at the heart of everyday problems of identity. All cultural identity is inseparable from its limits in that it is always constructed around the 'figures of its territorial edge'. The experience of alterity does not reside exclusively in the elite realm of artistic practice; rather it is always implicit in the mundane strategies through which domination is maintained. The issue of otherness lies not in the aesthetic realm, but at the heart of the process through which the marks of difference – sexual, racial, cultural – are routinely turned into signs of inferiority and the way in which cultural hegemony is maintained by setting the valorized culture over the other.

Thus the work on transgression overcomes the problematic quest of *Madness and Civilization* for a phenomenologically pure form of contestatory experience. However, by displacing the issue of the other into the realm of aesthetics, much of the force of the previous analysis of madness is sacrificed. *Madness and Civilization* highlights the way in which symbolic processes of representation are always implicated in material practices of oppression. The philosophical and political implications of this critique are lost in the transformation of the question of the other into a poetics of self-identity which privileges the artistic consciousness. By relying on an aestheticized notion of madness, Foucault forgets his insistence in *Mental Illness and Psychology* on understanding madness in relation to its social conditions of existence: 'Only the real conflict of the conditions of existence may serve as a structural model for the paradoxes of the schizophrenic world.'[103]

2

The Subject of Knowledge

Introduction

The Order of Things and *The Archaeology of Knowledge* continue the critique of the sovereign rational subject initiated in *Madness and Civilization* and the work on transgression. This critique, however, adopts a fundamentally different line of attack. In *Madness and Civilization*, Foucault was concerned to uncover an original experience of madness in order to undermine the illusion of a self-sustaining and impartial rationality. In *The Order of Things* and *The Archaeology of Knowledge* the problematic search for a phenomenologically pure experience is abandoned. Instead an attempt is made to unpack the notion of an atemporal, universally valid form of rationality by revealing its dependence on a deepseated set of discursive regularities which, in any era, determine what it is possible to think, say and experience. It is such an interpretative strategy based on the uncovering of deep-level structures constitutive of all thought that suggests the term archaeology. Foucault captures this methodological difference between the work on madness and archaeological analysis in a distinction between the history of the Other – the history of that which in any culture must be excluded and shut away – and the history of the Same – the history of the order and identity imposed on things.[1] By unpacking the discursive regularities that underlie the thought of the same, or the identity logic of Enlightenment rationality, Foucault hopes to contribute to its eventual dislocation: 'In attempting to uncover the deepest strata of Western culture, I am restoring to our silent and apparently immobile soil its rifts, its instability, its flaws; and it is the same ground that is once more stirring under our feet.'[2]

Despite the divergence in approach, however, Foucault's fundamental aim remains the same, namely the opening up of a space
in which to think 'difference' or 'otherness' through the critique of
rationality. In his view, the greatest problem of our time is the
inability to think difference: 'We are afraid to conceive of the
Other in the time of our own thought.'[3] In the light of this project,
there is no doubt that through the archaeological method Foucault
develops a broad array of critical tools that deepen the critique of
the constitutive subject of knowledge. Archaeological analysis
reveals that the notion of a subject who exists prior to language
and is the origin of all meaning is an illusion created by the
structural rules that govern discursive formations. However, by
confining archaeology to a purely formal style of analysis, an
understanding of discourse as a culturally specific formation is
precluded. Issues raised by a consideration of the necessary social
embeddedness of discourse, such as the question of how individuals come to occupy certain discursively constructed subject
positions, problematize the validity of Foucault's total rejection of
any notion of the subject.

Birth of the Clinic

The decisive move from the analysis of hidden, ontological
sources of meaning to the more objectivist archaeological method
occurs in Foucault's study of the development of the methods of
medical observation, *The Birth of the Clinic*.[4] Here Foucault focuses
on the rapid transformation that took place in clinical medicine
from the end of the eighteenth to the middle of the nineteenth
century. In less than half a century, the medical understanding of
disease was transformed from a classical notion of disease as a
pathological essence that could be conceived independently of its
concrete manifestations to the modern idea of disease as necessarily expressed in the human body. Foucault describes this
transformation as a shift from the 'language of fantasy' to a world
of 'constant visibility'. Conventional histories account for such a
change in terms of the inevitable development of science and its
greater approximation to the truth. In this view, the change constitutes an act of 'psychological and epistemological purification'
in which 'doctors, free at last of their theories and chimeras,
agreed to approach the object of their experience with the purity

of an unprejudiced gaze.'[5] Against such teleological accounts, Foucault argues that the development of clinical medicine should be understood not as an inevitable progression but as a transformation of deep-level structures of visibility and spatialization, as a 'syntactical reorganization of disease in which the visible and invisible follow a new pattern'.[6]

Through a detailed examination of the medical treatises of the period, Foucault elucidates the nature of the structural transformation that brought about the move from classical to modern medicine. Classical medicine was dominated by the notion of disease as a series of abstract and independent typologies whose localization in the human body was a subsidiary problem. The individual patient had no positive status; indeed, for an abstract diagnosis to be ensured it was necessary for doctors to abstract the patient from analysis so that the outlines of the essential disease should not be blurred. Modern medicine radically changes this perception by superimposing the space of configuration of the disease on to the space of localization of the illness in the human body. The move from a notion of disease in terms of a 'pathological garden where God distributed species' to an understanding of disease as ineluctably embedded in the social realm and the human body brings about a corresponding transformation of the medical gaze. The doctor's gaze no longer passively maps a predetermined illness, rather it attempts to ascertain the significance of the disease through an active interpretation of symptoms: 'the gaze is not faithful to truth, nor subject to it, without asserting, at the same time, a supreme mastery: the gaze that sees is a gaze that dominates.'[7]

The emergence of the dominatory medical gaze also signals a transformation in the understanding of space and in the structures of visibility or the relation that exists between the visible and invisible. The symptom no longer indicates an abstract, pathological essence beyond itself but is in fact integral to the disease itself. The disease is a collection of symptoms whose significance must be interpreted rather than immediately giving access to a self-evident truth. Thus the homogeneous, flat space of classical typologies is replaced by a vertical space of hidden depths and indecipherability that reaches its fullest expression in the birth of pathological anatomy. Here the gaze is expanded to include the non-visual order of touch; the body must be penetrated through the autopsy in order to determine the nature of the disease. The medical gaze becomes three-dimensional, travelling a vertical path from the manifest to the hidden, from the symptomatic to the tissual surface.[8] The classical idea of a pathological essence inserting itself into the body is definitively overthrown and replaced with the notion of the body itself that becomes ill.

A consequence of the reorganization of the relation between the visible and invisible from a horizontal to a vertical dimension is a transformation of the significance of death in medical knowledge. In classical medecine, death was the absolute, privileged point at which time stops, it is the 'night into which disease disappeared'. However, with the emergence of pathological anatomy, death becomes disease made possible in life. Through a notion of degeneration, death is no longer conceived as an absolute end, but as multiple and dispersed in time in the sense of an uneven and diffuse degeneration and cessation of bodily functions. Knowledge of life is not based on an 'essence of living' but on a principle of degeneration and death. Death is the third term in which the relation between disease and life is articulated in the singular space of the body.

Thus the idea that the individual has always been at the centre of medical thought is turned on its head and shown to be the final stage of a 'long movement of spatialization whose decisive instruments were a certain use of language and a difficult conceptualization of death'. In an argument that parallels the discovery of the transgressive moment in the dissolution of the subject of thought, Foucault traces the move from classical to modern medicine in terms of a process of internalization in which 'death left its old tragic heaven and became the lyrical core of man: his invisible truth, his visible secret.'[9]

By rejecting the 'confused, under-structured and ill-structured' approaches of traditional intellectual history, Foucault succeeds in defamiliarizing some of the central concepts of medical thought. The move from a surface-level study of the empirical content of specific knowledges ('*connaissance*') to an analysis of deep-level epistemic structures ('*savoir*') explains the development of medical knowledge not in terms of an enlightened positivism but as a transformation of relations of visibility and spatialization.[10] It is this distinction between surface-level knowledge and underlying governing structures that forms the basis of the archaeological method explicitly developed in *The Order of Things* and *The Archaeology of Knowledge*.

Archaeological method

The Order of Things is a study of the development of modern thought from the late seventeenth century to the present. Its ultimate aim is an analysis of the status and role of the human sciences in contemporary thought – hence the subtitle of the book, 'an archaeology of the human sciences'. However, like *The Birth of the Clinic*, *The Order of Things* is not a straightforward intellectual history. As Michel de Certeau has commented, Foucault's starting point is 'the result of an irritation or a weariness with the monotony of commentary'.[11] In the foreword to *The Order of Things*, Foucault explicitly counterposes archaeological analysis to traditional approaches in intellectual history. The latter privilege a self-reflective subject anterior to discourse who is the sole origin of meaning. They also attempt to restore what has eluded that consciousness through an exhaustive documentation of the submerged background or *negative unconscious* of a given knowledge, that is to say 'the influences that affected it, the implicit philosophies that were subjacent to it, the unformulated thematics, the unseen obstacles'.[12] Finally they place a tendentious emphasis on the teleological progression of knowledge towards a greater approximation to a notion of 'truth' or objectivity.

In contrast to such approaches, the archaeological method attempts to uncover a *positive unconscious* of knowledge. This term denotes a set of 'rules of formation' which are constitutive of the diverse and heterogeneous discourses of a given period and which elude the consciousness of the practioners of these different discourses. This positive unconscious of knowledge is also captured in the term *episteme*. The episteme is the condition of possibility of discourse in a given period; it is an *a priori* set of rules of formation that allow discourses to function, that allow different objects and different themes to be spoken at one time but not at another. The episteme is not to be confused with epistemology or other forms of reflexive knowledge. Epistemological enquiry reflects on empirical knowledge in order to explain how it is ordered, what principles it follows and why a particular order, rather than some other, has been established. Its investigations are conducted within the dynamic of the subject/object relation. The episteme is, however, anterior to such epistemological forms of reflection. The latter, along with empirical forms of knowledge, is

determined by the *a priori* rules of discursive formation. The episteme constitutive of such knowledge is situated in what Foucault
calls a 'middle region' between the 'encoded eye' (empirical
knowledge) and reflexive knowledge:

> This middle region, then, in so far as it makes manifest the modes of
> being of an order, can be posited as the most fundamental of all: anterior
> to words, perceptions, and gestures . . . in every culture, between the
> use of what one might call the ordering codes and reflections upon
> order itself, there is the pure experience of order and its mode of being.[13]

Drawing on the distinction introduced in *The Birth of the Clinic*,
the two words *savoir* and *connaissance* are used to differentiate
between historically determinate forms of knowledge and the
conditions of possibility of knowledge. *Savoir* refers to the implicit
level of knowledge which makes possible, at any given moment,
the appearance of a theory, an opinion or a practice (*connaissance*).
Savoir is the condition of possibility of the everyday forms of
connaissance.[14]

The archaeological method allows Foucault to bypass some of
what he regards as the central difficulties of more traditional
forms of intellectual history. First, an archaeological study of
knowledge is not restricted to discrete, disciplinary categories or
to the study of formal, as opposed to informal, types of knowledge. Traditional histories of science, for example, privilege the
discourses of pure reason – 'rigorous sciences, sciences of the
necessary, all close to philosophy' – to the exclusion of less
systematic and more empirically based types of knowledge,
which are seen as unreliable or irrelevant to developments in
formal knowledge.[15] Against this, Foucault proposes that less formal knowledge – 'naive notions' – obey the same 'well-defined
regularity' of epistemic rules as the most abstract and specialized
systems of knowledge. The archaeological quest to uncover the
common rules of formation underlying the heterogeneous
ensemble of discourses that make up a given era is thus described
as a 'history of resemblance, sameness and identity'.

The juxtaposition of formal with informal knowledges leads to
results that are strikingly different from those to be found in
traditional, single discipline studies. The boundaries between different types of knowledge are redrawn and things generally considered unrelated are found to be connected and vice versa. For
example, instead of relating the biological taxonomies to other

knowledge of living beings (the theory of germination, or the physiology of animal movement, or the statics of plants), they are compared with what was said about 'linguistic signs, the formation of general ideas, the language of action, the hierarchy of needs, and the exchange of goods'.[16]

The second problem that Foucault claims the archaeological method enables him to bypass is that of chronology. Orthodox intellectual histories invariably regard the contemporary moment as the culminating point of the process of thought set in motion by the Enlightenment. There are two points that Foucault takes issue with here: the notion of continuity and the notion of progress. With regard to the former, Foucault argues that, contrary to the common notion of the continuous development of the *ratio* from the Renaissance to the present, Western thought is in fact divided into three distinct and discontinuous epistemic blocks. Drawing on Gaston Bachelard's notion of the epistemic break, archaeological analysis discloses radical changes across distinct disciplines at certain crucial junctures.[17] Arising from the abandonment of the idea of an uninterrupted chronological development of thought is a corresponding rejection of a notion of progress. Like Thomas Kuhn's theory of paradigms, the archaeological method makes it possible to abandon a normative perspective which would see modern thought as advancing closer to the truth or an 'objectivity in which today's science can be finally recognized'.[18] Against such correspondence theories of truth, any system of knowledge must be studied in terms of its own internal and relatively contingent rules of formation.

Finally, an archaeological approach makes it possible to dispense with a conception of the sovereign subject as the source of all knowledge. The treatment of the history of thought in terms of individual intellectual biographies is, in Foucault's view, not adequate to describe the density of discourse in general and scientific discourse in particular. A privileging of the subject as the prediscursive origin of knowledge disregards the fact that the subject itself – 'its situation, its function, its perceptive capacities' – is in fact determined by regularities that are beyond the reach of a transcendental consciousness. As Foucault puts it:

> If there is one approach that I do reject ... it is that ... which gives absolute priority to the observing subject, which attributes a constituent role to an act, which places its own point of view at the origin of all historicity – which, in short, leads to a transcendental consciousness. It seems to me that the historical analysis of scientific discourse should, in

the last resort, be subject, not to a theory of the knowing subject, but rather to a theory of discursive practice'.[19]

Here Foucault attacks the 'great myth of interiority', where cultural artefacts ranging from archival material to works of art are invariably interpreted in terms of an originary, creative consciousness. In this view, the task of the critic is to uncover the expressive value or truth of a 'document' that is always referred back to a controlling notion of consciousness.[20] In contrast, archaeological analysis takes a step behind the notion of the author in order to examine the discursive structures that determine the utterances of the author. Archaeology also takes a step beyond the creating consciousness in order to examine the formal relations that exist between apparently disparate and unrelated utterances or texts.[21] If the role of the author is to be broached at all, it is not in terms of a constitutive subjectivity but in terms of 'the primordial function of the name', that is, the function that the 'name' plays in unifying texts and inserting them into relations of opposition and difference with other works.[22] From an archaeological perspective, the author and more generally the subject of knowledge is the 'anonymous one'.[23]

A further way in which the category of the subject is problematized relates not so much to the subject of knowledge but to an outcome of the archaeological rereading of the history of thought. Arising from the disclosure of the *a priori* rules of formation constitutive of thought is the revelation that the apparently 'eternal' notion of man – 'the study of whom is supposed by the naive to be the oldest investigation since Socrates'[24] – is in fact a recent construction conterminous with the decline of the classical episteme and the reflexive turn taken by thought since the beginning of the nineteenth century. 'But as things become increasingly reflexive, seeking the principle of their intelligibility only in their own development, and abandoning the space of representation, man enters in his turn, and for the first time, the field of Western knowledge.' If, from an archaeological perspective, the concept of 'man' is not the oldest problem of thought but in fact the most recent, it follows that it may also be only a transient preoccupation of contemporary thought. This leads to Foucault's famous declaration of the 'death of the subject' or the 'end of man':

As the archaeology of our thought easily shows, man is an invention of recent date. And one perhaps nearing its end. If those arrangements were to disappear as they appeared, if some event of which we can at the moment do no more than sense the possibility . . . were to cause them to crumble, as the ground of classical thought did . . . then one can certainly wager that man would be erased, like a face drawn in sand at the edge of the sea.[25]

From the Renaissance to the modern episteme

Having outlined the methodological principles and aims of the archaeological method, Foucault proceeds to remap Western thought in terms of three fundamental epistemic blocks. First, until the end of the sixteenth century, an episteme ordered around the principle of resemblance was determinant of knowledge in Western culture. Resemblance structured the exegesis and inter-pretation of texts, it organized the play of symbols and it controlled art. The term resemblance denotes the Renaissance belief that the world was related through similitudes which were discernible in the 'signatures' or 'hieroglyphs' that marked the face of the world. For example, Renaissance thinkers observed an affinity between aconite and the eyes that would have otherwise remained obscure if it were not for the sign, legible in the seeds of the aconite, which resemble the human eye. Furthermore, this sign indicates that a cure for diseases of the eye is contained in the seeds.[26]

Renaissance knowledge was a composite but coherent structure in which magic and science – complementary rather than compet-ing forms of knowledge – were caught up in the decipherment of signs or 'semiology of signatures' and the determination of their meaning – a 'hermeneutics of resemblance': 'the sixteenth century superimposed hermeneutics and semiology in the form of similit-ude. To search for a meaning is to bring to light a resemblance. To search for the law governing signs is to discover the things that are alike. The grammar of being is an exegesis of these things.'[27] It follows from this definition of Renaissance knowledge, that lan-guage was not valued for its representative function but because it itself is a 'thing' in nature. Like other objects, words were caught up in the doctrine of correspondences in that they were under-stood to have specific properties and virtues that draw together and repel each other.[28]

Within a few years, however, the Renaissance doctrine of resem-blance is abruptly overthrown and is replaced by the classical system of knowledge, which is ordered around an 'episteme of representation'. The qualitative, magical thought of the sixteenth century is replaced with the classical concern for a 'general science of order'. Cervantes' *Don Quixote* marks the transition from the Renaissance to the classical episteme. This book is the first work of modern literature because here writing is no longer understood as the 'prose of the world'; indeed, time and again, similitudes and resemblances are proved to be false. Words become autonomous and are no longer tied by a material link to the world. There ceases to be a resemblance between written words and things: 'language breaks off its old kinship with things and enters into that lonely sovereignty from which it will reappear, in its separated state, only as literature.'[29] Prominent thinkers of the classical age, such as Francis Bacon and Descartes, denounced Renaissance knowledge as a muddled and distorted body of learning. In place of resemblance, the classical age admitted only two forms of comparison: that of measurement and that of order. Identity, difference and exactitude replace the play of resemblance. Whereas during the Renaissance resemblances were probable in nature and potentially infinite in number, classical thought assumed that the elements that composed the social and natural worlds could be completely enumerated and exhaustively understood. *Mathesis* and *taxonomia* – the ordering of simple and complex natures respectively – were the central principles around which knowledge was organized.[30] Knowledge could, in principle, attain complete certitude.[31]

Just as the relation to interpretation was central to Renaissance knowledge, so the relation to order was central to the classical age: 'the ordering of things by means of signs constitutes all empirical forms of knowledge as knowledge based on identity and difference.'[32] The sign ceases to be a form of the world, to be bound to what it signifies by the 'solid and secret bonds' of resemblance and affinity. Language and sign systems are cut off from nature and become arbitrary. The primary question for the classical age is how adequately a sign system represents the nature of the world in terms of accurate depiction and universal veracity. In its perfect state, the system of signs should be invisible, it should be 'that simple and absolutely transparent language which is capable of naming what is elementary: it is also that complex of operations which defines all possible conjunctions.' The ternary Renaissance understanding of language as a formal domain of marks, the content indicated by them and the similitudes that link the marks to the things designated by them is replaced by the binary classical system of a transparent relation between signifier and signified. The analysis of the sign in the classical age permits direct connection of two terms precluding a third term as in the Renaissance notion of resemblance or a modern theory of signification. The consciousness of the subject is regarded as intrinsically representational.[33] The act of representation is thus naturalized or remains unrepresentable. The non- representability of classical forms of representation is illustrated in Foucault's analysis, at the beginning of *The Order of Things*, of Velasquez's painting *Las Meninas*. Here Velasquez depicts the discrete elements which constitute the process of representation, but he cannot portray the act of representation itself.

The end of classical thought coincides with a decline in the faith of the representational function of language or the 'emancipation of language with regard to representation'.[34] The work of De Sade is situated on the threshold between the classical and the modern episteme. On the one hand, De Sade's work belongs to the classical era in that the libertine, while yielding to every desire, must also meticulously record and represent the precise nature of these desires: 'There is a strict order governing the life of the libertine: every representation must be immediately endowed with life in the living body of desire, every desire must be expressed in the pure light of a representative discourse.'[35] On the other hand, the impossibility of capturing the ineffable quality of desire reveals the inadequacy of language: desire is necessarily that which exceeds representation. De Sade's writing not only signals the decline of the notion of absolute representation but also gestures towards a dark underside of language, an 'other' which continually escapes representation. After De Sade, Foucault claims, 'violence, life and death, desire and sexuality will extend, below the level of representation, an immense expanse of shade which we are now attempting to recover, as far as we can, in our discourse, in our freedom, in our thought.'[36]

The transition from the classical to the modern episteme has two stages. In the first phase, the fundamental categories of existence designated in the classical era – the analysis of wealth, general grammar and natural history – appear to remain unchanged. However, an imperceptible shift occurs within these categories towards the use of concepts that overflow or exceed the classical notion of knowledge as the representation of the visible. For example, in natural history, the classification of natural beings is no longer based on a principle of the identification of visible, external characteristics, but comes to depend on a notion of an inner organic structure. Likewise, the study of language increasingly relies on an idea of an internal architecture or inflectional system rather than on a notion of the adequacy or 'transparency' with which language represents reality. In the analysis of wealth, the value of objects comes to be assessed according to the 'invisible' concept of labour, rather than in terms of an explicit or discernible relation between a given object and an expressed need. In short, the concept of labour, like the concepts of organic structure or internal architecture, are not directly derivable from the notion of representation but are based on conditions exterior to representation – 'the dark, concave, inner side of their visibility'.[37] These displacements indicate that representation has lost the power to provide a foundation for thought; henceforth, any explanatory structure 'resides . . . outside representation, beyond its immediate visibility, in a sort of behind-the-scenes world even deeper and more dense than representation itself'.[38]

This 'miniscule displacement' of the primacy of representation initiated at the end of the eighteenth century had, by the beginning of the nineteenth century, deepened to a fundamental rejection. The horizontal schema of taxonomia around which classical knowledge is ordered is definitively overthrown and replaced by a vertical ordering of things in which 'what matters is no longer identities . . . but great hidden forces developed on the basis of their primitive and inaccessible nucleus.'[39]

The dissolution of the homogeneous field of orderable representations leads to the preoccupation of modern thought with the source and origin of representation. On the one hand, modern thought addresses the condition of possibility of representation from the perspective of its putative source: the transcendental subject of knowledge. On the other hand, it considers the conditions of possibility of representation from the perspective of the being itself that is represented: the object of knowledge. Within these parameters of the subject and object of knowledge, the themes of historicity and finitude come to dominate modern thought. In this respect, Foucault extends the argument in *The Birth of the Clinic*, where death becomes the source from which knowledge of life is derived. Thus, in economics, Ricardo transforms the classical analysis of wealth through the introduction of a value not fully representable in signs: labour.[40] A primary consequence of this substitution is that *homo oeconomicus* is no longer seen as a being who represents his own needs to himself but as a human being who spends, wears out and wastes life in evading the imminence of death, that is, 'man' as a finite being.[41]

The question of finitude also becomes a fundamental ordering principle in natural history where life and death constitute the themes against which animals as 'transient beings' are studied: 'Transferring its most secret essence from the vegetable to the animal kingdom, life has left the tabulated space of order and become wild once more.'[42] Similarly, in the study of language, Franz Bopp discovered the basis of language in a kind of *energia* or power of speech that eludes systematic representation.[43] In short, historicity permeated all aspects of Western thought. Knowledge of an object no longer consisted in the accurate representation of its constitutive elements, but rather in the study of its development according to laws springing from internal necessities.

The stress on historicity and finitude within the general understanding of knowledge in terms of the subject and object of thought leads to the emergence of the human sciences and the birth of the concept of 'man'. The object of the human sciences is not life, production or language but the being who represents these things to himself. Foucault argues that the 'analytic of finitude' that comes to dominate the human sciences crystallizes into three fundamental paradigms: the empirical and the transcendent, the cogito and the unthought, the retreat and return of the origin.[44]

The status of language also undergoes a transformation with the shift from the classical to the modern episteme. Freed from its representative function, from the necessity of having to provide a transparent grid in which to order the knowledge of things, language rediscovers what Foucault calls its 'ancient, enigmatic density'. No longer defined exclusively in terms of its representativeness, language becomes an object of study in its own right, acquiring a density and self-referential quality in which it folds back 'on the enigma of its own foundation'.[45] For Foucault, the most important consequence of the 'return of language' is the birth of modern literature. With the supercession of its representative function, the language of modern literature becomes radically intransitive. The word, in modern literature, refers to nothing but itself; it has 'nothing to do but shine in the brightness of its being'.[46]

-76?

The problem of historical method

Like *Madness and Civilization*, *The Order of Things* has aroused critical controversy with regard to the accuracy of Foucault's use of his historical material. G. S. Rousseau claims that whereas in *Madness and Civilization* Foucault was at least 'tied to solid facts and still concerned with historical accuracy', he has lost all sense of periodization in *The Order of Things*: 'chronological labels actually play no part in Foucault's hypothesis, and it is therefore a waste of time to examine them seriously.'[47] In a less disparaging fashion, George Huppert claims that Foucault's representation of the Renaissance episteme as a coherent and harmonious mix of scientific and magical thought – 'divinatio et eruditio' – is erroneous. In fact, the 'dominant and respectable' intellectual tradition during the sixteenth century was represented by a tradition of humanist and scientific learning which was highly critical of the magical thought and theories of correspondence and resemblance misleadingly highlighted by Foucault in order to maintain the distinction between the Renaissance and classical epistemes.[48]

In response to such criticisms, Foucault reaffirmed his aim to write history from a radically different perspective than the traditional, continuist one. The force of the archaeological conception of knowledge as distinct and incommensurable epistemes derives from its problematization of continuist historical perspectives and the resultant themes of progress and a recuperative macro-consciousness of history: 'continuous history is the indispensable correlative of the founding function of the subject: the guarantee that everything that has eluded him may be restored to him.'[49] The internalist analysis of each episteme in terms of its formal properties and the juxtaposition of one set of distinct epistemological concerns with another permits the denaturalization of concepts that each era takes to be self-evident.

However, a primary concern with epistemological breaks does not mean that Foucault denies completely the possibility of historical continuity.[50] In certain respects, the stress on discontinuity and breaks complements rather than opposes a continuist perspective in so far as it is a symmetrical effect of the same methodological renewal of history in general.[51] The continuist histories that are referred to here are those of the *Annales* school – Marc Bloch, Lucien Febvre and Fernand Braudel. By enlarging established historical periodizations, the *annales* historians at-tempt to shift the focus of history from the actions of individuals to a deeper, structural level which reveals large continuities and movements imperceptible at the level of actions and events.[52]

The stress on deep-seated continuity and on discontinuity and rupture are linked, therefore, to the extent that they replace an anthropological stress in history with a deep-level analysis of 'unities, totalities, series, relations'.[53] Thus it can be seen how, on the one hand, the category of the epistemological break enables Foucault to reveal continuity, at a diachronic level, in the descrip-tion of the transitional stage from one episteme to another. On the other hand, the notion of discontinuity reveals continuity, at the synchronic level, in the *a priori* formal similarities – 'the simultan-eous functioning' – between diverse and disparate forms of lan-guage in any given era.

The autonomy of knowledge

Other critiques of *The Order of Things* have tended to focus on some of the broader philosophical questions that it raises. One set of criticisms has centred on Foucault's definition of the episteme as an *a priori* set of rules which, at any given point, determines what can and cannot be thought and said. The notion of an *a priori* set of rules has exposed Foucault to the charge that he produces an unacceptably idealist account of knowledge. Perhaps the most well-known criticism on this count comes from Jean-Paul Sartre, who accuses Foucault of freezing history by replacing the 'cinema with the magic lantern'.[54]

Rather than lapsing into a quasi-Kantian idealism, Foucault makes use of the concept of the episteme to avoid a reductionist understanding of knowledge. Discourse and knowledge have their own specificity and are relatively autonomous: the structure of knowledge does not simply reflect in an unproblematic fashion the wider social structure in which it is ineluctably embedded:

> In wanting to engage in a rigorous description of the statements them-selves, it appeared to me that the domain of statements very much obeyed certain formal laws, that one could for example discover a single theoretical model for different epistemological domains and that one would, in this sense, infer an autonomy of discourse.[55]

The insistence on the autonomy of the episteme should be understood in the context of the late 1960s, when many French thinkers were attempting to develop an understanding of social and cultural phenonoma outside of the economic determinism of the dominant Marxist approach.[56] Foucault himself regarded some of his earlier work as replicating a reductionism similar to orthodox Marxist approaches in its failure to think through the complex nature of the relations between social systems and systems of knowledge:

> In *Madness and Civilization* and *The Birth of the Clinic* I wanted precisely to define the different relationships between these different domains. I took for example the epistemological domain of medicine and that of the institutions of repression . . . but I perceived that things were more complicated than I had believed in the first two works, that the discursive domains didn't always obey the structures that had common practical domains and associated institutions, that they obeyed on the other hand structures common to other epistemological domains.[57]

In this light, archaeology represents an attempt to avoid a materially reductionist account of knowledge in which knowledge and other social practices are understood to have an isomorphic structure. In a sense, archaeology resembles a realist approach in that some form of 'ontological hiatus' obtains between social practices and knowledge of those social practices. Such a hiatus helps to explain how it is that causal laws or determining social structures cannot simply be read off, in a one-to-one relationship, from empirical manifestations.

As well as the work on madness, the theoretical problems arising from reductionist accounts of knowledge are also illustrated in Foucault's later formulation of the relations between knowledge and power. In *Discipline and Punish* and *The History of Sexuality*, systems of knowledge are defined as ineluctably bound up with regimes of power. Systems of power bring forth different types of knowledge, which in turn produce material effects in the bodies of social agents that serve to reinforce the original power formation: 'power produces knowledge . . . power and knowledge directly imply one another . . . there is no power relation without the correlative constitution of a field of knowledge, nor any knowledge that does not presuppose and constitute at the same time power relations.'[58]

The complexities of the Foucauldian category of power/knowledge will be considered in the next chapter. The significant point here is that the establishment of an elliptical link between know-ledge and what is an essentially monolithic account of power as domination yields an undialectical and functionalist account of knowledge. With no autonomy from dominant power relations, knowledge is little more than an instrument and effect of domina-tion. The problem with such a reduction of all forms of knowledge and discourse to a level of positivity is that a certain critical or reflexive moment inherent to a more autonomous conception of knowledge is effaced. The idea that all thought is in the service of dominatory regimes cannot adequately explain how conflicting perspectives may arise in the same regime. Nor does it explain the emergence of counterfactuals or how knowledge is necessarily distinguishable from the rationalized systems through which so-ciety is ordered.[59]

The archaeological definition of knowledge runs counter to such an understanding of knowledge purely in terms of the role it plays in the reproduction of relations of domination. It seeks to attribute to systems of knowledge a specificity that is in excess of such functionalist definitions. Thus, in an interview, Foucault argues that in the analysis of discourse it is inconsistent, when confronted with a problem, to pass from one level of analysis of a statement to another exterior to it. Knowledge has an internal logic that is not entirely reducible to its social conditions of existence.[60]

However, although the episteme is a relatively autonomous formation, Foucault also stresses that 'there is no reason for describing this autonomous layer of discourse except to the extent that one can relate it to other layers, practices, institutions, social and political relations, etc.'[61] It is in the elaboration of the precise nature of these relations between the autonomous discursive realm and the institutional and social practices external to it that Foucault's work is marked by ambiguity. Such ambiguity mani-fests itself in relation to the concept of the epistemological break and the issues of change and causality that it raises.

The epistemological break

It has already been noted that the transition from one episteme to another is conceptualized not as a gradual process but as a sudden and complete rupture. In a matter of a few years, the cluster of problems and concepts that preoccupied a preceding era have been entirely abandoned and replaced by a new, incommensurable set of issues. Such an account of epistemic revolution inevitably raises the issue of causality. If the episteme is conceived as an internally consistent formation in that it comprises deepseated discursive *regularities*, then an explanation of the process of epistemic transformation in terms of an internally irregular movement of contradiction or displacement has, by definition, been foreclosed. It follows from this logic that the process of epistemic transformation must be initiated by a force external to the episteme: a non-discursive force.

Yet an elucidation of how discursive and non-discursive elements are implicated within each other in such a way as to explain a move from one episteme to another is persistently deferred by Foucault. He argues that the question of causality is beyond the scope of archaeology. An attempt to produce a definitive explanation of the rupture falls back into the problematic of traditional history: 'Only thought re-apprehending itself at the root of its own history could provide a foundation, entirely free of doubt, for what the solitary truth of this event was in itself.'[62] Yet, by according the moment of transition or break such a central place in the definition of the episteme and by failing to provide a plausible transformative principle, it would seem that the issue of causality is not as easily bypassed as Foucault would claim.

Such a gap in the account of epistemic change means that Foucault finishes by asserting rather than demonstrating the possibility of radical epistemic shift. To a certain extent, Foucault is justified in claiming that the demand to postulate a 'solitary truth' as the cause of the epistemological break would be to fall back into the reductionism of an expressive totality. Yet, by failing to provide a systematic account of the relation between the epistemic order and its sociohistorical context, Foucault himself becomes vulnerable to his own counter-accusation, in that the discursive formation becomes a hermetically sealed, self-sustaining 'expressive' totality. Replicating a weakness in Althusser's notion of the problematic, Foucault's episteme becomes a 'closed universe', unconnected with other realms of knowledge or social practice.[63] The notion of the episteme homogenizes the realm of knowledge to such an extent that the uneven, complex and often conflictual relations that exist between dominant, residual and emergent discourses are entirely effaced.[64]

Furthermore, if an analysis of language in terms of its formal properties can only be justified by taking into account 'its concrete functioning', then, on Foucault's own terms, there must be a fuller account of the connection between language as a formal structure and language in its social effectivity. In Foucault words: 'Language is very much a set of structures, but discourses are unities of function, and the analysis of language in its totality cannot fail to confront this essential demand.'[65]

From the episteme to the archive

The Archaeology of Knowledge represents an attempt by Foucault to overcome some of the theoretical confusions in *The Order of Things*, in particular the misinterpretation of the episteme as a reifying cultural totality.[66] The concept of the episteme is replaced, therefore, with the new category of the *archive*. Like the episteme, the archive is defined as the general condition of possibility – the system of discursive regularities – which determines what can and cannot be spoken in a given historical era. Foucault stresses, however, that the archive is composed of multiple and varying discourses; it is not, a limiting or constraining formation but an enabling system of rules which is never entirely complete and which is, therefore, always open to change. The archive is a regulative rather than a constitutive principle, the 'general system of the formation and transformation of statements'.[67]

Similarly, the set of discursive rules that the archive embodies does not amount to a *formal a priori*, a limiting and invariant set of rules 'whose jurisdiction extends without contingence'.[68] Rather the archive constitutes a *historical a priori*, that is a set of rules that are themselves historically determined and thereby capture a notion of change: 'this *a priori* . . . has to take account of the fact that discourse has not only a meaning or a truth, but a history, and a specific history that does not refer it back to the laws of an alien development.'[69] The neologism 'theoretico-active' – a modification of the Sartrean term 'practico-inert' – is used to capture the active, historical element of the discursive rules of formation.[70]

The archive of a given period is composed of the totality of discursive formations or ensemble of statements which constitute a given field of knowledge, for example, grammar, medicine or political economy.[71] The notion of the discursive formation is used to problematize the self-evident unity of such discourses: what is the unifying principle that enables us to identify a certain group of statements as, say, medicine rather than economics? Several conventional explanations of this unifying principle are assessed and discounted. A discursive formation cannot derive its coherence through reference to the same object because an object does not possess a prediscursive identity but rather is constituted by the discursive framework in which it is implicated. This argument amounts to a retrospective refutation of the approach adopted in *Madness and Civilization*, where, at points, it was assumed that madness is a historically constant, objective phenomenon which is worked upon by various disciplinary regimes. Against this, Foucault maintains that madness and its different forms – melancholia, hysteria, etc. – are the result of the different discourses that take it as an object of study.

The notions of style, concept and theme are also discounted as constituting potential principles of discursive unification. With regard to style, Foucault notes that a discourse, such as clinical medicine, is as much characterized by certain assumptions about life and death, 'of ethical choices, of therapeutic decisions, of institutional regulations', etc., as it is by a similarity of descriptive statement.[72] Similarly, an analysis of the use of concepts in a specific discourse reveals that they are not always logically connected and that concepts often arise that are heterogeneous and even incompatible with other concepts used in a given field. Finally, the notion of theme is discounted as a unifying principle because the same theme may occur in different discursive formations and contradictory themes may be employed in the same discourse.[73]

In place of these concepts, Foucault proposes the idea of a *system of dispersion* as the regulatory principle which makes it possible to distinguish one discursive formation from another. The system of dispersion is, in turn, governed by four sets of *rules of formation*: the formation of objects, the formation of enunciative modalities, the formation of strategies and the formation of concepts. If in the analysis of a group of dispersed statements the operation of any or all of these rules of formation can be discerned, then it can be concluded that a particular discursive formation has been identified. This relation is expressed in the following way:

> With the unity of a discourse like that of clinical medicine . . . we are dealing with a dispersion of elements. This dispersion itself . . . can be described in its uniqueness if one is able to determine the specific rules in accordance with which its objects, statements, concepts and

theoretical options have been formed: if there really is a unity, it does not lie in the visible, horizontal coherence of the elements formed; it resides well anterior to their formation, in the system that makes possible and governs that formation.[74]

The discussion of the rules of formation that govern the particular nature of the dispersion among a set of statements is detailed, and there is not space here to consider all the issues raised.[75] In order to clarify what is meant by a rule-governed system of dispersion, the set of rules of formation pertaining to the enunciative modalities will be considered – this is to say the rules which determine the positioning of the subject within a discursive formation.

The archaeological method is developed, as we have seen, to counter approaches to knowledge which privilege a 'sovereign' subject anterior to discourse. It is not the individual who imparts meaning to discourse, rather it is the discursive formation that provides an array of 'subject positions' which individuals may occupy. A series of dispersed statements may be unified, therefore, by a certain regularity in the way in which subject positions, or enunciative modalities, are distributed among them. The analytical steps to be taken in the identification of enunciative modalities are outlined. First it must be asked, who is speaking? It is necessary to examine who among the totality of speaking subjects is able to use a particular discourse. Thus, for example, the discourse of medicine generally permits only individuals of a certain status – doctors, nurses, etc. – to use it: 'Medical statements cannot come from anybody; their value, efficacy, even their therapeutic powers, and, generally speaking, their existence as medical statements cannot be dissociated from the statutorily defined person who has the right to make them, and to claim for them the power to overcome suffering and death.'[76] The examination of who is speaking involves, therefore, a consideration of the issues of criteria, institutional networks, pedagogic norms, etc.

Second, the institutional situation from which a given discourse derives its legitimacy and efficacy must be examined. The discourse of medicine, for example, is generally to be located in the hospital, the laboratory and the library. Each institutional site must be analysed in terms of its own internal structure as well as in terms of the position it occupies in an external network of social and institutional relations. Finally, the positionality of the subject is also determined by the field of potential relations that may be occupied with regard to the object or domain of knowledge. Thus it is possible to occupy the role of a listening subject, an observing subject, a questioning subject, etc., where each role is determined by a specific network of discursive relations.

The idea of enunciative modalities is used to demonstrate the redundancy of a notion of a unifying and originative subject of meaning in the analysis of discourse. The subject is in fact a discontinuous category composed of a dispersion of positions within a specific discursive formation: 'Thus conceived, discourse is not the majestically unfolding manifestation of a thinking, knowing, speaking subject, but, on the contrary, a totality, in which the dispersion of the subject and his discontinuity with himself may be determined. It is a space of exteriority in which a network of distinct sites is deployed.'[77]

The primacy of discourse

It should be apparent from the account of the systems that govern the dispersion of statements in discourse that archaeology is not simply a form of linguistic analysis. Rather it involves the analysis of a series of heterogeneous elements: institutions, techniques, social groups, perceptual organizations, etc. The discursive formation is not just of the order of language or representation, it is a structuring principle which governs beliefs and practices, 'words and things', in such a way as to produce a certain network of material relations.[78] For example, the process of 'hysterization' of the female body that is described in the first volume of *The History of Sexuality* refers to the inscription of material effects on the body by a series of moral and medical discourses and clinical practices.

The inclusion of a notion of material as well as linguistic practices in the definition of the discursive formation represents an attempt to overcome the criticism, levelled at the previous notion of the episteme, that history has been bypassed in favour of a quasi-Kantian idealism. It is the explicit aim to examine the interconnections between the discursive realm and non-discursive social practices – the imbrication of words with things – that distinguishes archaeological from structural analysis. Foucault vehemently rejects any similarities between archaeology and structuralism on the grounds that the former is explicitly counterposed to the formal type of analysis characteristic of the latter.[79] This formalist tendency has been noted by many commentators, who argue that the structural emphasis on the internal features of cultural symbolic forms forecloses a consideration of the socially structured contexts and processes within which these symbolic forms are embedded.[80] Thus, although archaeology is primarily oriented to the synchronic analysis of discursive formations – the mode of distribution of subject positions within a series of statements – these synchronic positions are not unrelated to the institutional siting of individuals. This, in turn, introduces a notion of mutability into the understanding of a discursive formation:

> Archaeology does not deny the possibility of new statements in correlation with 'external' events. Its task is to show on what condition a correlation can exist between them, and what precisely it consists of (what are its limits, its form, its code, its law of possibility). It does not try to avoid the mobility of discourses that makes them move to the rhythm of events; it tries to free the level at which it is set in motion – what might be called the level of – 'evential' *engagement*.[81]

The definition of the episteme as a hybrid formation of words and things raises the question of the form that relationship between discourse and external events or the non-discursive realm takes. What degree of autonomy does the discursive realm have with regard to the non-discursive or socioeconomic field? The strong claim of *The Archaeology of Knowledge* is that the discursive realm has priority in that it determines non-discursive events. This is to say that the social-institutional field only acquires a meaning or a unity once it is articulated within a particular discursive formation. Clinical medicine, for example, is not the result of a new technique of observation, rather it must be regarded as the result of the articulation, in medical discourse, of a relation between distinct elements such as the status of doctors, the institutions from which they speak and their position as perceiving, observing, describing subjects etc.: 'It can be said that this relation between different elements (some of which are new, while others were already in existence) is effected by clinical discourse: it is this, as a practice, that establishes between them all a system of relations that is not "really" given or constituted *a priori*.'[82]

The assertion of the primacy of the discursive over the non-discursive realm has evoked much controversy. Dreyfus and Rabinow have argued that in order for a discursive formation to develop, there would seem to have to be some already constituted coherence between institutional practices for the two realms to mesh. It may be possible to describe an institution such as a university as a discursive formation in the light of the specific network of relations it establishes between individuals and fields of knowledge. However, it is also possible to think of certain non-discursive circumstances – a feudal social and economic order – which would prohibit the establishment of a modern university.[83] Such an example would suggest that social and economic practices have some unity and force prior to discursive relations, thereby undermining the notion of the primacy of discourse.

From a different perspective, Ernesto Laclau and Chantal Mouffe argue that it is inconsistent of Foucault to establish a distinction between the categories of the discursive and the non-discursive. According to the notion of discourse that they derive from Foucault's work, the category of the non-discursive is tautological. If every object is constituted as an object of discourse in that it only acquires meaning within the discursive conditions of emergence, then the discursive formation necessarily includes a notion of the non-discursive.[84] It is therefore not necessary to make a distinction between the discursive and non-discursive: 'If the so-called non-discursive complexes – institutions, techniques, productive organization, and so on – are analysed, we will only find more or less complex forms of differential positions among objects, which do not arise from a necessity external to the system structuring them and which can only therefore be conceived as discursive articulations.'[85] In Laclau and Mouffe's view, the strength of the notion of the discursive formation is that it by-passes distinctions between the material and non-material, theory and practice and the related issues of determinism and priority. By establishing a distinction between discourse and the non-discursive, Foucault reinscribes such problematic dualisms into his work.

Despite these difficulties, however, Foucault adheres, in *The Archaeology of Knowledge*, to the claim of the primacy of discursive formations in the determination of non-discursive or socioeconomic experience. Yet a close reading reveals that, in practice, Foucault is unable to maintain this claim without a certain amount of theoretical ambiguity and, at points, contradiction. This is illustrated in his discussion of the second of the systems of formation that govern the dispersion of statements in discourse, the formation of objects. As we have already seen, Foucault discounts the notion that it is the focus on a similar object of study that may provide the unifying principle for a discursive formation. This is because a given object of study does not exist anterior to discourse but is constructed within discourse. Following from this, Foucault outlines three principles that determine the formation of objects within discourse. First, there is the 'surface of emergence' which denotes the complex of social and normative relations that allow an object to first appear in order to be taken up by a discursive formation. Second, the 'authorities of delimitation' are those groups of individuals or institutions that define a particular object. For example, the medical profession was the authority in society that 'delimited, designated, named and established madness as an object'. Finally, 'grids of specification' are those systems and forms of differentiation against which an object is classified, measured and defined. Thus madness was studied, in the nineteenth century, against the background of a hierarchically ordered soul and a conception of the body as a 'three-dimensional volume of organs'.[86]

The account of these rules of formation raises the problem of the nature of the relations that exist between the different planes of differentiation in which the object of discourse appears. The definition of planes of emergence and authorities of delimitation seems to attribute a greater weight to the role that the socio-institutional context plays in the formation of the object than to the role of discourse. Yet Foucault asserts that these planes of emergence do not provide objects 'fully formed and armed, that the discourse . . . has then merely to list, classify, name'.[87] However, the distinction and priority that Foucault has in mind between a plane of emergence and a process of formation remains obscure. The issue is further confused by a second distinction that is drawn between discursive rules of formation, '*primary* relations' and '*secondary* relations':

> These relations [rules of formation] must be distinguished first from what we might call 'primary' relations, and which, independently of all discourse or all objects of discourse, may be described between institutions, techniques, social forms, etc. . . . But we must also distinguish the secondary relations that are formulated in discourse itself: what, for example, the psychiatrists of the nineteenth century could say about the relations between the family and criminality does not reproduce . . . the interplay of real dependencies; but neither does it reproduce the interplay of relations that make possible and sustain the objects of psychiatric discourse. Thus a space unfolds articulated with possible discourses: a system of *real* or *primary relations*, a system of *reflexive* or

secondary relations, and a system of relations that might properly be called *discursive.* The problem is to reveal the specificity of these discursive relations, and their interplay with the other two kinds.[88]

Not only does Foucault fail to draw out the specificity of the interrelations between these three realms, but also, by introducing the terminology of primary, secondary, etc., he appears to contradict his main postulate that it is only through discourse that the socioeconomic realm acquires order and meaning. The argument here implies that the socioeconomic realm has a coherency and order that exists independently of the discursive realm and also that this realm is somehow prior to or hierarchically privileged over the discursive realm, hence the term 'primary' or 'real relations'.

The contradictions that manifest themselves here, and at other points in *The Archaeology of Knowledge,* indicate the extent to which the problematic of determination remains unresolved. Foucault claims that an archaeological focus on the formal, internal structure of discourse allows him to bypass the issue of determination altogether: 'This style of research . . . permits me to avoid every problem concerning the anteriority of theory in relation to practice, and the inverse. In fact, I deal with practices, institutions and theories on the same plane and according to the same isomorphisms, and I look for the underlying knowledge (*savoir*) that makes them possible.'[89]

Following this logic, some commentators have argued that the concept of discourse developed in *The Order of Things* and *The Archaeology of Knowledge* enables Foucault to bypass some of the problems of economic determinism inherent in a Marxist approach, most notably in the Marxist notion of ideology as an epiphenomenal layer of illusion or misperception.[90] However, the ambiguities in Foucault's exposition of the relation between a discursive formation and its socio-institutional context suggest that while a Marxist privileging of the economic realm is thrown into question, the problem of determination is not successfully rethought.[91] Indeed, rather than providing a thorough account of the precise relations that exist between the socioeconomic context and the discursive realm, the question of determinism is in fact simply deferred in the form of a juxtaposition of these two realms. Foucault slips from an explanation of the imbrication of the discursive within the non-discursive into an antinomic formulation of the relation between the two that replicates a tendency of the structural methods that he claims to reject.[92]

It is this antinomy in the conceptualization of the relation between discourse and the social that creates further problems in the archaeological method. By maintaining an antinomy rather than an interrelation, there is a slippage in Foucault's formulation in which qualities that are properly characteristic of the social realm are attributed to the realm of discourse. This slippage is exacerbated by Foucault's rejection of any notion of the subject which may serve as a mediatory category through which the relation between discourse and the non-discursive can be understood.

The principle of rarefaction

The problematic tendency in the analysis of the archive to prioritize the formal issue of the discursive rules of formation over issues connected to the archive's non-discursive elements such as power and social relations can be illustrated with reference to the idea of the *rarefaction of discourse*. Here the priority of the discursive over the non-discursive can only be maintained through an implicit slippage in which the issue of power is transfered from the realm of the non-discursive into a formal principle of discursive regulation. Such a slippage is indicative of the tendency to juxtapose rather than interrelate the discursive and non-discursive elements within the archive.

The principle of rarefaction is offered as an explanation of why it is that, in any era, everything that can be said is never said; that in relation to the wealth of possible statements that can be formulated in natural language, only relatively few things are actually said. Following on from Foucault's distaste for notions of hidden depth or interiority, the principle of rarefaction must not be understood as a principle of repression, that is, that at any given point there is a great unsaid waiting to be uttered. Rather, at any time, it is only possible to say and think a certain amount of things: 'We are not linking these "exclusions" to a repression; we do not presuppose that beneath manifest statements something remains hidden and subjacent . . . There is no subtext. And therefore no plethora. The enunciative domain is identical with its own surface.'[93]

The problem arising from the principle of rarefaction is that while it may describe a state of affairs, it cannot adequately explain why there should be a relative paucity of statements at a given point. Foucault defines the archaeological method as a 'pure description of the facts of discourse'. Following this definition, a formal, descriptive principle cannot have the causal efficacity that is also implicitly ascribed to it. The principle sets up as a cause – the fact of rarity – what is in fact more properly understood as an effect. Dreyfus and Rabinow regard this contradiction as a result of the failure of Foucault's bracketing method, which introduces a slippage from the descriptive to the prescriptive: 'Foucault illegitimately hypostatized the observed formal regularities which describe discursive formations into conditions of these formations' existence.'[94]

A possible way out of this dilemma may be to posit a causal dynamic through reference to the social context of asymmetrical relations in which any discursive formation is situated. This is to say that if, in any period, it is only possible to speak a few things, it is because the rarefaction of discourse is crucially linked to the reproduction of relations of social domination through the control of meaning. Discourses and meaning are the site of social struggle. The process through which hegemonic social relations are achieved and maintained often involves the stabilization of discursive relations and the fixation of meaning. The construction of racial or sexual identity through the 'stereotype' exemplifies such processes of fixation. Similarly, resistance to hegemonic meaning entails the contestation and disruption of naturalized forms of discourse.[95]

In short, the idea of what it is possible and not possible to say in any given era cannot be considered apart from issues of power and asymmetrical social relations. At points, Foucault does indeed note that the principle of rarefaction necessarily raises the question of power relations:

> It [discourse] appears as an asset – finite, limited, desirable, useful – that has its own rules of appearance, but also its own conditions of appropriation and operation; an asset that consequently, from *the moment of its existence poses the question of power*; an asset that is, *by nature*, the object of a *struggle*, a *political struggle*.[96]

However, although it is acknowledged that from 'the moment of its existence' the rarity of discourse necessarily encompasses the issue of political struggle, the problem of thinking through the relation of discourse to struggle is foreclosed through the assertion of the anteriority of discourse. Such an assertion transposes the issue of power into the formal discursive principle of rarefaction.

Dispersion of the subject

The definition of the rules of formation that determine the subject position in discourse ('modalities of enunciation') raises a similar issue, namely, the nature of the relations that exist between these rules and the socioeconomic context. We have already seen that the dispersion of the subject in discourse is governed by rules that involve asking who is speaking and from what institutional site they speak. As in the discussion of the rules of formation of the object, the implication is that the non-discursive realm has a coherence and determining force prior to the discursive realm. Again, however, an analysis of the nature of the precise relations that exist between discourse and its socioeconomic context is deferred. This results in a formal account of the construction of subject positions within discourse, while revealing little about why it is that certain individuals occupy some subject positions rather than others. By neglecting to analyse how the social positioning of individuals intersects with the construction of certain discursive subject positions, Foucault reinscribes an antinomy between subject positions and the individuals who occupy these positions. Thus archaeology provides a one-dimensional, formal account of the subject of discourse.

The one-dimensionality of the archaeological analysis of the subject in discourse can be broached through a critique made by Ernesto Laclau and Chantal Mouffe of the poststructuralist dissolution of the subject. The insight of the decentred nature of subject positions often slips into the postulation of the *effective separation* of these positions. This results in an 'essentialism of the elements' which endlessly postpones an explanation of how the individual, as an overdetermined complex of different subject positions, can begin to act at all in a relatively autonomous fashion.[97] Similarly, the archaeological insistence on the dispersion of subject positions within the discursive formation provides a formal description of the range of subject positions that can be occupied by an individual. However, it does not explain why certain individuals may occupy these subject positions and why others may not. This polarity where the formal issue of the construction of discursive positions blocks a consideration of the socially governed processes through which these positions are filled is manifest in Foucault's discussion of the enunciative function:

> So the subject of the statement should not be regarded as identical with the author of the formulation – either in substance, or in function. He is not in fact the cause . . . of the written or spoken articulation of a sentence; nor is it that meaningful intention which, silently anticipating words, orders them like the visible body of its intuition . . . It is a particular, vacant place that may in fact be filled by different individuals.[98]

On the one hand, this passage rightly problematizes the notion of the author or subject as the source of meaning anterior to discourse. Yet, on the other hand, the social processes that determine how individuals come to occupy the 'vacant place' of the author and also who these individuals may be is not considered. Discursive subject positions become *a priori* categories which individuals seem to occupy in an unproblematic fashion. Indeed, the term 'different individuals' creates difficulties because it implies that individuals have a unified, prediscursive existence which enables them to step freely in and out of the different available subject positions. There is no explanation of why it may be more difficult for a woman to assume a certain authoritative speaking position than a man. Nor is there an explanation of how a discursive formation may be internally dislocated by a woman assuming a subject position traditionally occupied by men. As Beverly Brown and Mark Cousins remark, Foucault elides 'subject positions of a statement with individual capacities to fill them'.[99]

Similarly, the archaeological approach does not explain how, despite the dispersion of subject positions in discourse, individuals do not necessarily experience this dispersion as such. Archaeology brackets off a consideration of how ideology and meaning is mobilized to maintain asymmetrical social relations through the suturing of dissonant subject positions and the effacement of contradiction. Thus many feminist theorists have noted that the experience of womanhood involves the assumption of conflictual and contradictory subject positions. Nevertheless, women do not necessarily experience their lives as inherently contradictory and fragmented and this is attributable, in some part, to the work of an ideology of femininity which conceals and naturalizes these dissonances.

Archaeological analysis can explain the construction of discrete subject positions within discourse but it offers no explanation of the social context in which these positions are embedded and

which govern how they are filled. Thus, despite the nominal
inclusion of non-discursive forces in the definition of the archive,
the socio-institutional context in which the enunciative modalities
are situated remains, in effect, unthought.

Thus there appears to be an antinomy between the theorized
notion of the enunciative position in discourse and the un-
theorized concept of the individual who fills these positions in a
seemingly straightforward fashion. This antinomy between the
subject and the individual derives, in part, from the treatment of
the archive as a structure rather than as an 'event'. The distinction
between the categories of structure and event is taken from an
essay by Paul Ricoeur, where he argues that the structuralist analysis of language is essentially antinomic because it artificially
separates language from speech.[100] The premises of structural analysis apply to language as an already constituted, finished and
closed system, but do not take into account language as an act of
speech, an utterance or an event. By failing to consider language
as a living medium of communication, it also brackets off a consideration of the historical issues relating to the diachronic development of language and the dynamism of speech and intention,
the *veut dire* of language which constitutes its essential 'openness
or opening'. Thus the plurivocity of discourse is not a function of
words in themselves but an effect of their context and the creative
nature of intersubjective communication. As Ricoeur puts it: 'For
us who speak, language is not an object but a mediation. Language is that through which, by means of which, we express
ourselves and express things. Speaking is the act by which the
speaker overcomes the closure of the universe of signs, in the
intention of saying something about something to someone.'[101]

A consequence of considering language as an event is that attention is directed towards the speaking subject at the centre of
discourse. This is not to oppose a phenomenology of meaning to
a structuralist science of language. Ricoeur stresses that it is
necessary to think the dialectical unity of the atemporal system of
possibility that is language and the transitory act of speech itself;
'to produce the act of speech in the very midst of language'.
Nevertheless, discourse has the act or event of speech as its mode
of presence and this necessitates consideration of the speaking
subject and the essentially creative and intersubjective nature of
the process of communication.

The problematic implications of the one-sided conception of
discourse as a formal structure of enunciative modalities are illus-

trated in the final passages of Foucault's essay 'What is an author?'. Having analysed the different ways in which the category of the author governs the circulation of discourse in society, Foucault concludes: 'What are the modes of existence of this discourse? Where has it been used, how can it circulate, and who can appropriate it for himself . . . And behind all these questions, we would hear hardly anything but the stirring of an indifference: What difference does it make who is speaking?'[102]

The work of recent postcolonial and feminist theory has illustrated that the subject of discourse cannot be bypassed so easily. These theorists claim that the poststructuralist dissolution of the subject, exemplified in the archaeological method, accurately problematizes the category of the unified subject but is tendentious in its total rejection of any substantive notion of the subject. This rejection is regarded as a Romantic gesture on the part of certain privileged white male thinkers who are the legitimate heirs of Enlightenment thought. The stress on the fragmentation of the subject denies those groups traditionally excluded from mainstream discourse the space in which to construct alternative identities for themselves.[103] The reformulation of the category of the subject is illustrated in work on subaltern identity and on the politics of location. Such projects do not seek to restore the subject in an unproblematic fashion; they are 'strategic' rather than 'essentializing'.[104] This is to say that, while acknowledging the 'necessarily fictional nature of the modern self', they also recognize the centrality of the idea of the subject in the formation of new political identities.[105] Such work makes it difficult to accept Foucault's assertion that in the analysis of discourse it does not matter who is speaking. The question of who speaks and the issues of power and communication it raises are as important as how it is that subjects are positioned in a discursive structure.

Ricoeur's notion of discourse as both structure and event highlights the one-sided and formal nature of archaeological analysis. On the one hand, the concept of the archive, unlike that of the episteme, captures a sense of the openness and mutability of discourse through an inclusion of non-discursive elements and its definition as a historical rather than a formal *a priori*. Yet, by failing to articulate successfully the relation between the archive's discursive and non-discursive elements, Foucault in fact produces a rigid taxonomy of discursive potentialities that says little about how discourse actually functions in a sociohistorical context. It is somewhat ironic, as Gillian Rose has pointed out, that the category of the archive finishes by replicating the aspiration of the classical episteme of instituting a universal *mathesis*.[106]

Other as epistemic break

The failure to provide a fuller analysis of the role of the subject in the discursive formation also creates problems in Foucault's conceptualization of the other. In his view, the central problem of contemporary thought is its inability to think the other: 'we are afraid to conceive of the Other in the time of our own thought.' A given epistemic order is ruled by a monolithic logic of the same: 'The history of the order imposed on things would be the history of the same.'[107] By disclosing the discursive regularities that structure and constrain thought, archaeology aims to dislocate the dominant logic of identity, thereby creating a space for the emergence of new ways of thinking. However, because of the formalist emphasis that renders archaeology unable to explain the imbrication of the discursive within the non-discursive, difference or alterity can only be thought in the problematic form of an epistemic break. The discursive regularities of the archive are hypostatized to the extent that the rule of identity logic becomes absolute and can only be contested from beyond.

Now, while hegemonic systems of thought undoubtedly operate through a logic of identity, the imposition of this logic is never total and nor, therefore, can the other be entirely external to the dominant system. As Laclau and Mouffe put it: 'A hegemonic formation also embraces what opposes it, insofar as the opposing force accepts the system of basic articulations of that formation as something it negates, but the *place of the negation* is defined by the internal parameters of the formation itself.'[108] By bracketing off questions of power, archaeology cannot think of difference in terms of antagonisms or systems of knowledge which may be marginal but also immanent in the episteme. The Romantic presentation of the other as a liminal figure hinders a recognition of the social and historical specificity of the other as the oppressed and derogated figures within a dominant system. The problem with Foucault's antinomic formulation of the relation between the dominant and its others is that it is unclear, given the absence of any interconnection or dialectical relation between the two moments, how the transition from a history of the same to an acceptance of difference is to be realized.

The conceptualization of difference as epistemic break raises a further set of problems which relate to the intrusion of a normative authorial presence. This is apparent at the end of *The Order of Things*, where Foucault considers the collapse of the modern episteme and the corresponding 'end of man'. In subsequent interviews, Foucault denies that he makes such a prediction, arguing that it would be false to view the contemporary preoccupation with the density of language as an indication of 'some new thought or new knowledge'.[109] Nevertheless, in the discussion of writers such as Antonin Artaud, Raymond Roussel, Georges Bataille and Maurice Blanchot whose work exemplifies the fascination with 'the being of language', Foucault states explicitly that 'man' has come to an end. The implosion of language in such literature indicates the limits of 'man's' identity:

> From within language experienced and traversed as language, in the play of its possibilities extended to their furthest point, what emerges is that man has 'come to an end', and that, by reaching the summit of all possible speech, he arrives not at the very heart of himself but at the brink of that which limits him ... It was inevitable that this new mode of being of literature should have been revealed in works like those of Artaud or Roussel – and by men like them.[110]

This passage is problematic because the intrusion of a normative authorial presence throws into question the claims of archaeology to be a neutral form of analysis which confines itself to a 'pure description of the facts of discourse'. Under the guise of a purely descriptive archaeological standpoint, Foucault's own normative position intrudes. This 'cryptonormativism' is apparent in the slip from a quasi-objective tone to a conspiratorial 'we', in which it is assumed that the end of man is something 'whose promise we fear today, whose danger we welcome'.[111] The archive is defined as a set of rules that are not accessible to consciousness.[112] Such a definition, however, throws into question the critical standpoint from which Foucault is able to discern these subconscious structures in order to predict their collapse. As Michel de Certeau puts it:

> Who is he to know what no one else knows, what so many thinkers have "forgotten" or have yet to realize about their own thought? He acts as though he were omnipresent (since all the heteronomies of history

constitute the only account his thought will relate), but he is absent (since he has designated his own place nowhere in that history).[113]

The intrusion of a normative authorial presence undermines the opposition that distinguishes archaeology from epistemology. Epistemological investigations of knowledge are conducted through the notions of an originative subject of thought and associated concepts such as reason, objectivity and truth.[114] In contrast, archaeology eschews such normative analytical categories confining itself to a purely descriptive analysis of knowledge. However the intrusion of Foucault's own normative position dissolves the distinction between epistemology and archaeology and, in the final analysis, undermines the claims of archaeology to be a neutral and objective mode of analysis.

Bypassing of the subject

In the final analysis, the conception of difference or otherness in terms of a radical epistemic break – discernible only in a certain literary canon – is questionable because it replaces the 'ordinary' or 'pragmatic' subject of resistance by an aestheticized and ostensibly 'subjectless' practice. From this perspective, innovation and resistance cannot be initiated from below at the level of ordinary, everyday actions but must come from above in the form of an elite, poetic practice, what Michel Pecheux has called: 'the solitary, heroic moment of theory and poetry . . . as the "extraordinary work" of the signifier'.[115]

The implicit elitism of this theoretical position has been addressed by Pecheux, who regards this as a result of the abandonment, in archaeological analysis, of any notion of the subject. Like Ricoeur, Pecheux argues that discourse must be understood not as a subjectless epistemic structure, but as an event which invokes a notion of discourse as a spoken, everyday practice. Against a rule-governed, formalized notion of discourse, Pecheux argues that day-to-day discourse is marked by a profound interpretative ambiguity. Discourse takes the form of an event which has a sociohistorical specificity rather than the abstract form of a synchronic structure.

To illustrate the notion of discursive ambiguity, Pecheux cites the catchphrase of the socialist election victory in France in 1981, 'on a gagné'(we have won/one has won/it is won). The ambiguity of the phrase occurs on several levels; the subject of the statement (that is, who has won, the left, the rank and file, the party, etc.) and the object of the statement (what has been won – the election, power, what sort of power, etc.). This ambiguity arises because the phrase 'we have won' is immersed in a heterogeneous series of statements, functioning at various discursive levels with a variable logical stability. Yet, after the event, the essential ambiguity of the statement is logically stabilized and, henceforth, may be univocally responded to (yes or no, x or y).[116] In a logically stabilized discursive space, every statement reflects structural properties that are independent of the enunciation of the statement.[117] This logically stabilized discursive space forms a 'cover' over the heterogeneous regions of the real. This cover is not understood as a kind of ideological deception or mystification. Rather, in order to cope with the conflicting and diverse exigencies of everyday life, ordinary people – 'pragmatic subjects' – have a need for logical homogeneity or a semantically normalized world. Thus the boundaries of the logical cover coincide with the multiplicity of 'things to be known', the diverse and conflicting reserves of accumulated knowledge which are necessary for ordinary people to negotiate the threats and obstacles of everyday life.[118]

In order to study these multiple 'things to be known', it is necessary to recover the ambivalence and heterogeneity of everyday discourse. The recognition of the constitutive heterogeneity of everyday language leads to an understanding of utterances as always carrying the 'virtual presence' of the other, the mark of the ambiguous other meaning. This virtual presence of otherness – described by Pecheux as the 'law of social space and historical memory' – occurs at the point prior to archaeological analysis or the process of logical stabilization, where 'any utterance is intrinsically able to become other than itself, to split discursively from its meaning, to be diverted toward another'.[119] Attempts to unify this multiplicity of things to be known, to efface the essential ambiguity of everyday discourse by representing it as a homogeneous and logical structure, is to fall into the trap of a conceptually rigorous 'royal science' of structure. The 'narcissism of structure' characteristic of structural and archaeological analyses leads to a form of overinterpretation in which the ambivalences and indeterminacy of everyday language are persistently transposed into conceptually balanced, logically stabilized, subjectless discourse.[120]

There is not space here to consider Pecheux's method of discourse analysis in detail. It is of significance because it highlights certain problems with Foucault's archaeological method. Like Foucault, Pecheux is concerned to avoid the analysis of discourse in terms of a philosophy of consciousness or a phenomenology of speech. Nevertheless, he is also anxious to avoid what he regards as an analytic contempt for the ordinary that arises from the replacement of the ordinary or 'pragmatic' subject of discourse with the unified and subjectless space of a self-sustaining structure. While Pecheux counterposes the event to structure, Foucault's archaeological method effaces the singularity of the event through the superimposition of a formal system of regularities. It does not yield either an understanding of the subject of discourse or a principle of change and transformation other than the problematic idea of the epistemic break. *The Archaeology of Knowledge* provides an array of critical tools indispensable for the formal study of discourse. However, it remains a one-dimensional mode of analysis in its failure to tease out the issues of power ineluctably provoked in a consideration of the social context of discourse.

3

From Discipline to Government

Introduction

Foucault conceded, in retrospect, that the weak point of the archaeological method was its failure to incorporate a theory of power into the analysis of discourse.[1] This gap in archaeological analysis was rectified with the subsequent shift to a genealogical method, which yielded a radical reformulation of the theory of power. It is perhaps this phase of all Foucault's work that has attracted the most critical attention. His reconceptualization of power as a positive rather than as a purely negative force has had a significant impact on many different fields of study. It has also attracted a great deal of criticism, much of which focuses on a central tension in his work manifested in a slippage from the central insight of power as a positive force to a negative and monolithic notion of power as a dominatory force. This slippage generates a further series of theoretical difficulties and aporia.

Foucault's subsequent work on the idea of 'governmentality' overcomes some of the limitations of the previous notion of bio-power. The idea of governmentality broadens the category of power by distinguishing more clearly between violence, domination and the type of power relations that characterize relations between individuals. Also, power is defined both as an objectivizing and a subjectivizing force. This is to say that it is no longer understood to operate in a unidirectional fashion through the inscription of material effects upon the body. Rather, it is conceptualized as an 'agonistic struggle' that takes place between 'free individuals'. This allows Foucault to explain systems of social regulation in terms less one-dimensional than as 'an endless play of dominations'.

The order of discourse

The shift from an archaeological to a genealogical style of analysis
is signalled in Foucault's inaugural lecture at the Collège
de France, 'The order of discourse'.[2] Here Foucault begins with
the same problem that informed both *The Order of Things* and *The
Archaeology of Knowledge*, namely that given the potential for an
infinite production of meaning in discourse, there is in fact a
relative paucity or rarity of what it is possible to think and say at
any one time. However, instead of analysing this phenomenon
with reference to internal rules of formation, Foucault outlines a
series of external social forces – processes of control, selection,
organization and distribution – that govern the rarefaction of
discourse.

Firstly, discourse is controlled through procedures of exclusion
which function via strategies of prohibition, division and rejection
or the imposition of a 'will to truth'. Prohibitory strategies, for
example, operate in the realm of sexual discourses in the form of
taboos on the object of speech, constraints on the circumstances of
speech and a delimitation or authorization of certain speaking
subjects (the doctor, the sex therapist, etc.). The principle of division and rejection, illustrated in *Madness and Civilization*, refers to
the way in which 'rational' discourse necessarily derogates and
excludes the discourses and experiences of the 'other' in order to
maintain the integrity of its own identity. Finally, any society – but
especially modern industrial societies – is typified by a 'will to
truth' which establishes a distinction between truth and falsehood
and hence determines how knowledge is put to work, valorized
and distributed. For example, the modern penal system is justified
through notions of truth constructed in sociological, medical, psychological discourses as if, in Foucault's words, 'even the word of
the law could no longer be authorized, in our society, except by a
discourse of truth.'[3]

Corresponding to these external processes of discursive regulation are a series of internal procedures of rarefaction which control
and delimit discourse. The idea of 'commentary' governs discourse through a constantly revised process of differentiation between primary and secondary works which sets up a textual
hierarchy determinant of what can be said or thought about literature. Similarly, the category of the 'author' confines reception

of texts to the terms of authenticity, intentionality and creativity: 'the commentary-principle limits the chance-element in discourse by the play of an identity which would take the form of repetition and sameness. The author-principle limits this same element of chance by the play of an identity which has the form of individuality and the self.'[4] The notion of 'disciplines' keeps the production of discourse and circulation of meaning within narrow confines, pushing a 'whole teratology of knowledge beyond its margins'.[5]

A further set of procedures which control the social production of discourse operates through a rarefaction or delimitation of speaking subjects. An individual is unable to occupy a certain discursive position without, first, satisfying certain requirements. Constraints are exerted through the imposition of speech rituals, through the belonging to societies of discourse (for example, the difference between a published writer and any other writing subject) or doctrinal groups and through the social appropriation of discourse (for example, systems of education determine the extent of such appropriation). The idea of the rarefaction of speaking subjects overcomes, in part, the antinomic and formalist archaeological analysis of the enunciative modality.

These principles of constraint and rarefaction are reinforced by certain dominant philosophical themes which idealize and obscure the ineluctable embeddedness of discursive formations in social relations of power. These themes, familiar from *The Archaeology of Knowledge*, are those of a founding subject and an originating experience which tie interpretation to a phenomenology of meaning and to a Hegelian idea of a universal mediation in which events 'imperceptibly turn themselves into discourse as they unfold the secret of their own essence'.[6]

While 'The order of discourse' reiterates some of the themes of the archaeological phase, it provides a significant new inflexion to these themes. The emphasis on discourse as an internally regulating formation is replaced by a notion of discourse as determined by and also constitutive of the power relations that permeate the social realm. The rarefaction of discursive formations is fundamentally related to the maintenance of asymmetrical social relations. Entry to these discursive formations is influenced by relations of power which also overdetermine access to certain social goods and resources. There is, then, a decisive move from the archaeological postulation of the anteriority of discourse to an understanding of non-discursive relations forming the conditions of possibility of discourse.

Having outlined the structures that govern discursive rarefaction, Foucault goes on to propose an alternative set of methodological principles which yield a different conception of discourse. Firstly, there is a principle of reversal which involves regarding conventional notions of the author, disciplines, etc., not in a positive relation to meaning but in a negative relation connected to the 'cutting up' and rarefaction of discourse outlined above. The principle of specificity counters correspondence theories of truth and representation in the conception of discursive production not as an act of decipherment of a prediscursive truth but as constitutive of its objects; it is a 'violence which we do to things'. Finally, the principle of exteriority means that discourse is not analysed in terms of a hidden nucleus of meaning but in terms of its external conditions of existence, that is, the power relations in which it is embedded.

→ 90

Genealogy, the event and the body

The methodological principles outlined in 'The order of discourse' yield a form of analysis which is both critical and 'genealogical' and whose aim is to problematize the 'will to truth' and restore discourse to its character as an 'event'. The notion of genealogy and the category of the event are central to Foucault's work on power and it is in the essay 'Nietzsche, genealogy, history' that they first emerge as significant concepts.

 Traditional historiography, Foucault argues, seeks to represent the passage of time as a logical flow of causally connected events, each of which has a discrete significance and forms part of an overall pattern or meaning to history, a 'formless unity of a great becoming'.[7] Events are inserted into universal explanatory schemas and thereby given a false unity. The interpretation of events according to a 'transcendental teleology' deprives them of the impact of their own singularity and immediacy: 'The world we know is not this ultimately simple configuration where events are reduced to accentuate their essential traits, their final meaning, or their initial and final value. On the contrary, it is a profusion of entangled events.'[8] Foucault sees traditional history as falsely celebrating great moments and situating the self-reflexive subject at the centre of the movement of history. Privileging of the individual actor places an emphasis on what are considered to be immutable elements of human nature. History is implicitly conceived in terms of a macroconsciousness; it is interpreted as the unfolding and affirmation of essential human characteristics.[9] It also places historiography within a logic of identity, that is, history is read narcissistically to reconfirm one's present sense of identity and any potentially disruptive awareness of alterity is suppressed.[10]

Against traditional types of history, Foucault poses the notion, derived from Nietzsche, of 'effective' history or 'genealogy', which is connected to the idea of an 'analysis of descent' or 'emergence'. This should not be confused with a search for origins, which, in Foucault's view, is a metaphysical project which attempts to capture the exact essence of things, 'their purest possibilities and their carefully protected identities'.[11] Abandoning a faith in metaphysics, the genealogist discovers that historical events have no essence, or rather that their essence is fabricated in a haphazard fashion from 'alien forms'. Far from being teleologically governed, the historical processes that give rise to the emergence of events are in fact discontinuous, divergent and governed by chance (*aléa*): 'What is found at the historical beginning of things is not the inviolable identity of their origin, it is the dissension of other things. It is disparity.'[12] Genealogy or 'the philosophy of the event' is the method of analysis which traces the uneven and haphazard processes of dispersion, accumulation and overlapping that are constitutive of the event: it is a 'materialism of the incorporeal'.[13]

From the idea of genealogical analysis arise the concepts of power and the body. Adopting Nietzsche's conception of the primacy of force over meaning, Foucault opposes 'the hazardous play of dominations' and 'the exteriority of accidents' to the conception of an immanent direction to history. History has no immanent teleology but is based on a constant struggle or warfare between different power blocs which attempt to impose their own system of domination: 'Humanity does not gradually progress from combat to combat until it arrives at universal reciprocity, where the rule of law finally replaces warfare; humanity installs each of its violences in a system of rules and thus proceeds from domination to domination.'[14]

The human body is at the centre of this struggle between different power formations. Historical forces act upon and through the human body in a manner which cannot be explained from a totalizing historical perspective. The replacement of the self-thematizing subject with a notion of the body as the pivot of history results in a change in the historian's methodology. Historical development is no longer hermeneutically interpreted in terms of the meanings it reveals but is understood as a conflict between different power blocs, that is, permanent warfare. As the centre of the struggle for domination, the body is both shaped and reshaped by the different warring forces acting upon it. The body, then, is conceived of in radically anti-essentialist terms: 'Nothing in man – not even his body – is sufficiently stable to serve as a basis for self-recognition or for understanding other men.'[15] The body bears the marks, the 'stigmata of past experience', on its surface:

> The body is the inscribed surface of events (traced by language and dissolved by ideas), the locus of a dissociated self (adopting the illusion of a substantial unity), and a volume in perpetual disintegration. Genealogy, as an analysis of descent, is thus situated within the articulation of the body and history. Its task is to expose a body totally imprinted by history and the processes of history's destruction of the body.[16]

'Nietzsche, genealogy, history' is significant because it sketches some of the major themes around power and the body that are to be elaborated in the subsequent works, *Discipline and Punish* and the first volume of *The History of Sexuality*. Deriving from the idea that there is no immanent teleology to history, that history is rather a process of struggle between different power blocs, is the notion that power relations permeate all levels of social existence. This idea of the ubiquity of power relations necessitates a radical reconceptualization of the concept of power in general. According to Foucault most social analysts tend to regard power in an essentially negative manner, as a repressive force which is the property of an elite and is used to maintain social hierarchies. Foucault rejects such a uni-directional and repressive notion of power, replacing it with a concept of power as an essentially *positive* force which permeates all levels of society, engendering a multiplicity of relations other than those simply of domination:

> Power must be analysed as something which circulates, or rather as something which only functions in the form of a chain. It is never localised here or there, never in anybody's hands, never appropriated as a commodity or piece of wealth. Power is employed and exercised through a net-like organisation. And not only do individuals circulate between its threads; they are always in the position of simultaneously undergoing and exercising this power.[17]

This formulation does not deny the phenomenon of repression, but it does deny it theoretical primacy. Repression is not the paradigmatic form of power; it is only one in a multiplicity of positive and negative effects generated through the interplay of power relations.

It follows from this understanding of power as a positive and diffuse phenomenon that the study of power relations must be decentred. Power can no longer be analysed either in terms of intentionality – 'who then has power and what has he in mind?' – or by focusing exclusively on legitimate and institutionalized centres of power, such as state apparatuses.[18] This can only lead to an oversimplified and functionalist understanding of power. Foucault has in mind, in particular, orthodox Marxist accounts which locate the *raison d'être* of all manifestations of power at the level of the economy and class relations, and are, therefore, necessarily reductionist.[19] It is necessary to avoid 'the limited field of juridical sovereignty and State institutions' and instead to conduct an 'ascending analysis' of power.[20] This is to say that if power generates a multiplicity of effects, then it is only possible to discern these effects by analysing power from below, at its most precise points of operation – a *'microphysics'* of power. The human body is the most specific point at which the microstrategies of power can be observed. It is a microphysical analysis of the operations of power upon the body that yields the notion of 'disciplinary' or 'bio' power explored in detail in *Discipline and Punish*.

Discipline and punishment

Discipline and Punish is famous for its gruesome opening depiction of the public torturing and dismemberment of Damiens the regicide in 1757. This account is immediately followed with a description of the monotonous and regimented daily routine of a Parisian prison for young offenders some eighty years later. These sharply differing approaches to punishment frame the parameters of Foucault's enquiry in *Discipline and Punish*, namely to explore the implications of the shift from a system of justice that expresses itself in the violent spectacle of the public execution to one that unites punishment with incarceration.

This transformation in penal methods is usually attributed to the advent of the Enlightenment, when the feudal spectacle of the public execution came to be deemed uncivilized and reformers insisted on more humane forms of punishment. As in *Madness and Civilization*, Foucault throws into question this progressionary interpretation. While reformers attacked the feudal system of justice for the excessive nature of its punishments, this notion of excess is bound up not so much with an objection to the abuse of power to punish, but with a dislike for the irregularity or inefficiency of the feudal regime of punishment.[21] The main impetus underlying penal reform stems, in Foucault's view, not from an enlightened form of rationality, but from the necessity to ensure a more efficient and rationalized legal and social field. In a Weberian fashion, Foucault claims that an expanding capitalist system has a fundamental reliance on a social network that is completely calculable, dependable and efficient with regard to all aspects of the production of human labour power and the extraction of surplus value. A central weakness of a feudal, monarchical regime is that it is based on an exorbitant and spectacular use of power whose effects on its subjects are uneven and dysfunctional. The objective of the penal reform system was, therefore, not to establish a new right to punish based on more equitable principles, but to set up a new economy of power which was better distributed, more efficient and less costly in both economic and political terms: 'the power to judge should no longer depend on the innumerable, discontinuous, sometimes contradictory privileges of sovereignty, but on the continuously distributed effects of public power.'[22]

In certain respects, Foucault's study of the penal system resembles a Marxist view in so far as social transformation is connected to a fundamental economic need for a rationalized superstructure. However, as in the Weberian perspective, the economic realm is not granted any ontological or causal priority. Rather, the reforms in the penal system represent the institution of a new form of power or way of organizing social relations, which Foucault calls 'disciplinary' power. Disciplinary power is as fundamental to the growth of capitalism in the West as the development of techniques for the accumulation of capital.[23] This new regime of power centres around the production of 'docile bodies': the organization, disciplining and subjection of the human body in such a way as to provide a submissive, productive and trained source of labour power. The economic take-off of the West was only possible because the human body was already implicated in a network of power relations which both disciplined its unruly forces and increased its capacity for controlled productivity:

The body is . . . directly involved in a political field; power relations have an immediate hold upon it; they invest it, mark it, train it, torture it . . . This political investment of the body is bound up, in accordance with complex reciprocal relations, with its economic use; it is largely as a force of production that the body is invested with relations of power and domination; but, on the other hand, its constitution as labour power is possible only if it is caught up in a system of subjection . . . the body becomes a useful force only if it is both a productive body and a subjected body.[24]

The emergent prison regimes of the eighteenth century are the principal site where methods for the 'political investment' of the body are developed and refined. Order is ensured in these regimes through the control of space in strategies such as the separation of individuals, the homogenization of physical being and activity and the installation of permanent and intense forms of surveillance. Disciplinary techniques are also developed in other emergent institutional regimes, such as the school, the factory, the army, the hospital and so forth, which all form part of a 'carceral archipelago'. As Foucault puts it: 'Is it surprising that prisons resemble factories, schools, barracks, hospitals, which all resemble prisons?.'[25] In these diverse institutions key disciplinary strategies can be seen to function: the reliance on a strategy of 'enclosure', in which a space heterogeneous to all others is set apart to facilitate the operations of a 'disciplinary monotony'; a strategy of 'partitioning' within enclosed space, in which each individual is designated their own place to eliminate their imprecise circulation and possible disappearance; a 'rule of functional sites', in which particular activities are confined to particular spaces; and finally, a ranking or hierarchization of different activities that ensures the insertion of bodies and individuals within a specific network of disciplinary relations.[26]

The distillation of these disciplinary techniques is found in Bentham's Panopticon, a circular architectural structure where cells are arranged around a central viewing tower in such a way as to ensure permanent visibility. Without reliance on any physical instrument of control other than architecture and geometry, the Panopticon installs a repressive system based on a principle of permanent surveillance which ensures the functioning of power. Here Foucault extends to the theme of discipline the idea of the dominatory gaze first introduced in *The Birth of the Clinic*: 'the panoptic schema makes any apparatus of power more intense: it assures its economy . . . it assures its efficacity by its preventative character, its continuous functioning and its automatic mechanisms . . . it is a way of making power relations function in a function, and of making a function function through these power relations.'[27]

The efficacity of the panoptic principle of permanent visibility ensures its extension from enclosed disciplinary regimes to more diffuse forms of social control. Modern society is a disciplinary society based around the 'indefinitely generalizable mechanism of "panopticism".'[28] Panopticism does not simply ensure the regular and efficient distribution of bodies in space, however. The panoptic idea of permanent visibility also encompasses a notion of constant assessment or judgement: control through normalization. In a modern penal regime, for example, the prisoner is subjected to surveillance arising not only from the requirements of physical constraint but also from a set of 'assessing, diagnostic, prognostic' and normative knowledges, such as criminology, psychology, medicine, etc. These knowledges produce the pathologized subject of the 'delinquent', which in turn make it possible to police low-level criminality.

The category of the delinquent establishes divisions between the normal and the abnormal, the legal and the illegal, which implicate the subject within a set of normalizing assumptions. These normalizing assumptions are reflected in the aims of the modern penal system, which is not simply to judge the truth of a crime but to determine the reasons for a crime, why it occurred and how the offender can be rehabilitated. Attention is increasingly paid to the individual details of each case and how they can be corrected or effaced most effectively. The psychology of the individual criminal is put under scrutiny: intention rather than transgression becomes the central criterion of guilt. In Foucault's words: 'the sentence that condemns or acquits is not simply a judgement of guilt, a legal decision that lays down punishment: it bears within it an assessment of normality and a technical prescription for a possible normalization. Today the judge – magistrate and juror – certainly does more than judge.'[29]

Modern disciplinary society operates fundamentally through analogous strategies of normalization. The 'judges of normality', in the figures of the social worker, the teacher, the doctor, are everywhere assessing and diagnosing each individual according to a normalizing set of assumptions, or what Foucault calls the 'carceral network of power-knowledge'. Individuals are controlled through the power of the norm and this power is effective because it is relatively invisible. In modern society, the behaviour of individuals is regulated not through overt repression but through a set of standards and values associated with normality which are set into play by a network of ostensibly beneficent and scientific forms of knowledge. It is this notion of disciplinary power as a normalizing rather than repressive force that lies at the base of Foucault's assertion that power is a positive phenomenon, and it is explored most fully in the first volume of *The History of Sexuality*.

Power and repression

In order to validate the reconceptualization of power as a positive force, Foucault begins by unpacking the conventional notion of power as a purely repressive entity. In *The History of Sexuality*, Foucault conducts a genealogical analysis of the emergence of modern understandings of sexuality, beginning in the nineteenth century, which is commonly regarded as an era of extreme sexual repression. A slowly intensifying curve of repression is held to start at the beginning of the seventeenth century, to reach its peak in the restrained Victorian era and to decline progressively throughout the twentieth century with the growth of more liberal attitudes to sex.

Foucault questions the assumption that there should be such a sudden rupture between the Victorian era of intense repression and the permissive era of the twentieth century.[30] He claims that if the documentation on sex in the Victorian era is analysed, far from confronting a discursive paucity and even silence on that topic, a 'veritable discursive explosion' is in fact revealed. The Victorian era represents the culminating moment of an obsessive interest, first emerging in the early eighteenth century, with sex as a political and social problem: 'There was a steady proliferation of discourses concerned with sex . . . an institutional incitement to speak about it, and to do so more and more; a determination on the part of the agencies of power to hear it spoken about, and to cause it to speak through explicit articulation and endlessly accumulated detail.'[31] This proliferation of discourses on the subject of sex took the form principally of medical and psychiatric discourses on 'deviant' and marginal sexualities; the privileging of sex as a theme of confession both in a religious and clinical context; a judicial preoccupation with 'heinous' sexual crimes; an intense concern with infantile sexuality, a fixation on female fecundity, and so forth.

The obsession with the verbalizing or 'putting into discourse' of sex was not simply a quantative phenomenon but had the tacit aim of reducing or excluding forms of sexuality that 'were not amenable to the strict economy of reproduction'.[32] For example, the intense interest of the Victorians in 'deviant sexualities' results in what Foucault calls the 'perverse implantation'. This is to say that the Victorians did not suddenly discover a variety of unorthodox behaviours that had previously existed but remained unrecognized. Rather, the polymorphous conducts that constituted the object of interest were in fact extracted from or imposed on the bodies under surveillance by the network of medical, educational and psychiatric discourses in which they were implicated. This recalls Foucault's earlier point in 'The order of discourse' that discourse does not passively reflect a pre-existent reality but is a 'violence which we do to things'.

> These polymorphous conducts were actually extracted from people's bodies and from their pleasure, or rather, they were solidified in them; they were drawn out, revealed, isolated, intensified, incorporated by multifarious power devices. The growth of perversions is not a moralising theme that obsessed the scrupulous minds of the Victorians. It is the real product of the encroachment of a type of power on bodies and their pleasures.[33]

The perverse implantation has several regulatory effects. It instituted a tendency towards the *medicalization* of sexuality; sexual irregularity became linked with mental illness or deviancy and thus the sexual instinct became a legitimate object of scientific and medical study. Correlative to this process of medicalization, sexuality became implicated in a network of truth. The web of scientific and medical practices operating on the body produced a field of knowledge, a *'scientia sexualis'*, which constructs sexuality as an ostensibly empirical and 'natural' object of scientific study. The truth of individuals is held to reside in their sexuality: sexuality is regarded as the secret essence of the individual. The job of science, medicine and psychoanalysis was to uncover that truth. Truth, then, is ultimately a historically specific and relative category, the product of the effects of the various discourses – which together constitute the 'will to truth' – on the body. The body has no inherent truth; rather truths are constructed through the various categorizing strategies of a modern biopower: 'and so, in this question of sex . . . two processes emerge . . . we demand that sex speaks the truth . . . and we demand that it tells us our truth.'[34]

The sexual saturation of the bodies of individuals through discourse has a correlative effect in that individuals eventually internalize this obsession and become 'self-policing' subjects. The phenomenon of self-regulation is extorted through the tactic of the *confessional*, which, in modern society, becomes the general standard governing the production of 'the true discourse on sex'.[35] Tracing its roots back to a transformation in Catholic confessional practices in the seventeenth century, Foucault shows that sex has always been a privileged theme of confession in as much as sexual pleasure was thought to lie at the base of all sin. With the historical development of confessional practices, there is a gradual shift in focus from a relatively objective account of the acts *per se* towards a more subjective itemization of the private feelings surrounding them. During the nineteenth century, the practice of the confessional disseminates from a religious context and becomes a central tactic of secular institutional practices. In educational, psychiatric, medical, legal procedures, etc., individuals are solicited and encouraged to divulge their innermost feelings in the presence or virtual presence of an authority who has the power to 'judge, punish, forgive, console and reconcile'.[36]

Foucault regards psychoanalysis as the paradigm of the secularized, modern confessional.[37] Here, confession is not extracted from the subject under analysis; rather the urge to confess is so deeply embedded in the modern subject that it is no longer perceived as coerced but is regarded as a voluntary act of disencumberment or liberation from psychical repression. However, in Foucault's view, the disclosure of one's inner self and desires does not lead to greater self-knowledge, but merely imbricates the subject further in a network of disciplinary power relations: 'The obligation to confess is now relayed through so many different points, is so deeply ingrained in us, that we no longer perceive it as the effect of a power that constrains us; on the contrary, it seems to us that truth, lodged in our most secret nature, demands only to surface.'[38]

Control in modern societies is achieved, therefore, not through direct repression but through more invisible strategies of normalization. Individuals regulate themselves through a constant introspective search for their hidden 'truth', held to lie in their innermost identity. In so far as it is associated with the most intimate knowledge of the self, sexual identity is a linchpin of these normalizing strategies. The introspective search for a hidden essence prevents individuals from recognizing the essentially 'constructed' nature of their sexuality and, hence, from seeing the potentiality for change and experimentation.

Foucault's enquiry into the effects of the proliferation of discourses on sex results in a reformulation of the relation between power and sexuality. The prevailing idea that power merely controls or represses an 'unruly sexuality', that the relation between the two phenomenon is negative, is illusory. The idea of power as a pure limit set on freedom – the 'juridical' notion of power as law – is the dominant fiction that ensures its acceptability in modern society and disguises the productive nature of power.[39] In fact, power and sexuality are not ontologically distinct; rather sexuality is the result of a productive 'biopower' which focuses on human bodies, through a network of interconnecting mechanisms, inciting and extorting disparate sexualities.[40]

The conceptualization of the relation between power and sexuality in terms of 'immanence' rather than exteriority represents the first of four methodological rules outlined by Foucault in an understanding of power.[41] The second and third rules refer to the notion of power as a heterogeneous and uneven force. The distribution of power is constantly open to modification ('rule of continual variation') and the relation between its microscopic and macroscopic elements exceeds any notion of simple determination or reciprocity ('rule of double conditioning'). Finally, the rule of the 'tactical polyvalence of discourses' denotes the way in which the discursive formations that transmit and produce power relations are potentially reversible. This will be considered in more detail later on.

In Foucault's conception, sexuality becomes a dense transfer point for relations of power: 'Sexuality is not the most intractable element in power relations, but rather one of those endowed with the greatest instrumentality: useful for the greatest number of manoeuvres and capable of serving as a point of support, as a linchpin, for the most varied strategies.'[42] In modern society, this 'deployment of sexuality' takes four principal forms. First, there is the 'hysterization of women's bodies', whereby the female body was construed as being 'thoroughly saturated with sexuality'. Second, there is the 'pedagogization of children's sex', where the assertion that children are prone to sexual activity permits the installation of an array of neurotic practices to prevent this activity and its perceived harmful moral and physical effects. Third, there is a 'socialization of procreative behaviour', which, through various strategies, legitimates the heterosexual couple as the norm for reproduction. Finally, there is a 'psychiatrization of perverse pleasure', through which sexual 'irregularity' is pathologized.[43] These four strategies form part of an overarching tendency towards an increasing 'intensification of the body', which is the basis of modern power techniques. The control of the 'sexual' body, either through an individualizing 'anatamo-politics' or through a more generalized 'biopolitics of the population', ensures social regulation through the distribution of individuals in the domains of value and utility. Modern biopower operates through a 'life administration' which is fundamentally normalizing and regulatory: 'A normalising society is the historical outcome of a technology of power centred on life.'[44]

It is difficult to overestimate the impact that Foucault's idea of the positive nature of power and his study of this positivity in relation to the body and sexuality has had on various fields of contemporary thought. Two aspects of his thought have been particularly significant. First, the notion of a type of power which acts principally through the human body – a biopower – has provided a forceful alternative to Marxist conceptions of power, which ultimately deprive the issues of sexuality and the body of any specificity by reducing them to secondary effects of a fundamental class struggle. Foucault's theory of biopower is not meant to replace a Marxist conception. Indeed, in *Discipline and Punish*, Foucault draws heavily on a conventional Marxist account of the rise of capitalism. However, his work on power and the body has been extensively drawn on to great effect by a large number of historians and social and cultural theorists seeking an analytical framework in which to deal with cultural issues, such as sexuality, other than as secondary-level or epiphenomenal effects.

Second, Foucault's fundamentally anti-essentialist conception of the sexual body has had a significant effect on various types of feminist theory. The problem of theorizing the sexualized body without positing an original sexual difference is one that has preoccupied feminist thinkers and informs current debates over essentialism. On a fundamental level, a notion of the body is central to feminist analysis of the oppression of women because it is on the biological difference between the male and female bodies that the edifice of gender inequality is built and legitimated.

However, although the oppression of women is based on the appropriation of their bodies by patriarchy, it does not follow that oppression derives from the body or sex in any straightforward fashion. Social asymmetries cannot be reduced to an *a posteriori* effect of a natural sexual difference. In this respect, Foucault's idea that sexuality is not innate but an effect inscribed upon the body through various discursive formations seems to provide some way out of this dilemma.

The amount of academic work that has been generated from these convergences is too vast to be considered here and has been extensively documented elsewhere. However, as well as having a stimulating effect on many diverse fields of study, Foucault's theory of power is riven by certain theoretical aporia. These aporia derive from an inability to sustain the central insight of power as a positive force, and a consequent slippage into a more conventional notion of power as a negative or dominatory force. It is some of the theoretical difficulties that arise from this slippage that will be examined in the next few sections.

Discipline and resistance

While Foucault's account of a normalizing disciplinary power offers a compelling account of tendencies immanent in societal modernization, the derivation of a general paradigm of social power from the disciplinary model is contentious. One difficulty arising from such a derivation is that it leads to a slippage from a positive to an essentially dominatory model of power. As many commentators have pointed out, Foucault fails to distinguish between the totally reified power relations that characterize the 'complete and austere' institutions from which his model of disciplinary power is derived and the more open and reciprocal forms of power relations that tend to operate within other institutional sectors of society.[45] Anthony Giddens, for example, contrasts Foucault's problematic positing of the total institution as the paradigm of all social relations with Erving Goffman's treatment of the issue. In *Asylums*, Goffman shows that total institutions, by virtue of their all-embracing character and the process of 'civil death' that entry into these regimes involves, are demonstratively different from other social contexts. Taking into account these fundamental differences, total institutions can be said only to represent 'aspects of surveillance and discipline' found in other social contexts in a highly distilled form.[46]

The tendency to fall back on a negative notion of power that ensues from the generalization of the idea of discipline is exacerbated by Foucault's one-sided analysis of institutional power. Power relations are only examined from the perspective of how they are installed in institutions and not considered from the point of view of those subject to power. Peter Dews has pointed out that Foucault's analysis of the disciplinary techniques within the penal system is skewed towards the official representatives of the institutions – the governors, the architects, etc. – and not towards the voices and bodies of those being controlled. Failure to take into account any 'other' knowledges – such as a prison subculture or customs inherited from the past – which those in control may have encountered and come into conflict with means that Foucault significantly overestimates the effectiveness of disciplinary forms of control.[47]

This slippage from a theory of power as positive to an implied history of unmitigated domination has problematic implications for Foucault's postulation that resistance or counter-discourses arise at the very points where power relations are at their most rigid and intense. Following on from the idea that power is a positive force is the idea that all power relations are potentially reversible and unstable. Wherever domination is imposed, resistances will inevitably arise (the rule of the tactical polyvalency of discourses). Repression and resistance are not ontologically distinct; rather repression produces its own resistance: 'there are no relations of power without resistances; the latter are all the more real and effective because they are formed right at the point where relations of power are exercised.'[48] In this way, Foucault circumvents the problematic tendency, characteristic of his earlier work, to posit resistance in the form of a radical rupture or as an 'extra-social' force.

On this view of resistance, the sexed body is to be understood not only as the primary target of the techniques of disciplinary power, but also as the point where these techniques are resisted and thwarted. The sexed body may have been 'driven out of hiding and constrained to lead a discursive existence', but, at the same time, 'discourse transmits and produces power; it reinforces it, but also undermines and exposes it, renders it fragile and makes it possible to thwart it.'[49] Thus, on the one hand, the 'perverse implantation' of the nineteenth century – the massive proliferation of discourses on 'deviant' sexualities – served to reinforce social controls in the area of 'perversity' and to legitimate a notion of 'normal' heterosexuality. Yet, on the other hand, this very multiplication of controlling discourses created a counter-vocabulary or 'reverse discourse', which could be used by those labelled deviant to establish their own identity and to demand certain rights: 'homosexuality began to speak in its own behalf, to demand that its legitimacy or "naturality" be acknowledged, often in the same vocabulary, using the same categories by which it was medically disqualified.'[50]

Yet, despite Foucault's assertions about the immanence of resistance to any system of power, this idea remains theoretically underdeveloped, and, in practice, Foucault's historical studies give the impression that the body presents no material resistance to the operations of power. In *Discipline and Punish*, Foucault argues that disciplinary methods intensify the link between an 'increased aptitude' and an 'increased domination', producing 'subjected and practised bodies, "docile bodies"'.[51] In *The History of Sexuality*, bodies are 'saturated' with disciplinary techniques, sex is 'administered' by a controlling power that 'wrapped the sexual body in its embrace'. Individuals live 'under the spell' of telling the truth about sex; they cannot resist or even identify the 'imperious compulsion' to confess.[52] In short, Foucault tends to highlight disciplinary practices at the expense of a consideration of the various other practices that also constitute the social realm. Such practices might include the everyday activities of individuals who resist, in a mundane and 'invisible' fashion, the normalizing pressures exerted over their lives.[53] As Michel de Certeau observes, beneath the 'monotheistic' apparatuses of the panopticon, a 'polytheism of scattered practices survives'.[54]

Docile bodies and the exclusion of experience

Problems with Foucault's theory of resistance can be linked to a failure to elaborate a more rounded theory of subjectivity arising from the substitution of the concept of the person with the concept of the body. While Foucault's critique of the constitutive subject of action and knowledge is forceful, he neglects to develop an alternative conception of subjectivity, relying instead on a problematic inversion of the Cartesian body/soul dualism. In *Discipline and*

Punish, it is claimed that the human soul – and associated concepts of personality, psyche, subjectivity, etc. – are little more than the result of the operations of power upon the body. This argument is extended in *The History of Sexuality*, in the idea of the confessional that produces self-policing subjects. The effects of power on the body give rise to a certain system of knowledge, which in turn reinforces and strengthens its effects on the body through the retroactive creation of the notion of the soul. For example, the signs of 'sexual deviance' are implanted in the body through various discursive strategies. They are then retrospectively naturalized as the result of a 'perverted' personality, which in order to 'cure' itself, must confront the 'truth' of its inner nature in order to eradicate such desires. The category of the soul is, therefore, instrumental in the process through which disciplinary power converts itself into an insidious, normalizing regime of truth:

> Rather than seeing this soul as the reactivated remnants of an ideology, one would see it as the present correlative of a certain technology of power over the body . . . it is the element in which are articulated the effects of a certain type of power and the reference of a certain type of knowledge, the machinery by which the power relations give rise to a possible corpus of knowledge, and knowledge extends and reinforces the effects of this power. On this reality reference, various concepts have been constructed and domains of analysis carved out: psyche, subjectivity, personality, consciousness, etc.[55]

The advantage of such a view is that it denaturalizes understandings of human subjectivity by drawing attention to its essentially constructed nature and, by implication, its open-endedness and mutability. The problem, however, with such a conception is that it tends to reduce all forms of psychic inner life and the diversity of human experience and creativity to the effects of a unifying bodily discipline. Subjects are understood as arbitarily constructed and manipulable 'docile' bodies, rather than as persons with the capacity for autonomous experience and action. As some critics have argued, the construction of the subject cannot be explained simply through reference to bodily experiences, but must be understood as a complex and often contradictory amalgam of legal, social and psychological constructs. Too great an emphasis is placed on the effects of a corporeally centred disciplinary power at the expense of an analysis of how other forms of power – such as legal definitions of the person – contribute to the construction of the modern individual.[56] Furthermore, Foucault provides no way of going beyond the minimal notion of the subject as a purely determined category to a fuller understanding of the subject as a thinking, willing, responsible agent of choice. As Christopher Norris observes, the subject is little more than a 'place-filler, a recipient of moral directives which issue from some other, heteronomous source of authority, and which cannot be conceived as in any way belonging to a project of autonomous self-creation.'[57]

This filtering out of experience is epitomized in Foucault's critique of psychoanalysis. While its anti-repressive effects are conceded in passing, Foucault tends to dismiss psychoanalysis as directly implicated in networks of social control through its naturalization of the link between law and desire. Psychoanalysis always unfolds 'within the deployment of sexuality, and not outside or against it.'[58] The extent to which psychoanalytic theory and practice has led to an increase in the freedom and expressive possibilities for modern individuals, particularly women, in regard to their sexuality cannot be fully considered because an adequate theory of the subject around which to articulate such a notion of experience is not provided.[59] As a result, Foucault simplifies the process through which hegemonic social relations are maintained and also effaces the different types of experiences of individuals in modern society. As Axel Honneth has pointed out, Foucault's reduction of the subject to an effect of techniques of corporeal discipline resembles a crude behaviourism that 'represents psychic processes as the result of constant conditioning'.[60]

Undoubtedly, Foucault's analysis of the disciplined body provides some important insights into the way in which individuals are controlled in modern society. However, Foucault slips too easily from describing disciplinary power as a *tendency* within modern forms of social control, to positing disciplinary power as a fully installed monolithic force which saturates all social relations. This leads to an overestimation of the efficacy of disciplinary power and to an impoverished understanding of the individual which cannot account for experiences that fall outside the realm of the 'docile' body.

Marxist critique of Foucauldian power

Many of the problems that arise with Foucault's theory of power are related to the fact that a multiplicity of divergent phenomena are subsumed under a totalizing and essentially undifferentiated notion of power. In short, the concept of power is generalized to such an extent that it loses any analytic force. Many Marxists have accused Foucault of a lack of differentiation in his theory of power which results in a reductionist and functionalist account of processes of social control. There is a certain irony to these criticisms in so far as Foucault elaborated his theory of power in contradistinction to the economic reductionism that, in his view, hampered Marxist analysis. Nicos Poulantzas is more sympathetic to Foucault's work than many Marxists in that he recognizes the force of the idea that power does not work simply through techniques of repression or ideological inculcation but also through less visible strategies of normalization. However, Poulantzas goes on to argue that the Foucauldian notion of power lapses into a 'neofunctionalism' that arises from the term's lack of internal differentiation. By positing a 'metaphysical' notion of power as the original source of all forms of social control, Foucault obviates a more complex form of analysis which addresses the institutional specificity of power and the forms of its spatial and temporal mediation in the state, relations of production and the social division of labour.[61]

The problems immanent in such a diffuse concept of power have been further drawn out by Jürgen Habermas. According to Habermas, Foucault implicitly derives his concept of power from the theory of the 'will to truth', the ceaseless drive to establish normalizing regimes of truth that is characteristic of modern societies. As Foucault puts it: 'Truth is a thing of this world: it is produced only by virtue of multiple forms of constraint. And it induces regular effects of power. Each society has its regime, its "general politics" of truth: that is, the types of discourse which it accepts and makes function as truth.'[62] A result of this 'concealed derivation' of a theory of power from a dominating will to knowledge is that power is also a de-differentiated concept, understood purely as the violent installation of systems of domination.

In Habermas's view, this undifferentiated concept of power is unable to account for the complex dialectical character of modern society. In a Weberian fashion, *Discipline and Punish* shows that the rationalization of disciplinary power simply produces ever more insidious forms of bodily control. While the negative effects of the forces of rationalization on modern society cannot be denied, Habermas also argues that the rationalization of the social world has generated increasingly complex forms of freedom and individual empowerment. The individualizing formative processes that penetrate ever broader social strata are both regulatory and also constitutive of reflexive and autonomous modes of identity. Where Habermas sees the dialectic of freedom, Foucault sees the progressive subsumption of bodies under an inexorable disciplinary regime.[63]

This one-dimensional view of individuation as constraint is curious given that elsewhere Foucault asserts that freedom and constraint are inextricably linked.[64] Such a view accords with Foucault's understanding of power as a positive phenomenon. If power is to be conceived as an enabling force that permeates the social realm, then autonomy and liberation cannot be conceived in contradistinction to power. However, by levelling down the concept of power to an essentially technical notion of bodily control, the dialectic of individuation is obliterated. It is not until the development of a more differentiated theory of power and the self in his later work that Foucault is able to theoretically sustain the insight that the very means through which subjects are constrained may also constitute the means through which they may creatively express themselves.

The categorical poverty of the Foucauldian theory of power also filters out the complex and often contradictory relations that exist between different forms of institutionalized power. For example, Foucault's dismissal of juridical forms of power as a smokescreen for the covert operations of disciplinary power greatly simplifies the paradoxical role of legal power in capitalist societies. The shift from a feudal system of capital punishment to the establishment of the modern judicial order is interpreted one-sidedly by Foucault as the spread of a normalizing biopower. However, as Habermas has pointed out, if Foucault had paid attention to the development of the legal system that governs and regulates the penal process, he might have been forced to admit into the bleak vision of carceral society the undeniable gains in liberality, legal security and the expansion of civil rights guarantees. As Habermas says: 'In the welfare-state democracies of the West, the spread of legal regulation has the structure of a dilemma, because it is the legal means for securing freedom that themselves endanger the freedom of their presumptive beneficaries.'[65] The simplified account of biopower effaces the complex relations that exist between legal and other forms of institutional power and reduces the associated issues of legitimacy and illegitimacy to a technical issue of control.[66]

Ideology and discourse

A concept of ideology or any similar symbolic or non-material definition power is also sacrificed through the elision of biopower with a technical notion of control, or what Habermas calls the 'uncircumspect levelling of culture and politics to immediate substrates of the application of violence'.[67] Foucault's critique of ideology is well known and need only be briefly summarized here. Theories of ideology are rejected primarily because they necessarily imply a pre-existent truth situated elsewhere which is finally revealed with the demystification of ideological fictions.[68] The distinction between science and ideology is rejected and, therefore, the idea that there are discernible, objective truths. In Foucault's view, all science has an ideological function. The production of knowledge is ineluctably bound up with historically specific regimes of power; every society produces its own truths which have a normalizing and regulatory function. It is not surprising, for example, that political economy 'has a role in capitalist society, that it serves the interests of the bourgeois class, that it was made by and for that class, and that it bears the mark of its origins even in its concepts and logical architecture'.[69] By establishing a connection between science and ideology, questions of validity and truth are suspended. Rather, it is the task of the genealogist to discover how these discourses or 'regimes of truth' operate in relation to the dominant power structures of a given society. As Foucault puts it: 'the problem does not consist in drawing the line between that in a discourse which falls under the category of scientificity or truth, and that which comes under some other category, but in seeing historically how effects of truth are produced within discourses which in themselves are neither true nor false.'[70]

Related to the refusal of the assumed primacy of truth over ideology is the rejection of theories of ideology because they always stand in a secondary relation to some anterior determining material realm. For Foucault, as for many social theorists, the reduction of cultural phenomena to secondary or derivative effects of a primary economic realm is untenable. The third reason that theories of ideology are rejected is because they are understood to refer to 'something of the order of the subject'. Objections here arise from the notion of a constitutive and unified subjectivity that underlies the categories of true and false consciousness.[71]

In place of a concept of ideology, Foucault substitutes a notion of discourse which has been revised from its initial archaeological definition. As was indicated in 'The order of discourse', the move to genealogy overturns the anteriority accorded to discourse over non-discursive practices. This is not to say that Foucault reverses the priority and falls back into a crude material determinism. Rather, the discursive and the material are linked together in the symbiotic relationship of the power-knowledge complex. On the one hand, all knowledge is the effect of a specific regime of power, and, on the other hand, forms of knowledge constitute the social reality which they describe and analyse: 'power and knowledge directly imply one another . . . there is no power relation without the correlative constitution of a field of knowledge, nor any knowledge that does not presuppose and constitute at the same time power relations.'[72]

The effects of the power-knowledge complex are relayed through different discourses: 'it is in discourse that power and knowledge are joined together.'[73] Thus discourse, or a particular discursive formation, is to be understood as an amalgam of material practices and forms of knowledge linked together in a non-contingent relation. This connection is most clearly expressed in the notion of the *apparatus* (*dispositif*) as a system of relations that is established between heterogeneous elements so as to realize a 'dominant strategic function'. The apparatus of sex denotes the complex of medical, legal, educational and psychiatric discourses and practices that constructed sexuality as a crucial element in a network of social control. A monocausal conception of the apparatus as a consciously articulated strategy of repression is circumvented by emphasizing that, despite a moment of 'functional overdetermination', the effects generated by the heterogeneous elements may be discontinuous, uneven and conflictual.[74]

It is by linking the material and non-material together in a theory of discourse that Foucault hopes to bypass some of the problems immanent in theories of ideology. With respect to the problem of determinism, there is no prior determining moment in the theory of discourse because the effects of knowledge and power have a mutually determining and productive role.[75] With regard to the problem of truth, discursive analysis does not seek to pierce a mystificatory realm of ideas in order to uncover an objective truth; rather it examines the particular way power-knowledge complexes operate at a microsocial level in order to produce regimes of truth. With respect to the problem of the subject, genealogical analysis is conducted not in terms of the subject as the transcendental source of events, but rather in terms of the constitution of the subject within a historical framework.[76]

However, the tendency to define discursive regimes only in terms of their material or regulatory effects on the body means that Foucault finishes by presenting a reductionist notion of power as a type of material or technical control. Despite its many problematic implications, the concept of ideology provides some way of understanding power as a symbolic or non-material force. In this way it is possible to explain the maintenance of asymmetrical relations not solely through a notion of insidious bodily control but through an 'unperceived' process in which individuals are complicit, in the sense that they neither submit to a material constraint nor do they freely adopt dominant values.[77]

One set of problems that may arise from the jettisoning of a notion of ideology in favour of a materially reductionist notion of power-knowledge has been highlighted by Gayatri Spivak. She criticizes the conclusion reached by Foucault and Deleuze on the role of the intellectual in politics, that it is no longer possible to speak of representation. The intellectual should not function as a representing and representative consciousness for other political groups: 'A theorising intellectual, for us, is no longer a subject, a representing or representative consciousness. Those who act and struggle are no longer represented, either by a group or a union that appropriates the right to stand as their conscience.'[78] Such a statement is based on the belief that collectivities are formed out of struggle and not out of a language of substitution that preempts the experiences of one social group with categories derived from another. However, this seemingly altruistic gesture on the part of the intellectual is problematic because it uncritically valorizes the concrete experience of the oppressed and attributes to them precisely the form of expressive subjectivity or full self-presence that Foucault relentlessly deconstructs throughout the rest of his work. By rejecting any notion of representation, Foucault and Deleuze fall back on a crude distinction between abstract 'pure theory' and concrete applied practice – 'there is no more representation; there's nothing but action' – which itself rests on a problematic fetishization of a notion of 'Desire'.[79] Desire is presumed to provide the motivating force behind individual actions in a way that circumvents an analysis of the specific and often contradictory relations that exist between desire, need and interest. In an elliptical move, desire is accorded an apodicticism or self-evident radicality that leads directly to revolutionary political behaviour.[80]

Spivak's point is that the oppressed cannot always speak directly of their oppression and this is because of the constitutive contradictions in capitalist society which structure desires and experience and which are mediated and effaced through the work of ideology. In short, there is no necessary and direct link between the contradictory aspects of individuals' lived experience and a revolutionary awareness of the position they occupy within a capitalist system of exploitation: 'However reductionist an economic analysis might seem, the French intellectuals forget at their peril that this entire overdetermined enterprise was in the interests of a dynamic economic situation requiring that interests, motives (desires), and power (of knowledge) be ruthlessly dislocated.'[81] A theory of ideology provides a way of accounting for subject formations that articulate and conceal, on a micrological level, the macrological interests of multinational capitalism. It also offers a more complex explanation of the levels of dislocation between exploitation, experience and consciousness (knowledge) than the short-circuited link between desire, oppression and action proposed by Foucault and Deleuze: 'Reality is what actually happens in a factory, in a school, in barracks, in a prison, in a police station.'[82]

Foucault's materially reductionist or technical conception of power cannot explain how it is that the construction of subjectivity may be both determined by and also in excess of the material conditions of existence. The category of the subject is simply conflated with material processes of subjection. Foucault finishes by juxtaposing macrophysics of power to the microphysics of bodily discipline without providing any mediatory category which would explain how these two moments are held together. As Habermas puts it: 'Disciplinary power functions without the detour through a necessarily false consciousness . . . The discourses of human sciences merge with the practices of their application into an opaque power complex on which the critique of ideology makes no impression.'[83] While by no means unproblematic, the notion of ideology at least begins to address the dislocations in the formation of the subject between unconscious and conscious desires, desire and interest, experience and knowledge, etc.

Social cohesion and norm

A further problem arising from the tendency to address all sociocultural phenomena in terms of a certain level of material positivity is that the theory of power cannot provide a satisfactory account of social cohesion. Without such an account, Foucault's work finishes in an unresolved contradiction between a view of social relations as fragmented and contestable and a vision of a totally administered society. In 'Nietzsche, genealogy, history', social relations are conceptualized in terms of a dynamic of constant struggle or warfare between different power blocs.[84] Inverting Clausewitz's aphorism, Foucault argues that politics is war continued by other means, and, furthermore, that it is the function of political power to reinscribe its dynamic of struggle on to the rest of the social domain:

> If it is true that political power puts an end to war, that it installs . . . the reign of peace in civil society, this by no means implies that it suspends the effects of war or neutralises the disequilibrium revealed in the final battle. The role of political power . . . is perpetually to reinscribe this relation through a form of unspoken warfare; to re-inscribe it in social institutions, in economic inequalities, in language, in the bodies themselves of each and every one of us.[85]

This Lockean view of the social as a state of perpetual and ubiquitous struggle poses the problem of how these diffuse forms of struggle crystallize into the relatively permanent and enduring hierarchies that elsewhere Foucault regards as characteristic of contemporary social relations. The developmental logic of Foucault's theory of power, which moves from the theoretical postulation of power relations as an atomized and perpetual process of struggle to the description, in *Discipline and Punish*, of a petrified society with a 'carceral texture', implicitly raises but also defers an explanation of this problem.[86]

The analysis of power in terms of its institutionalized forms in state structures or in terms of its manipulation by various 'elite' groups is, as we have already seen, rejected by Foucault. Theories of ideology or any notion of symbolic power which might explain social cohesion at the level of belief, values or tradition are also rejected. In place of such concepts, Foucault substitutes the notion of the normalizing force of power understood as the imposition of 'regimes of truth' through the operations of power upon the body. Yet, as a result of this insistence on the material nature of power, the concept of norm that Foucault employs is also quite circumscribed. Norm does not refer to the force of tradition, collectively generated systems of values or patterns of moral action. Rather it refers to the routinized modes of behaviour that are so deeply inscribed on the body by disciplinary modes of power that they seem natural or normal. By norm, then, Foucault means normalizing. Indeed, as Nancy Fraser points out, there is a tendency in Foucault's work to elide the first notion of norm as collectively generated moral values with the second notion of a normalizing force to the extent that the first has no meaning outside of the second: the normative is inevitably normalizing.

The problem with such a limited definition of the concept of norm is that it smuggles back in, on an implicit level, a notion of violence or domination as the element which must ensure social cohesion. According to Axel Honneth, the stabilization of power struggles into an ordered system of social relations presupposes the cessation of the struggle through the means either of a normatively motivated agreement, or of a pragmatically aimed compromise, or of a permanently installed use of force.[87] By explicitly rejecting the first two explanations, Foucault necessarily relies implicitly on the third notion of the use of force or violence. The concept of violence is a logical corollary of an understanding of the social in terms of warfare and, as we have seen, permeates the description of disciplinary regimes. The notion of violence is not explicitly used by Foucault but constitutes the unthought background on which the theory of power relies. It is only with the covert notion of violence that, in the absence of any other principle of cohesion, the move from viewing the social in terms of strategic conflict to a notion of the enduring character of certain features of modern life can be explained. Yet, at the same time, a reliance on the category of violence reinstals the central dilemma of the Foucauldian theory of power, which is that, despite its positive definition, it is in fact conceived as a negative and dominatory force. As Honneth puts it: 'Contrary to his own claims, the social-theoretic determination of the character of modern techniques of power contains nothing more than the conceptually differentiated but nonetheless fundamentally reductionist idea of a one-sided rule of force.'[88]

Having outlined some of the central difficulties with the theory of disciplinary biopower, it will be shown in the remainder of this chapter how the subsequent theory of government overcomes some of these problems.

Governmentality

Foucault worked on the idea of government from the late 1970s until his death in 1984. In a key lecture entitled 'Governmentality', Foucault undertakes a genealogical analysis of the emergence of the theme of the 'art of government' in the mid- sixteenth century, where it was the dominant concern of numerous political treatises.[89] The conjuncture of two major social transformations during this period generated the intense interest in questions of government. The two transformations were the shattering of feudal social structures, which led to the establishment of the modern state, and the Reformation and Counter-Reformation. From the convergence of these tendencies towards state centralization, on the one hand, and religious dissidence, on the other, the problematic of government arose. The topic of government was considered in relation to a wide range of issues: from the issue of the correct government of one's self to the pedagogic question of the government of children and the question of the government of the state by the monarch. As Foucault puts it: 'How to govern oneself, how to be governed, how to govern others, by whom the people will accept being governed, how to become the best possible governor – all these problems, in their multiplicity and intensity, seem to me to be characteristic of the sixteenth century.'[90]

Foucault conducts his discussion of the art of government through a reading of Machiavelli's *The Prince* and shows how the notion of governmentality arose in explicit opposition to the conception of sovereign power proposed by Machiavelli. The notion of government derived from *The Prince* is one of an essentially *transcendent* relationship between the prince and the principality over which he rules. Regardless of the means through which the prince acquires his principality – through violence, treaty or inheritance – the link remains a purely synthetic one: 'there is no fundamental, essential, natural and juridical connection between the prince and his principality.'[91] The prince stands in a relation of singularity and externality to his principality. A corollary of the external nature of the link between the prince and the principality is that the link is also fragile and continually under threat. The prince's main objective in the exercise of power must be to strengthen and reinforce the principality, understood not as 'the objective ensemble of its subjects and the territory' but rather as 'the prince's relation

with what he owns, with the territory he has inherited or acquired, and with his subjects'. The art of government consists in
identifying dangers and manipulating the relations of force that
allow the prince to ensure the protection of his principality. In short, it
amounts to the prince's ability to keep his principality.

The idea of the arts of government is formulated in opposition
to this monarchical notion of power. For the anti-Machiavellians,
the ability to retain one's principality does not amount to the same
thing as possessing the art of governing. A key difference is that
whereas the prince is in a position of singularity and transcendence *vis-à-vis* his principality, practices of government are *multifarious* and *immanent* in the state and society: 'the multiplicity and
immanence of these activities distinguishes them radically from
the transcendent singularity of Machiavelli's prince.'[92] A further
difference is that, in the juridical theory of sovereignty, a radical
discontinuity is established and constantly redefined between the
legitimate power of the prince and other 'illegitimate' forms of
power. In contrast, a continuity is maintained between the different forms of power that compose the arts of government. There is
an upward continuity in the sense that the person who governs
the state well must first learn how to govern himself correctly, and
a downward continuity inasmuch, as when a state is well run, the
head of a family will know how to look after his family, and
individuals, in general, will behave correctly. Foucault labels this
downward continuity as *'police'*, a category which, as we shall see
later, will assume some significance in the theory of government.

The central problem for theorists of the art of government was
that of the government of the family, also known as 'economy'. In
anti-Machiavellian literature, discussions of the art of government
revolve around the question of 'how to introduce economy' – that
is, the correct and most efficient management of individuals'
goods and wealth in order to make the family prosper. Related to
this is a further preoccupation with the possibility of transposing
the meticulous attention paid by the father in the government of
the family to the management of the state – that is, the introduction of economy into political practice:

> To govern a state will therefore mean to apply economy, to set up an
> economy at the level of the entire state, which means exercising towards
> its inhabitants, and the wealth and behaviour of each and all, a form of
> surveillance and control as attentive as that of a head of a family over
> his household and his goods.[93]

A further difference between the Machiavellian notion of juridical sovereignty and the arts of government emerges in connection with the nature of the object over which power is exercised. For the prince, sovereignty is exercised over territory and, consequently, over the subjects that inhabit it. In contrast, in the definition of governmentality, power is exercised over a complex of men and their 'relations to things'. This complex can be illustrated in the example of the ship, where its correct government consists not just in the management of the crew, but also in the care of the boat and its cargo, the reckoning with the wind, rocks and storms and all eventualities that may befall the ship. Government is a general form of management in which the issues of sovereignty and territory are only secondary matters in relation to the efficient management of 'men and things':

> What government has to do with is not territory but rather a sort of complex composed of men and things. The things with which in this sense government is to be concerned are in fact men, but men in their relations, their links, their imbrication with those other things which are wealth, resources, means of subsistence, the territory with its specific qualities, climate, irrigation, fertility, etc.; men in their relation to that other kind of things, customs, habits, ways of acting . . . lastly, men in relation to that other kind of things, accidents and misfortunes...[94]

The aim of this form of government is the most efficient and productive disposal of things. In this sense, government resembles discipline, in that disciplinary techniques aim to maximize the utility and productive output of the human body. This contrasts with the finality of sovereignty, which is grounded in the idea of the sovereign's right to rule in so far as he bears the common good in mind. This notion of the common good is, in turn, based on an idea of obedience to the law: '"the common good" means essentially obedience to the law, either that of their earthly sovereign or that of God, the absolute sovereign.'[95] The ends and justification of sovereignty are essentially circular or self-referential: 'the end of sovereignty is the exercise of sovereignty. The good is obedience to the law, hence the good for sovereignty is that people should obey it.'[96] Against the self-referential juridical notion of sovereignty, the ends of government rest in the disposal of things in the most correct and efficient manner through the deployment of a plurality of tactics. Whereas the end of sovereignty is internal to itself in the form of obedience to the law, for government the law has no significance. Its finality is instrumental in that it resides in 'the things it manages and in the pursuit of the perfection and intensification of the processes which it directs; and the instruments of government, instead of being laws, now come to be a range of multiform tactics.'[97]

The preoccupation with government arose with the decline of the belief in divine or natural right that underpinned the feudal order, and its replacement with a notion of the state believed to possess its own immanent rational principles of order. Initially, however, the notion of the reason of the state was conceived in terms of the exercise of sovereignty and this hindered the development of the theory of the arts of government: 'so long as the institutions of sovereignty were the basic political institutions and the exercise of power was conceived as an exercise of sovereignty, the art of government could not be developed in a specific and autonomous manner.'[98] However, with the demographic expansion of eighteenth century and the growth of capitalism, the science of the arts of government was recentred from the theme of the family to that of the *population*. With the displacement of the model of the family by that of the population, new forms of study arose which led to the analysis of population in terms of its own regularities, its own cycles of scarcity, its own rate of death and diseases, etc. Arising from these new knowledges, a range of techniques of government are developed whose principal aim is to manipulate populations in such a way as to increase their wealth, longevity, health, productivity, etc.

Here Foucault extends the theme, first introduced in *The History of Sexuality*, of the biopolitical control of populations. On the one hand, biopower focuses on the individual human body as a machine and tries to extort from it greater efficiency, productivity and economy of movement. On the other hand, biopower takes as its target the biological processes of the collective social body by attempting to increase life expectancy, birthrate, levels of health, etc.[99] With the shift from biopower to governmentality, this theme of the efficient management of the population acquires new centrality:

> The population ... is ... the object in the hands of government, aware, *vis-à-vis* the government, of what it wants, but ignorant of what is being done to it. Interest at the level of the consciousness of each individual who goes to make up the population, and interest considered as interest of the population regardless of what the particular interests and aspirations may be of the individuals who compose it, this is the new target and the fundamental instrument of the government of population: the

birth of a new art, or at any rate of a range of absolutely new tactics and techniques.[100]

It is with the recentring of the art of government from the problem of the family to that of the population that the modern under-standing of the 'economic' emerged in the sense of the recognition of continuous and multiple networks of relations between popu-lation, territory and wealth.[101]

Governmentality and the modern state

From the study of the theme of government in sixteenth-century political theory, Foucault develops a new paradigm in which to understand the operations of power in modern society. The notion of government does not replace the theory of disciplinary bio-power; rather modern societies are characterized by a triangular power complex: sovereignty–discipline–government or *govern-mentality*.

The notion of governmentality is counterposed to statist concep-tions of power, which, in Foucault's view, erroneously dominate modern understandings of social relations. It has been noted al-ready that Foucault's work on discipline subsumes a critique of the notion of the state under a more general attack on the notion of sovereignty. Foucault argues that the state and sovereignty both rely on juridical conceptions of power as a negative or re-pressive force. The limited conception of power as an institutional and prohibitory phenomenon cannot adequately explain the range of infinitessimal power relations that permeate the body, sexuality, the family, kinship, discourse, etc. Although these realms stand in some kind of 'conditioning-conditioned' relation to a prohibitory state power, this relation is not one of direct causality but is sustained, in an indirect and erratic fashion, through a multiplicity of mediatory power networks: 'this meta-power with its prohibitions can only take hold and secure its footing where it is rooted in a whole series of multiple and indefinite power relations that supply the necessary basis for the great negative forms of power.'[102]

The notion of governmentality extends this critique of the state. According to Foucault, the state figures in two basic forms in modern thought, both of which attribute excessive importance to the concept. On the one hand, certain types of liberal thought conceive the state as a reified *'monstre froid'*, against which civil society – understood in oppositional terms as embodying values such as the freedom and autonomy of the individual – is pitted.[103] On the other hand, there are more functionalist conceptions, for example Marxist views, where the state is understood as the body which ensures the maintenance and reproduction of capitalist relations of production: 'This reductionist vision of the relative importance of the state's role nevertheless invariably renders it absolutely essential as a target needing to be attacked and a privileged position needing to be occupied.'[104]

The state, in Foucault's view, does not have the 'unity', 'individuality' or 'rigorous functionality' accorded to it by either of these conceptions. In place of such a 'mythicized abstraction' which leads to the *'étatization of society'*, he proposes that the state be conceived as a composite reality expressed in the formulation of the *'governmentalization of the state'*. This denotes the way in which, historically, the modern state has adapted and strengthened itself through the adoption of multifarious techniques of government which are not necessarily immanent in the state or deployed in an intentional fashion. This is to say that although strategies of government may result in the efficient management of the population, there is not necessarily a causal link between these strategies and a centralized state power. Like the notion of the *dispositif*, governmentality refers, therefore, to a series of regulatory strategies that are heterogeneous and indirect:

> If the state is what it is today, this is so precisely thanks to this governmentality, which is at once internal and external to the state, since it is the tactics of government which make possible the continual definition and redefinition of what is within the competence of the state and what is not, the public versus the private, and so on; thus the state can only be understood in its survival and its limits on the basis of the general tactics of governmentality.[105]

Police and pastoral power

In the lecture entitled 'Omnes et singulatim: towards a criticism of political reason', Foucault provides an illustration of techniques of government which are also designated through the term *'ap-*

paratuses of security'.[106] The idea of the 'police' denotes a cluster of apparatuses of security that are central to the governmental techniques of the modern state. Tracing its emergence in the work of French and German political thinkers of the seventeenth century, Foucault shows how the category of the police was understood not as an institution primarily concerned with the enforcement of the law but in more diffuse terms. In a discussion of the constitution of the state, Turquet de Mayenne delineates four grand officials besides the king: one each in charge of justice, the army, the exchequer and the police. The function of the official in charge of the police is broadly defined as fostering among the nation's subjects 'modesty, charity, loyalty, industriousness, friendly cooperation, honesty'.[107]

Emphasis is placed on a particular phrase used by Turquet, that 'The police's true object is man', referring again to the governmental notion of the efficient management of the population through the manipulation of 'men' in their relation to things. The aim of the management of men in their relations to things is firstly, to provide the city with 'adornment, form and splendour' and, secondly, to ensure 'communication' in the sense of working and trading relations between men: 'Men and things are envisioned as to their relationships: men's coexistence on a territory; their relationships as to property; what they produce; what is exchanged on the market. It also considers how they live . . . What the police see to is a live, active, productive man.'[108]

From the work of these early political thinkers, Foucault derives a notion of the police as a form of rational intervention that exerts a political power over men. By efficiently managing the communication of men – their activities such as work, production, exchange, consumption, etc. – human beings are supplied with a 'little extra life', and simultaneously the state is supplied with a 'little extra strength': 'life is the object of the police: the indispensable, the useful, and the superfluous. That people survive, live and even do better than just that, is what the police has to ensure.'[109]

A further cluster of apparatuses of security, which are central to modern governmental techniques, are denoted in the idea of *pastoral power*. The theme of *'pastorship'* illustrates the idea of a form of regulation that is originally extraneous to the realm of the state but is eventually absorbed into governmental techniques.[110] The notion of pastorship also expresses the central dynamic of the concept of governmentality – a dynamic that distinguishes it from the earlier theory of biopower – namely that it is a form of power that is both *totalizing* and *individualizing*. On the one hand, the type of power exercised in pastorship can be related to the totalizing interests of the centralized state in that it can be characterized as 'power techniques intended to rule [individuals] in a continuous and permanent way'. At the same time, however, pastoral power is constitutive of the individual in a way which exceeds any understanding in straightforward terms as a 'state apparatus': 'If the state is the political form of a centralized and centralizing power, let us call pastorship the individualizing power.'[111] The significance of this twofold dynamic will be considered more fully later on in the chapter.

The notion of pastorship – the idea of the deity, the king or the leader as a shepherd in charge of a flock – first appears in Hebrew thought and is subsequently intensified in the Christian tradition. Several themes run through the Hebrew notion of pastorship. Firstly, it is the relation of the shepherd to his flock rather than to the land which is primary. Secondly, the shepherd gathers together and unifies his flock, which, without his presence, would consist only of dispersed individuals. Thirdly, the shepherd's role is to ensure the salvation of his flock through 'constant, individualized and final kindness'.[112] Finally, the shepherd should watch over his flock with scrupulous and detailed attention.

Under Christianity, these elements in the theme of pastorship are intensified. The idea of the shepherd's responsibility for his flock is deepened to encompass the notion that the shepherd must render an account not just of each sheep but also of all their actions, 'all the good or evil they are liable to do, all that happens to them'.[113] The relation between shepherd and flock is transformed, in the Christian conception, from one of obedience to one of absolute individual dependence: 'In Christianity, the tie with the shepherd is an individual one. It is personal submission to him. His will is done, not because it is consistent with the law . . . but principally, because it is his will.'[114] Christian pastorship implies, therefore, a peculiar type of individualized knowledge between the shepherd and each of his sheep. The shepherd is not just aware of the state of his flock as a whole but is aware of what occurs in the soul of each of its members. To acquire such knowledge, classical techniques of self-examination and of the guidance of the conscience are transposed into a Christian thematics which establishes a link between total obedience, knowledge of oneself and confession to someone else. These techniques of examination, confession, guidance and obedience are constitutive of Christian identity based on a notion of 'mortification' or ascetic renunciation of the world and oneself, an 'everyday death': 'Christian mortification is a kind of relation from oneself to oneself. It is a part, a constitutive part of the Christian self-identity.'[115]

It is the Christian notion of pastoral power which, during the course of the eighteenth century, is assimilated into governmental apparatuses of security and is to become a fundamental regulatory technique in contemporary society, that is, the confessional. The dissemination of pastoral power into the arts of government involves a corresponding shift in focus from a spiritual to a secular end. It is no longer a question of ensuring the salvation of individuals in the next world, but rather of augmenting their existence in this world. Converging with the governmental concern with efficient management, salvation takes on a new meaning in a series of worldly aims such as health, well-being (in the sense of sufficient wealth and standard of living), security, protection against accidents.[116]

Totalization and individualization

The notions of the police and pastoral power both illustrate the paradoxical nature of modern techniques of government. On the one hand, governmental strategies seek to augment the happiness of citizens in terms of the conditions and quality of life. On the other hand, the achievement of such ends results in an intensification of regulatory controls over citizens: 'to develop those elements constitutive of individuals' lives in such a way that their development also fosters that of the strength of the state.'[117] It is the tension between these two aims that captures the essential dynamic of modern power as a force which is simultaneously individualizing and totalizing. This is to say that power takes as its immediate objects the individual and everyday life, drawing out their peculiarities and idiosyncracies. The very process of drawing out the individual and devoting attention to his or her well-being also serves to implicate them further within the large-scale normalizing structures that underpin society: 'This form of power applies itself to everyday life which categorizes the individual, marks him by his own individuality, attaches him to his own identity, imposes a law of truth on him which he must recognize and which others have to recognize in him.'[118]

It may seem initially that the notion of governmentality as a form of power which is both individualizing and totalizing does not substantively differ from the earlier notion of a disciplinary biopower. The key technique of biopower – the confessional – also deploys a dynamic which is at once individualizing and totalizing. Through various techniques – interrogation, hypnosis, the questionnaire – individuals are induced to reveal the most intimate and precise details about the nature of their desires, etc. 'The truthful confession was inscribed at the heart of the procedures of individualization by power.'[119] The knowledge acquired from the confessional is then recodified into the discourses of medicine, psychiatry, etc., which establish a normalizing field – a regime of truth – in which individuals are categorized as deviant, normal, etc.[120]

Despite the apparent similarity in dynamic, however, there are important differences between the theories of biopower and governmentality. One such difference turns around a shift from the conceptualization of power as an *'objectivizing'* force – a process that involves the transformation of individuals into objects or docile bodies – to viewing power also as a *'subjectivizing'* force:

> In the second part of my work, I have studied the objectivizing of the subject in what I shall call 'dividing practices'. The subject is either divided inside himself or divided from others. This process objectivizes him . . . Finally I have sought to study . . . the way a human being turns him – or herself – into a subject'.[121]

In an early interview, Foucault explains that, in the analysis of disciplinary forms of power, it is not necessary to consider the question of its mediation through the subject's consciousness because biopower takes hold of the subject's body directly: 'power relations can materially penetrate the body in depth, without depending even on the mediation of the subject's own representations. If power takes hold on the body, this isn't through its having first to be interiorised in people's consciousness.'[122]

As we have seen, the one-sided emphasis on the material effects of power on the body leads to an impoverished notion of subjectivity. Although governmentality is partially a material form of power in that it operates through the ordering of men in relation to things, it also achieves its ends, in a more indirect fashion, through the manipulation of the consciousness of individuals:

'this form of power cannot be exercised without knowing the inside of people's minds, without exploring their souls, without making them reveal their innermost secrets. It implies a knowledge of the conscience and an ability to direct it.'[123] To a certain extent, this subjectivizing element in governmental power is understood in a straightforward way as a manipulation of consciousness. This negative understanding is captured in the definition of the constitution of subjectivity as a process of subjection either to an external party or in the form of an internalization of social norms: 'It [pastoral power] is a form of power which makes individuals subject: subject to someone else by control and dependence, and tied to his own identity by a conscience or self-knowledge. Both meanings suggest a form of power which subjugates and makes subject to.'[124] Furthermore, what renders the modern state so powerful is its successful annexation of such techniques of subjectivization: 'one could say that power relations have been progressively governmentalized, that is to say, elaborated, rationalized, and centralized in the form of, or under the auspices of, state institutions.'[125] The power imputed to the state here intensifies the negative interpretation of a subjectivizing power as subjection.

Yet, unlike the earlier notion of the disciplinary control of the body, the government of individualization is not understood simply in terms of domination. The process of subjectification through which individuals are regulated also provides the basis from which resistance to such government can be articulated. This formula recalls the earlier rule of the tactical polyvalency of discourses, in which resistance arises at the points where power relations are the most intense. However, the replacement of the notion of docile bodies with a more active understanding of the subject renders the idea of resistance more plausible. Individuals are explicitly endowed with the capacity for rational and purposive action and this provides the basis for Foucault's argument that resistance to the 'government of individualization' is one of the most pressing tasks of modern times. It is necessary to explore forms of identity that escape the double bind of the individualizing and totalizing forces of modern power structures. The aim of such an exploration is not to discover what we are, but to refuse what we are:

The political, ethical, social, philosophical problem of our days is not to try to liberate the individual from the state, and from the state's institutions, but to liberate us both from the state and from the type of individualization which is linked to the state. We have to promote new forms of subjectivity through the refusal of this kind of individuality which has been imposed on us for several centuries.[126]

This resistance to the government of individualization gives rise to the project of an ethics of the self, which will be considered in more detail in the next chapter.

Discipline and communication

A correlative of broadening the concept of power to include objectivizing and subjectivizing moments is a more precise distinction between violence, domination and other types of power. The primacy accorded to the notion of discipline undermined the idea of power as a positive force, rendering it little more than a theory of domination tacitly sustained by a notion of violence. Although the theory of governmentality retains the idea of discipline, it is no longer implicitly generalized as the paradigmatic form of modern power relations. This extension of the concept of power to government makes it possible to admit other models of power into a theory of social regulation. Previously, disciplinary power was defined in opposition to all non-material forms of power, such as communication, language, symbolism.[127] However, the notion of government distinguishes between directly imposed relations of force and symbolic mediums such as relations of communication, which relay relations of power in an indirect and diffuse fashion:

> It is necessary also to distinguish power relations from relationships of communication which transmit information by means of a language, a system of signs, or any other symbolic medium. No doubt communicating is always a certain way of acting upon another person or persons. But the production and circulation of elements of meaning can have as their objective or as their consequence certain results in the realm of power; the latter are not simply an aspect of the former . . . power relations have a specific nature.[128]

Emphasis on the specificity of different types of power relation leads to a corresponding stress on the complexity of their interrelations. This is to say that social control is not always achieved through a monotonous logic of domination but is often realized indirectly through a convergence of different social practices. Thus systems of communication cannot be viewed as direct forms of domination but may produce oppressive effects through a modification of the field of information between individuals.[129]

The broadening of the concept of government to include symbolic, communicative and other forms of power provides a framework in which to explain social cohesion without relying on an implied notion of violence. This is not to say that Foucault adopts a quasi-Habermasian notion of social cohesion immanent in the principles of communicative rationality. Foucault remained critical of the idea that normatively reached agreement or consensus is a potential means through which social cohesion may be achieved. In his view, the notion of consensus is based on a fundamental misunderstanding of power relations as purely negative. Furthermore, as an ideal to be striven towards, the idea of pure consensus may be totalitarian in its effacement of difference:

> The thought that there could be a state of communication which would be such that the games of truth could circulate freely, without obstacles, without constraint, and without coercive effects, seems to me to be Utopia. It is being blind to the fact that relations of power are not something bad in themselves, from which one must free one's self. I don't believe there can be a society without relations of power.[130]

Yet, at the same time, Foucault is also suspicious of the notion of permanent dissensus: 'one must not be for consensuality, but one must be against nonconsensuality.'[131] Characteristically, Foucault did not overcome this equivocation. The theory of government does not present a definitive solution to this dilemma, it merely hints at a possible way forward. By expanding the conception of power to include techniques of regulation other than those of discipline, a theoretical space is cleared in which social cohesion may be explained in terms other than the imposition of force or 'endless play of dominations'.

The attempt to map more precisely the complex relations that exist between different power formations leads Foucault to use the notion of discipline in a more circumscribed sense. Discipline is no longer used as a general exemplar of all power relations; rather it indicates a certain freezing of the disequilibrium that normally exists between different power formations and systems of communication. A disciplinary regime represents a 'blockage' in the system where communication, power and the adjustment of abilities 'constitute regulated and concerted systems'.[132] For example, in the ordering of its space, its internal regulations, its hierarchical relations, etc., an educational institution indicates a relatively immobile and enduring system of power relations, a 'block of capacity-communication-power'.[133] Rather than being monolithically constitutive of the social realm, disciplines represent, in the form of 'artificially clear and decanted systems', the *potential* for the reification or welding together of systems of communication and power.[134] Discipline is not understood as the reduction of individuals to docile bodies, but as indicative of tendencies immanent in the process of societal rationalization which, when realized, align more 'efficiently' the diverse relations of power and communication:

> What is to be understood by the disciplining of societies in Europe since the eighteenth century is not, of course, that the individuals who are part of them become more and more obedient, nor that they set about assembling in barracks, schools, or prisons; rather that an increasingly better invigilated process of adjustment has been sought after – more and more rational and economic – between productive activities, resources of communication, and the play of power relations.[135]

From the imposition of violence to the exercise of freedom

The circumscription of the notion of discipline yields a further distinction between the unidirectional imposition of dominatory relations reliant on force and the horizontal exercise of power that characterizes relations between individuals. A relation of power is distinct from the imposition of violence, in that the former does not act 'directly and immediately' on others, but rather is an action that has an effect on the actions of others: 'what defines a relationship of power is that it is a mode of action which does not act immediately and directly on others. Instead it acts upon their actions: an action upon an action, on existing actions or on those which may arise in the present or future.'[136] In contrast, an act of violence imposes itself directly on the body or things: 'A relationship of violence acts upon a body or upon things; it forces, it bends, it breaks on the wheel, it destroys, or it closes the door on all possibilities.'[137] Violence allows no opposition to arise and, should resistance occur, it seeks to crush it: 'Its opposite pole can only be passivity, and if it comes up against any resistance it has no other option but to try to minimize it.'[138]

A power relation, however, only occurs where there is the potentiality for resistance, that is to say it only arises between two individuals each of whom has the potential to influence the actions of the other and to present resistance to this influence:

> A power relationship can only be articulated on the basis of two elements which are each indispensable if it is really to be a power relationship: that 'the other' (the one over whom power is exercised) be thoroughly recognized and maintained to the very end as a person who acts and that, faced with a relationship of power, a whole field of responses, reactions, results, and possible inventions may open up.[139]

The idea that a relation of power is constituted between subjects only by virtue of their acting or being capable of action signals the introduction of concepts that had not figured in the previous definition of biopower, namely those of freedom and autonomy. The notion of freedom is crucial to understanding the concept of government in so far as it refers not only to a process of social regulation, but also to a process in which free individuals attempt to govern others by influencing their actions. Government is *'la conduite de la conduite'* ('the conduct of conduct').[140] The absence of freedom to resist or act otherwise implies a state of absolute domination or physical constraint:

> Power is exercised only over free subjects, and only insofar as they are free. By this we mean individual or collective subjects who are faced with a field of possibilities in which several ways of behaving, several reactions and diverse comportments may be realized. Where the determining factors saturate the whole there is no relationship of power; slavery is not a power relationship when man is in chains. (In this case it is a question of a physical relationship of constraint.)[141]

The reformulation of power in terms of the concepts of freedom and autonomy is tantamount to a retrospective critique of the notion of disciplinary power in which the concepts had only figured in the form of covert normative assumptions. As many commentators have pointed out, the force of Foucault's analysis of the 'carceral' texture of disciplinary society derives in large part from a tacit appeal to concepts such as autonomy, dignity and human rights.[142] In the work on government, the ideas of autonomy and freedom are explicitly developed categories and, as such, go some way in overcoming the theoretical impasse reached with the one-dimensional categories of the body and discipline.[143]

The introduction of the categories of freedom and autonomy make it possible to sustain the original insight that the social realm is permeated with power relations which are enabling, unstable and reversible: 'In a society such as ours, but basically in any society, there are manifold relations of power which permeate, characterise and constitute the social body.'[144] With only docile bodies as the supports of the social system, the idea that power is everywhere in modern society meant that domination is universal. With the idea of the 'free individual', power relations become the necessary precondition for the establishment of social relations. States of domination are characterized by power relations which are asymmetrical and irreversible. However, the nature of normal power relations is that they are unstable and changeable. An element of freedom is inherent to all power relations in the sense that they can only operate between free individuals, and are, therefore, unfixed, fluid and reversible. Freedom and power are not ontologically distinct entities; rather freedom consists in the ability to exercise one's power autonomously: 'there is no face-to-face confrontation of power and freedom which is mutually exclusive (freedom disappears everywhere power is exercised), but a much more complicated interplay. In this game freedom may well appear as the condition for the exercise of power.'[145]

The interplay of power and freedom characteristic of relations between individuals is described by Foucault as a process of 'permanent provocation' that involves 'the recalcitrance of the will and the intransigence of freedom'. The process through which individuals seek to influence each other should not be seen as a face-to-face confrontation which paralyses both sides, but rather as an agonistic struggle in which individuals seek to refuse imposed forms of identity and also communicate their differences or 'otherness' to each other. Transposed from the realm of relations between individuals to the realm of institutional power, this process of permanent provocation takes the form of an assertion of the individual's autonomy in the face of intransigent and normalizing social structures: a struggle against the 'government of individualization'.[146]

This 'recalcitrance of the will' which is the motivating force behind political action is illustrated in Foucault's discussion of the social security system in France. On the one hand, the social security system has 'perverse effects' in that it renders individuals institutionally dependent and marginalizes them from the mainstream of social activities.[147] Nevertheless, on the other hand, the social security system also has the potential to accommodate the demand for a security 'that opens the way to richer, more numerous, more diverse, and more flexible relations with oneself and with one's environment, while guaranteeing to each individual *real autonomy*'.[148] While the demand for autonomy remains as yet unmet within the existing social security system, in Foucault's view individuals are far from passive victims of the system. They have an awareness of the problems concerning dependence and autonomy that arise from state assistance: 'From the 1950's onwards . . . the notion of security has begun to be associated with the question of independence. This development has been an extremely important cultural, political, and social phenomenon. One cannot now not take it into account.'[149] Furthermore, the capacity of those subject to the system to demand changes on their own behalf should not be underestimated: 'What we must try to appreciate is people's capacity for assuming such a negotiation and the level of compromise of which they are capable.'[150] This example of the struggle for the right to autonomy in the face of intransigent social institutions illustrates Foucault's claim that it is the 'intransitivity' of the individual's freedom that constitutes the 'permanent political task inherent in all social existence'.[151]

Foucault and liberal thought

The adoption of the concepts of the free individual, autonomy and will is somewhat surprising given their association with liberal humanist thought against which Foucault's whole oeuvre is pitched. Indeed, some commentators have taken this as a sign of defeat in that the thinker who once proclaimed the death of the subject finishes by restoring the free individual in what appears to be a retreat to a form of neoliberal thought. The use of such concepts signals an important shift in Foucault's work, but this should not be seen as a retraction of previous thought; rather it is a rethinking of the relation between his work and Enlightenment thought in general.

This rethinking takes two significant directions. On the one hand, as we shall see in the next chapter, Foucault attempts to

re-evaluate some of the central philosophical terms of Enlightenment thought with regard to the formulation of a contemporary
'ethics of the self'. On the other hand, the work on governmentality signals, not an allegiance to neoliberal thought, but rather an
analysis of liberalism as a technique of government. The liberal
notions of laissez-faire, the free individual, autonomy, etc., exem-
plify the idea of an indirect form of rule that Foucault tries to
capture in the notion of government. The dilemma for modern
systems of government, in Foucault's view, is that if one governs
too much, one finishes by not being able to govern at all. The aim,
then, of modern government is to create 'a system of regulation of
the general conduct of individuals whereby everything would be
controlled to the point of self-sustenance, without the need for
intervention'.[152] In the light of this dilemma, liberal theory provides a paradigm of modern power in that its philosophical discussions make explicit certain techniques of government that
would normally remain unrecognized. As Foucault puts it:

> It is here that the question of liberalism comes up. It seems to me that at
> that very moment it became apparent that if one governed too much,
> one did not govern at all – that one provoked results contrary to those
> one desired . . . From the moment one is to manipulate a society, one
> cannot consider it completely penetrable by police. One must take
> into account what it is. It becomes necessary to reflect upon it, upon its
> specific characteristics, its constants and its variables.[153]

Thus, while Foucault is interested in liberalism in so far as it
articulates certain dilemmas of government, there remain substantive differences between his work and liberal thought. First,
Foucault's assertion that power and freedom are inextricably mixed
differs fundamentally from the liberal view that places power and
freedom in opposition. Whereas liberal theorists posit a separation between the freedom of civil society and state intervention-
ism, Foucault rejects all such distinctions as failing to understand
the way in which power permeates the social realm. Power is the
precondition of freedom, and just as power is a system that is
never fully stabilized, so freedom, *contra* the liberal conception, is
never guaranteed or definitive. There is no static essence to freedom; rather freedom or liberty is a form of practice which must
ceaselessly challenge that which is taken to be normal or inevitable.

> Liberty is a practice . . . The liberty of men is never assured by the
> institutions and laws that are intended to guarantee them. This is why

almost all of these laws and institutions are quite capable of being turned around. Not because they are ambiguous, but simply because 'liberty' is what must be exercised.[154]

The insistence on liberty as a process of permanent contestation evokes the earlier notion of transgression as an endless principle of non-positive affirmation, an evocation that is most pronounced in the final work on ethics of the self. In his final interview, Foucault illustrates what he means by the non-definitive nature of liberty with reference to the example of sexuality. In order for people to choose freely different types of sexual behaviour, there needs to be in place already a certain state of liberation, that is, a loosening of the bonds of 'compulsory heterosexuality'. However, the consequent emergence of alternative sexual practices should not be seen as indicative of a fixed and assured state of liberation. Rather these practices have to be ceaselessly worked on and modi fied in order to ensure the continuation of a state of liberation: 'This liberation does not manifest a contented being, replete with a sexuality wherein the subject would have attained a complete and satisfying relationship. Liberation opens up new relationships of power, which have to be controlled by practices of liberty.'[155]

The second respect in which Foucault's work differs from liberal thought is in the conceptualization of the individual. Although the work on government relies on terms such as the free individual and will, they cannot be conflated with corresponding liberal notions. The individual is accorded greater autonomy than in the previous theory of biopower, but Foucault is adamant that this does not represent a retreat to a liberal view of the constitutive subject. Consistent with his earlier work, Foucault still understands the individual as an effect of power relations rather than as a 'primitive atom' upon which 'power comes to fasten or against which it happens to strike'.[156] Individuals are the vehicles of power, not its points of application.

> I . . . believe that there is no sovereign, founding subject, a universal form of subject to be found everywhere. I am very sceptical of this view of the subject . . . I believe, on the contrary, that the subject is constituted through practices of subjection, or, in a more autonomous way, through practices of liberation, of liberty'.[157]

Individuals may struggle against the government of individualization, but it is through those same normalizing strategies that they are first constituted as individuals. Unlike the theory of biopower, however, the idea of government indicates possible ways in which these power relations may fold back on themselves, opening up a space for action.[158] In short, a more dialectical view of constraint is elaborated, where it is regarded simultaneously as the precondition of and a threat to individual liberty: 'the important question . . . is not whether a culture without restraints is possible or even desirable but whether the system of constraints in which a society functions leaves individuals the liberty to transform the system.'[159]

The elaboration of the relation between individual practices of liberty and overarching social constraints is far from systematic and results in several difficulties which will be considered in the following chapter. Because of this ambiguity, Foucault's work appears, at points, to lapse into a straightforward opposition of individual to state power, echoing a classic liberal dilemma. Despite this, it must be emphasized that while Foucault was undoubtedly drawn towards certain aspects of liberal thought in his final years, the work on governmentality does not simply recapitulate its central themes. Rather, liberal thought is treated as an exemplary model of the dilemma that lies at the heart of the problem of social control in modern societies, namely the possibility of government without intervention.

4

Aesthetics as Ethics

Introduction

The idea of governmentality or the conduct of conduct designates a broad array of different relations: the relation between the state and its subjects, between 'men and things', between free individuals and the relation with the self. It is this last category of the relation with the self that yields the idea of an *'ethics of the self'*, which is developed at greater length in the second and third volumes of *The History of Sexuality – The Use of Pleasure* and *The Care of the Self*, respectively. Through the formation of a 'critical ontology of the self' it is possible to formulate an alternative ethical standpoint from which individuals can begin to resist the normalizing force of the 'government of individualization'. The idea of an ethics of the self redefines Foucault's relation with a tradition of Enlightenment thought which he rereads through the figures of Kant and Baudelaire. From this reinterpretation, Foucault is able to deploy the concepts of autonomy, reflexivity and critique and, thereby, overcome some of what have been regarded as the nihilistic implications of his earlier work on discipline.

The idea of ethics of the self partially overcomes some of the difficulties, identified in the previous chapter, arising from Foucault's insistence on individuals as docile bodies rather than as agents with the capacity for autonomous action. The idea is not, however, without certain theoretical problems, which are related to the emphasis on contemporary ethics as a form of aesthetic practice or an *aesthetics of existence*. Some critics have argued that the notion of an aesthetics of existence, understood as a stylization of daily life, amounts to an amoral project for privileged minorities. Rather than representing a rarefied morality, Foucault draws on the utopian and non-instrumental moment that the category of the aesthetic has embodied in a certain tradition of Western thought. Problems arise, however, from the centrality that is accorded in the idea of aesthetics of existence to the notions of mastery of the self derived from Ancient Greek thought and of a heroization of the self derived from Baudelaire. There are also difficulties arising from Foucault's reliance on a theoretically underdeveloped notion of aesthetics. By failing to situate a notion of an aesthetics of existence in the context of a more sustained analysis of contemporary social relations, Foucault finishes by asserting rather than justifying the radical force he imputes to the idea of ethics of the self. The ethical moment amounts in fact to little more than a fetishization of a notion of aesthetic practice.

The emergence of the self

The notion of the self emerges in conjunction with the idea of governmentality and forms part of the self-critique conducted by Foucault on his earlier work on power and the body. Foucault concedes that the emphasis he placed there on the effects of power on the body resulted in a one-dimensional account of social agents as 'docile bodies' and a correspondingly monolithic account of power. In order to obtain a fuller understanding of the modern subject, an analysis of *techniques of domination* must be counterbalanced with an analysis of *techniques of the self*.[1]

The idea of techniques of the self complements Foucault's earlier studies of the ways in which the subject is constituted as an object of knowledge ('objectivization') with an analysis of how individuals come to understand themselves as subjects ('subjectivization'). The notion of techniques or practices of the self is illustrated in Foucault's study of Ancient Greek and Roman morality in *The Use of Pleasure* and *The Care of the Self*. Foucault observes that, from a certain perspective, Ancient Greek and early Christian moral injunctions around sexuality appear similar. Not only did both cultures share injunctions relating to the prohibition of incest, to male domination and to the subjugation of women, but they also shared similar attitudes and anxieties about sex. Both Greek and Christian cultures expressed fear about the deleterious effects of uncontrolled sexual activity on the health of the individual.[2] Both cultures valorized fidelity within marriage as a manifestation of the virtue and inner strength of the partners involved. Although Greek culture was more tolerant of homosexual relations, it was possible to discern, nevertheless, the beginnings of 'intense negative reactions' and 'forms of stigmatization' in literary and artistic images which would extend to the Christian period.[3] Finally, both cultures privileged an ascetic ideal in which abstention from sexual activities and other pleasures was linked to a 'form of wisdom that brought them into direct contact with some superior element in human nature and gave them access to the very essence of truth'.[4]

However, despite these continuities which appear at the level of themes or injunctions, Foucault claims that at the level of individual everyday practice there is a key difference between classical and Christian moralities relating to the degree of self determination or autonomy tolerated within each system. Whereas in Christian thought the demands of austerity were compulsory and universal, in classical thought the demands of austerity were not grounded in a unified, authoritarian moral system, but constituted more a 'supplement' or 'luxury' to the commonly accepted morality. Individuals were allowed much greater freedom in the interpretation and application of the demands of austerity to their own lives:

> It did not speak to men concerning behaviors presumably owing to a few interdictions that were universally recognised . . . It spoke to them concerning precisely those conducts in which they were called upon to exercise their rights, their power, their authority and *their liberty* . . . These themes of sexual austerity should be understood, not as an expression of, or commentary on, deep and essential prohibitions, but as the elaboration and stylisation of an activity in the exercise of its power and the *practice of its liberty*.[5]

The difference that Foucault perceives between the classical and Christian moral systems gives rise to a distinction between *morality* as a set of imposed rules and prohibitions and *ethics* as the 'real behaviour' of individuals in relation to the rules and values that are advocated to them: 'the manner in which they comply more or less fully with a standard of conduct, the manner in which they obey or resist an interdiction or prescription'.[6]

Techniques or practices of the self are situated at the level of ethical practice. It is through a series of different practices or 'arts of existence', ranging from the concrete techniques used to order

daily existence to the spiritual significance attached to these activities, that individuals seek to interpret their experiences. Arts of
existence are, in Foucault's words, 'those intentional and voluntary actions by which men not only set themselves rules of conduct, but also seek to transform themselves, to change themselves
in their singular being, and to make their life into an œuvre that
carries certain aesthetic values and meets certain stylistic criteria'.[7]

The Use of Pleasure and *The Care of the Self* provide an extensive
analysis of Ancient Greek and classical Roman arts of existence in
relation to the formation of the desiring subject. The principle of
self-mastery or moderation which governed the daily conduct of
the Greeks was ordered around two variables: a notion of intensity of practice and a distinction between activity and passivity.[8]
With regard to the first principle, what distinguished men from
each other is not how they chose to live their lives or what objects
they desired but the intensity with which they carried out certain
practices. Immorality was associated with excessive or un-
restrained behaviour: the moral individual exercised self-restraint
and moderation in relation to all sensual activities. The second
principle pertaining to activity and passivity arises out of this
notion of moderation. For the Greeks, *aphrodisia* – loosely understood as sexual activity – was thought of as an activity involving
two actors, each with a clearly defined role and function – the one
who performs the activity and the one on whom it is performed.
The division between activity and passivity fell mainly between
adult men and women, but there was also a second division
between adult free men and a category including women, boys
and slaves. The ethical man not only exercised self-restraint in his
sensual activities but also assumed the active role. Inversely: 'For
a man, excess and passivity were the two main forms of immorality in the practice of the aphrodisia.'[9]

These two dualisms of restraint/excess and activity/passivity
constituted the moral framework within which the Greek notion
of the ethical self was situated and governed activity in the four
main areas of daily life: dietetics (bodily regimen), economics
(marriage), erotics (boys) and wisdom. In relation to dietetics,
sensual pleasure was defined by the Greeks in terms of a certain
way of caring for the body based on a distrust of excessive
regimes. Sexual conduct was considered in relation to phenomena
such as the weather and alimentary prescriptions and was ordered in closest conformity to what the Greeks considered nature
demanded. In relation to sex, there was an ambiguous borderline

between excess and restraint. Excessive indulgence could harm the body, but so too could rigorous restraint.

With regard to marital relations, the principle which obligated men not to have extramarital liasons was not one of fidelity but rather of self-mastery. Women were obliged to be faithful because of their inferior status and because they were under the control of their husbands. Men were faithful because it was a manifestation of their self-control: 'For the husband, having sexual relations only with his wife was the most elegant way of exercising control.'[10] For example, Nicocles, King of Cyprus, is faithful to his wife not out of some heteronomously prescribed sense of duty, but because as a king who commands others he must also demonstrate that he commands himself. Ethical worthiness was manifested through a public, theatrical display of self-limitation or a 'stylization of dissymetry'.

The self-conscious stylization of the asymmetrical power relations in marriage was connected to the isomorphic relation that was perceived between the household and the state. The free man respects his wife in a similar fashion to the respect he accords his fellow citizens: 'The double obligation to limit sexual activities relates to the stability of the city, to its public morality, to the conditions of good procreation, and not to the reciprocal obligations that attach to a dual relation between husbands and wives.'[11] The obligation of a husband to a wife inheres not in a personal commitment but in a deliberate limitation of power which connects the sexual self to the ethical and political self. Thus, despite the potential to tyrannize one's inferiors immanent in the structures of Greek society, the ethical individual who adhered to an aesthetics of existence refrained from such behaviour. The Ancient Greek principle of self-limitation has a voluntary aspect which distinguishes it from a universally imposed Christian notion of duty or charity. In the classical case, aesthetic and political behaviour were directly linked. If the king wants people to accept him, he must create a glory that will survive and this glory is inseparable from aesthetic value.

Unlike the relationship between husband and wife, which was regulated by the institutional constraints of the *oikos*, the principles that governed relations between men had to be drawn from the relationship itself. Whereas in the areas of dietetics and marriage, it was the man only who exercised dominating self-restraint, in the relation between men, the male loved object was also supposed to exercise self-restraint:

In economics and dietetics, the voluntary moderation of the man was based mainly on his relation to himself; in erotics, the game was more complicated; it implied an ability on the part of the beloved to establish a relation of dominion over himself; and lastly, it implied a relationship between their two moderations, expressed in their deliberate choice of one another.[12]

It is this relation of mutual self-limitation that introduces an element of anxiety into the relation between men in so far as it blurs the crucial distinction between active and passive role-playing. On the one hand, as the object of love and desire, the boy had to occupy a passive role in sexual relations. Yet, on the other hand, as a mature free man, the boy was expected to assume the active role central to masculine self-restraint. The 'antinomy of the boy' refers to this contradictory position whereby the boy had to occupy the role of object of pleasure without acknowledging that he was in that position: 'The relationship that he was expected to establish with himself in order to become a free man, master of himself and capable of prevailing over others, was at variance with a form of relationship in which he would be an object of pleasure for another.'[13]

The problem presented by the antinomy of the boy produced an ambivalence in Greek thought on the moral status of the love for boys. While ostensibly the sex of the loved object was irrelevant, emphasis was increasingly placed on how love for boys could not be morally honourable unless immanent in that relation were elements that could change it into a socially valuable tie.[14] Foucault shows how this antinomy remained unresolved until it was taken up later in Socratic and Platonic reflections on love, which problematized the desire for boys in a new way. Platonic erotics responded to the difficulties inherent in the love between men by shifting the question of love away from the object itself to an interrogation of the subject of love and to the relation between love and truth. There is a move from the deontological question about what constitutes proper conduct to an ontological inquiry into the nature and origin of love itself. The problem of the asymmetrical power relation immanent in the love between men is bypassed and replaced by a Platonic notion of convergence in true love. In so far as love is drawn to truth, it is the person who is more in love and, therefore, nearer the truth who becomes the central figure in the relationship. The master of truth takes the place of the lover and the love of the master replaces the previous concern with the status of the boy. In Foucault's view, the Platonic reformulation of erotics initiates the slow transformation towards the Christian preoccupation with the self and the renunciation of desires.[15]

The third volume of *The History of Sexuality* – *The Care of the Self* – shows how by the time of the Roman Empire this move from a deontological concern with pleasure and the aesthetics of its use to an ontological inquiry into the desiring subject has become more entrenched. In Hellenistic Rome a new way of conceiving the relationship with the self in terms of one's status, functions and activities emerges. Classical ethics had established an isomorphic relation between power over oneself and power over others. Such issues began to assume less importance in Graeco-Roman ethics and a greater emphasis was placed on the establishment of a relation with self that relied as little as possible on external signs of respect and power over others: 'It is then a matter of forming and recognising oneself as the subject of one's own actions, not through a system of signs denoting power over others, but through a relation that depends as little as possible on status and its external forms, for this relation is fulfilled in the sovereignty that one exercises over oneself.'[16]

The intensification of the relation with the self altered the daily aesthetics of existence in the four realms of the body, marriage, erotics and truth. With regard to one's physical regimen, a correlation was established between care of the self and medical practice, which was expressed through an intense form of attention to the body. It was believed that the ills of the body and soul could communicate with each other and exchange their distresses. As a result, an image arose of the adult body as fragile and threatened, and there was an increased anxiety about the ill effects on the body of sexual activity. Sexual abstinence was viewed in an increasingly positive light and there was a move towards the 'conjugalization' of sexual relations. Within marriage, there was an increased austerity in sexual relations which attempted to limit them and valorize them in relation to a 'procreative finalization'.[17] The relation between husband and wife was no longer subordinated to the needs of the *oikos* and the principle of self-mastery. Instead, there was a move towards the establishment of a more reciprocal and voluntary union between the two partners – a 'stylistics of the individual bond' – which incorporated mutual love and respect. The intensification of the concern for the self necessarily involved an increased valorization of the other.

Resulting from the privileging of the relation between men and women was a philosophical disinvestment in the love for boys.[18]

Emphasis was placed on abstention from loving boys and this abstention was no longer linked to a notion of virile self-mastery. Rather, abstention became connected to the idea of the protection of a virginal integrity from the deleterious effects of sexual activity on the body and soul.[19] In short, the Roman Empire introduced the beginnings of a universal ideal of the subject. Nature and reason became the standards against which the individual's concern for self was judged. There was an increased sense of the frailty of the self in comparison with the standards of truth against which it was assessed. Implicit in this universalization of the sexual subject was an intensification of the code element in morality. The freedom of individual ethical conduct tolerated in ancient Greek morality was replaced by more absolute notions of prohibition and obedience. Although this tendency towards the absolutization of morality does not yet compare with the levels of constraint reached in Christian morality, a certain threshold in relation to the problematization of the self has been crossed:

> One is still far from an experience of sexual pleasure where the latter will be associated with evil, where behaviour will have to submit to the universal form of law, and where the deciphering of desire will be a necessary condition for acceding to a purified existence. Yet one can already see how the question of evil begins to work upon the ancient theme . . . of art and *techne*, and how the question of truth and the principle of self-knowledge evolve with the ascetic practices.[20]

Foucault's study of the differences between Ancient Greek and Hellenic Roman practices illustrates how the relationship between codes of behaviour and forms of 'subjectivization' vary from era to era. Hellenic Roman practices are similar to subsequent Christian practices in that both are based on a morality that is oriented more towards moral codes than ethics. This is to say that the emphasis within that morality is on the individual's conformity to externally imposed codes of behaviour; subjectivization occurs basically 'in a quasi-juridical form, where the ethical subject refers his conduct to a law, or set of laws, to which he must submit at the risk of committing offences that may make him liable to punishment'.[21]

Counterposed to moralities which emphasize codes are moralities oriented towards ethics exemplified in classical Greek thought. In this second type of morality, there is a element of dynamism in so far as there exists a more flexible relation between a system of laws and an individual's actual ethical behaviour.

Rather than conformity towards the law, emphasis is placed on the formation of a relationship with the self and on the methods and techniques through which this relationship is worked out: 'the will to be a moral subject and the search for an ethics of existence were, in Antiquity, mainly an attempt to affirm one's liberty and to give one's own life a certain form.'[22] In short, this second type of morality oriented towards ethics permits a greater element of freedom in individual behaviour in relation to general rules of conduct. Individuals are relatively free to interpret the norms of behaviour in their own style, rather than conform exactly to these norms.

It is this notion of a morality oriented towards ethics, exemplified in classical practices of self-formation, that Foucault draws on to develop the notion of a modern ethics of the self. He does not believe, however, that Ancient Greek ethics can be simply transported into contemporary society as a blueprint for behaviour. Indeed, he is adamant that it is not possible to 'find the solution of a problem in the solution of another problem raised at another moment by other people'.[23] Nevertheless, in a manner reminiscent of both postmodern and pragmatist rejections of grand narratives, Foucault claims that contemporary society has reached such a degree of scepticism with regard to large-scale systems of belief that any form of contemporary ethics must arise from a more individual or localized basis. It is in this respect that Foucault is of the opinion that it is possible to learn something from the moral perceptions of the Greeks: 'And if I was interested in Antiquity it was because, for a whole series of reasons, the idea of a morality as obedience to a code of rules is now disappearing, has already disappeared. And to this absence of morality corresponds, must correspond, the search for an aesthetics of existence.[24]

What Foucault values most highly in the Ancient Greek ethics of existence is the degree of autonomy exercised by the individual in relation to the more general social and moral codes. In *Madness and Civilization, Discipline and Punish* and the first volume of *The History of Sexuality*, attention is drawn to the pernicious tendency in contemporary society to embed social norms and rights in what are erroneously believed to be the rational and objective structures of the law and science. This, in turn, leads to the individual being caught up within insidiously normalizing regimes of truth. Foucault rejects Christian ascetics, indeed Christianity as a whole, because it is a heteronomous system inasmuch as it requires the absolute subordination of the individual's moral conduct to an externally contrived set of principles. The pressure to conform obliterates the autonomy of the individual. In many respects, modern secular ethics are more insidious because they are no longer grounded in religion, but in the 'so- called scientific knowledge of what the self is, what desire is, what the unconscious is'. Modern power operates through the related techniques of individualization and totalization, where, as we have seen, the 'truth' of the individual is extracted through various disciplinary techniques and then is incorporated into normalizing structures of knowledge which efface idiosyncracies and limit individuality to a set of very specific patterns. This corresponds to Foucault's understanding of the subject as subject to someone else by control and dependence, and also as tied to their own identity by a conscience or self-knowledge. In this dual conception, the term subject suggests a form of power which subjugates and makes subject to.[25]

In contrast, Foucault regards Ancient Greek ethics as free from such normalizing pressures. Although they operate around certain central moral imperatives, the privileged moment within these ethics is what Foucault calls a 'certain practice of liberty', whereby the Ancient Greek was free to establish a relation with himself, to idiosyncratically stylize his existence in order to maximize the pleasure, beauty and power obtainable from life. It is this principle of an autonomous aesthetics of the self that is presented as an antidote to the normalizing tendencies of modern society. As we saw in the previous chapter, Foucault regards as one of the most pressing political struggles for modern individuals the 'struggle against the forms of subjection', that is, against the regulated forms of identity and sexuality that are tolerated in contemporary society:

> The political, ethical, social, philosophical problem of our days is not to try to liberate the individual from the state, and from the state's institutions, but to liberate us both from the state and from the type of individualization which is linked to the state. We have to promote new forms of subjectivity through the refusal of this kind of individuality which has been imposed on us for several decades.[26]

It is this struggle against the 'government of individualization' that lies at the heart of Foucault's notion of a modern ethics of the self. In the essay 'What is Enlightenment?', Foucault draws on the work of Kant to define the critical attitude that he sees as typifying an ethics of the self. The title 'What is Enlightenment?' is borrowed from a minor article of Kant's where he defines the Enlightenment as a break from traditional systems of thought and as a heightened critical awareness of today as difference in history. Although generally considered to be one of Kant's marginal texts, Foucault argues that 'What is Enlightenment?' is of great significance because it is the first time that a philosopher has considered his work not just as a quest for universal values, but also as a deliberation on the specific historical moment at which he is writing. Kant's text gives birth to the idea of critical reflection on the present as a motive for a particular philosophical task: 'it seems to me that with this text on the Aufklärung we see philosophy . . . problematising its own discursive contemporaneity.'[27] 'What is Enlightenment?' inaugurates the first philosophical consideration of modernity; as Habermas puts it, 'Foucault discovers in Kant the first philosopher to take aim like an archer at the heart of a present that is concentrated in the significance of the contemporary moment.'[28]

It is Kant's treatment of the Enlightenment as an attitude of critical self-awareness that Foucault regards as relevant to the formation of a modern ethics of the self. Unlike Kant, however, Foucault does not attempt to ground this critical ethos in *a priori* universal structures of rationality or morality. In a movement that parallels the earlier distinction between morality and ethics, Foucault attempts to discard the transcendental foundations of Kantian morality in the categorical imperative in order to retrieve a more embedded and historical notion of practical reason in which to base a concept of ethics. What Foucault rejects about Enlightenment thought is the linking of moral codes to a notion of a universally valid rationality. Following a Weberian argument, discourses of universal reason are regarded as indissolubly linked to the permeation of society by a pernicious instrumental or rationalizing logic in society: 'The relationship between rationalisation and excesses of political power is evident. And we should not need to wait for bureaucracy or concentration camps to recognise the existence of such relations.'[29]

The freedom of the individual from oppressive aspects of modern society is not contingent, therefore, on any metanarrative of justice or morality grounded in an idea of transcendental rationality. One such metanarrative that Foucault rejects is the discourse of humanism, which, he argues, bolsters a certain, fixed conception of human nature. It is Foucault's rejection of humanist values which have led critics to label him an anti-Enlightenment thinker. Foucault argues, however, that the Enlightenment is not coextensive with humanism. Rather, the two are in a state of tension, because while the former fosters static conceptions of human nature, the latter encourages a process of critical self awareness and self overcoming.[30] It is this second element of Enlightenment thought – 'the principle of a critique and a permanent creation of ourselves in our autonomy' – that Foucault attempts to salvage, while rejecting the humanist theme of a fixed human nature which lends itself to modern practices of the normalization and the homogenization of individuality.

Although a belief in a universally valid form of rationality is rejected, what is retained from Enlightenment thought is the notion of autonomy, which is regarded as essential to a state of positive liberty, defined as the individual's ability to exercise critical judgement free from the influence of dominant beliefs and desires. Again, for Enlightenment thinkers, this notion of autonomy is bound up with a theory of the rational and unified subject of knowledge. Ensuing from the rejection of a foundational rationality, Foucault argues that there are instead multiple and historically specific forms of rationality: 'I do not believe in a kind of founding act whereby reason, in its essence, was discovered or established . . . I think, in fact, that reason is self-created, which is why I have tried to analyse forms of rationality: different foundations, different creations, different modifications in which rationalities engender one another, oppose and pursue one another.'[31]

This does not mean, however, that it is not possible to use reason to criticize other 'rational' practices. Critique is a necessary moment in the formation of autonomy, and Foucault retains, therefore, some notion of transcendence in the sense of being able to go beyond the limits that historically have been imposed on us. Critique is directed towards an investigation of the self that is primarily historical and practical rather than ontological in a transcendental sense. For Kant, autonomy and enlightenment consisted, in part, in the 'mature' use of reason defined as the moment when 'humanity is going to put its own reason to use, without subjecting itself to any authority'.[32] It is this notion of the mature and autonomous use of reason that Foucault salvages:

> It seems to me that a meaning can be attributed to that critical interrogation on the present and on ourselves which Kant formulated by

reflecting on the Enlightenment . . . the critical ontology of ourselves . . . has to be conceived as an attitude, an ethos, a philosophical life in which the critique of what we are is at one and the same time an historical analysis of the limits that are imposed on us and an experiment with the possibility of going beyond them.[33]

Foucault redefines the concept of autonomy as a process in which the interrogation of the established limits of identity leads to an increased capacity for independent thought and behaviour. The aim of this autonomy is not to achieve a state of impersonal moral transcendence, but rather to refuse to submit to the 'government of individualization' by constantly interrogating what seems to be the natural and inevitable in one's own identity: an interrogation of the 'contemporary limits of the necessary'.[34] A Foucauldian ethics of the self is not based on adherence to externally imposed moral obligations, but rather on an ethic of who we are said to be, and what, therefore, it is possible for us to become. In this respect, John Rajchman sees Foucault's ethics as furthering the modern ethical tradition, initiated by Sartre, which revolves around the question of a 'modern praxis' grounded in a principle of freedom rather than in any postulation of nature or essence.[35]

Limit, transgression and aesthetics

The idea of an ethics rooted in an interrogation of the limits of identity recalls Foucault's early work on transgression. As we saw in the first chapter, Foucault argues, following Bataille, that in a rationalized contemporary world it is only within the realm of sexuality that the possibility of the experience of transgression remains: 'at the root of sexuality . . . a singular experience is shaped: that of transgression.'[36] Modern sexuality is 'denatured' and it is only by pushing it to its limits that a transgressive or a radically challenging experience can be undergone. Ethics of the self is also primarily a 'limit experience'. Established patterns of individualization are rejected through the interrogation of what are held to be universal, necessary forms of identity in order to show the place that the contingent and the historically specific occupy within them. For the individual, freedom from normalizing forms of individuality consists in an exploration of the limits of subjectivity. By interrogating what are held to be necessary boundaries to identity or the limits of subjectivity, the possibility of transgressing these boundaries is established and, therefore, the potential of creating new types of subjective experience is opened up:

> But if the Kantian question was that of knowing what limits knowledge has to renounce transgressing, it seems to me that the critical question today has to be turned back into a positive one: in what is given to us as universal, necessary, obligatory, what place is occupied by whatever is singular, contingent, and the product of arbitrary constraints? The point, in brief, is to transform the critique conducted in the form of necessary limitation into a practical critique that takes the form of a possible transgression.[37]

As in the earlier principle of non-positive affirmation, Foucault stresses that an ethics of the self does not accede to a definitive knowledge of the self. It is not a process that involves a liberation of a true or essential inner nature; rather it confronts individuals with an obligation to endlessly reinvent themselves. 'Modern man', he says, 'is not the man who goes off to discover himself, his secrets and his hidden truth; he is the man who tries to invent himself. This modernity does not "liberate man in his own being"; it compels him to face the task of producing himself.'[38]

The theory of an ethics of the self also recalls the work on transgression in the insistence on a certain notion of aesthetics. The experience of transgression is understood as primarily an aesthetic experience in that it occurs at the points where language and, therefore, identity break down. Literature is the privileged site of this dissolution of the subject. With the notion of ethics of the self, the aesthetic re-emerges as a central theme in the idea of a reinvention of the self that takes the form of an *'aesthetics of existence'*. Through a process of 'stylization', the individual takes the self as an object of 'complex and difficult elaboration', like a work of art: 'From the idea that the self is not given to us, I think that there is only one practical consequence: we have to create ourselves as a work of art.'[39] The kind of relation the individual has to himself or herself is understood as a type of 'creative activity'.

The insistence on the aesthetic element in ethics of the self has provoked accusations that Foucault retreats into an elitist and amoral aestheticism. The elevation of an experimental self-stylization over other forms of political and cultural struggle has been condemned as a 'project for privileged minorities, liberated from all functions in the material reproduction of society'.[40] More bluntly, in *The Ideology of the Aesthetic*, Terry Eagleton describes Foucault's theory as being little more than a celebration of 'public school virtues'.[41]

Although such criticisms are not without force, the emphasis on the aesthetic element in Foucault's ethics of the self is more complex than these commentators allow. Rather than retreating into an amoral, elitist ethics, Foucault is more concerned with rethinking the notions of creativity and aesthetics by removing them from their high cultural niche. What interests Foucault in this idea of an aesthetic reinvention of the self are the moments when art passes over into the sphere of life and gives birth to life-forms directly: 'What strikes me is the fact that in our society, art has become something which is related only to objects and not to individuals, or to life. That art is something which is specialized or which is done by experts who are artists. But couldn't everyone's life become a work of art?'[42]

Foucault's radicalization of the notion of aesthetics can be seen as an attempt to perform a task abandoned by other radical thinkers inasmuch as there is a tendency to dismiss the category of aesthetics as a repository for bourgeois values.[43] With the idea of an aesthetics of existence, Foucault draws on the critical and utopian function that the category of aesthetics has frequently performed in Western thought to the extent that the imaginative creation of other worlds has led to a powerful indictment of existing society. As Raymond Williams has observed, the history of the aesthetic response is, in a large part, 'a protest against the forcing of all experience into instrumentality . . . and of all things into commodities.'[44] The insistence on the aesthetic element in an ethics of the self represents an attempt to free the moral imagination from the mere imitation of reality and establish, in Bachelard's words, 'imagination in its living role as the guide to human life'.[45] Far from an elitism, then, it is this utopianism that the idea of an aesthetics of existence aims to activate.

Foucault combines the utopian moment present in the idea of aesthetics with a notion of the 'everyday'. As both Charles Taylor and Henri Lefebvre have remarked, a notion of the 'everyday' has come increasingly to replace more abstract concepts as the focus of philosophical concern with morality.[46] According to Lefebvre, from Plato and Aristotle to Kant, philosophy tended to bypass a consideration of the quotidian on the grounds that it was vulgar or represented the contrary of complete truth. With the advent of Marx, however, and an insistence on the centrality of work, labour and productive activity to an understanding of the human condition, a notion of the everyday has increasingly come to occupy a central place in modern philosophical thought.

The concept of the everyday has a paradoxical status. Lefebvre explains how, on the one hand, the intensification of capitalism since the Second World War and its extension into the smallest details of everyday life has meant that the everyday is the point at which forms of social control and exploitation are most noticeable: 'The huge multinational corporations are introduced into the economy by everyday life.'[47] On the other hand, the everyday becomes a potential site for opposition to the increasing administration of society along the lines of commodity fetishism. The very repetitiveness of everyday life gives rise to a profound dissatisfaction, an 'aspiration for something else'. It is from this malaise or second order alienation that the project of transforming everyday life arises. This process of the transformation of everyday life is crucial to any project of wider social change. As Lefebvre remarks: 'A revolution cannot just change the political personnel or institutions; it must change *la vie quotidienne*, which has already been literally colonized by capitalism.'[48]

In a similar fashion, Foucault argues that it is at the level of the most mundane and routine experience – at the level of a microphysics of existence – that the normalizing effects of power are most insidiously deployed. Thus what Foucault calls the 'cult of the self', the preoccupation of the modern individual with discovering the truth or essence of their identity, can only be countered through a process of critique and denaturalization of phenomena that appear obvious and inevitable – an aesthetic stylization of the self. In an article entitled 'The problem of style', George Simmel makes a similar point, arguing that the notion of style encapsulates a principle of generality that provides relief from the 'exaggerated subjectivism' of modern times.[49] The aesthetic emphasis in Foucault's ethics does not necessarily signal a retreat to a form of elitism. Rather, by drawing on a notion of the non-productive quality of art, Foucault aims to rethink a type of ethical action that escapes the instrumental rationality or utilitarian logic that structures contemporary social experience. The creation of the self as a work of art is not intended as a gesture of withdrawal; it emphasizes instead that, far from being inevitable, one's life and identity involve a process of self-creation and therefore are open to change and re-creation.

Problems with the idea of an ethics of the self do not arise, therefore, from the aesthetic element *per se*. Difficulties do arise, however, from the way in which the idea of an aesthetics of existence is elaborated through a Baudelairean notion of the hero-ization of the self. The idea of a heroization of the self is a development of the theme of 'virile self-mastery' that charac-terized the classical practices from which the model of an ethics of the self is originally derived. By failing to problematize these themes of heroization and self-mastery, Foucault's theory of an ethics implicitly relies on a conventional notion of the sovereign self, which in turn rests on an unexamined fantasy of male agency. This considerably undermines the radical force that is imputed to the idea of an ethics of the self.

Heroization and mastery of the self

For Foucault, it is Baudelaire 'the dandy' who is the paradigmatic modern individual and exemplar for the 'mode of relationship that has to be established with oneself'.[50] Baudelairean *dandysme*, or the *heroic* transfiguration of the ephemeral and fleeting mo-ment, embodies the experimental attitude – 'the difficult interplay between the truth of what is real and the exercise of freedom' – that lies at the heart of a contemporary ethics of the self: Baude-laire is modern in that he does not seek to uncover an essential inner self but rather produce or invent a new self.[51]

It is, however, the centrality that is accorded to the figure of Baudelaire that undermines the radical force that is claimed for the notion of an ethics of the self. From a feminist perspective, for example, what is problematic is the way in which the discussion of a contemporary ethics of the self is deflected on to the figure of a 'lyric poet in the era of high capitalism'. It is not simply that the choice of Baudelaire is problematic because of the misogyny that permeates his work, although that has been well documented.[52] Rather, the choice of Baudelaire raises the question of how, in the light of his radical critique of sexuality, Foucault is able to cel-ebrate, in a relatively uncritical fashion, a certain tradition which normalizes as *the* experience of modernity a *particular* and gen-dered set of practices.

Much radical work has been devoted to 'unpacking' the myth of the artist as a marginal figure with a heightened sensibility, which arose during the nineteenth century and of which Baudelaire is a paradigmatic example. Cultural critics have demonstrated how the romanticized notion of the artist as 'genius' arose in response to the dramatic expansion in capitalism and the corresponding division and deskilling of labour, which resulted in a reattribution of certain categories of skill to a redefined notion of the arts. Art gained meaning in opposition to technology, to industry and to the worker. Feminist critics have also pointed out that the conception of the artist as a free agent of creativity is based not only on a mystification of the social conditions of privilege that led to such a notion, but also that it is a profoundly gendered category. Concomitant with the reorganization of wage labour under the expansion of capitalism was an intensification and consolidation of gender relations socially organized along the rigid distinction between the public and private, the world of work and domesticity.[53] Griselda Pollock has shown how a notion of the artist both draws on and obfuscates the inscription of gender relations in heavily demarcated social space. Thus the idea of the artist as a free-floating individual steeped in the underworld of urban life drew on bourgeois norms of masculinity that allowed men to step easily between the two realms of public and private in a way that was infinitely more problematic for women. Similarly, a notion of the artist as an ungoverned agent exercising a liberated sexuality – a theme which goes from Baudelaire, through the surrealists to Cocteau – may problematize conventional notions of masculinity in certain respects. However, at the same time it reaffirms conventional notions of masculine self-determination and power: 'art was a kind of parthenogenesis uniting reason and fertility, offering a dream to men of wholeness and confirmation of their universality.'[54] Such a combination of masculinity and femininity contributes to the romantic status of the male artist but is deemed 'unnatural' in the female artist.

Foucault's indifference to the implications of gender on his work has been noted by many feminists writers.[55] Meaghan Morris has commented that: 'any feminist drawn in to sending love letters to Foucault would be in no danger of reciprocation. Foucault's work is not the work of a ladies' man.'[56] The final work on the self is no exception in this respect. However, this desexualized perspective – or in Braidotti's words the problem of Foucault's 'impersonal style' – goes beyond a case of simple 'gender blindness'. Rather, the failure to analyse more thoroughly the implications of presenting the Baudelairean dandy as the paradigm of modern ethics results in tensions and aporia which undermine Foucault's explicit arguments.

For example, Foucault insists that the starting point for an ethics of the self is a critical ontology or politics of location that is as 'precise as possible', that is oriented to the 'contemporary limits of the necessary'. Yet, having stressed the necessity for a rigorous and detailed form of self-critique, the detail that remains significantly unaddressed in Foucault's own politics of self-location is the deflection or identification that permits him to situate a conventional and gendered notion of the 'heorization' of the self at the centre of a radical ethics. As Bourdieu puts it, in a critique of both objectivist and subjectivist modes of thought: 'the unanalyzed element in every theoretical analysis . . . is the theorist's subjective relation to the social world and the objective (social) relation presupposed by this subjective relation.'[57] As in the archaeological phase of Foucault's work, there is a curious absenting or denial of a normative authorial presence on an explicit level, only for it to re-emerge in an implicitly gendered subtext.

Foucault insists that an ethics of the self embodies a 'limit attitude', and yet the frontiers of identity are located, somewhat problematically, in a figure whose work embodies an established canon of male avant-garde literature. As in his earlier work, the radicality of such a tradition of high modernist art is assumed rather than critically examined. Indeed, it may be argued that more forceful and relevant examples of a contemporary exploration of identity can be drawn from the cases of women who, increasingly, step into social settings in which the only available identities are those offered by dominant, masculine stereotypes.[58] Furthermore, Foucault fails to consider the dissonance that arises from a contemporary morality that addresses itself to women as ethical subjects but draws, nevertheless, on a tradition in which woman has historically been positioned as the 'beautiful object'.[59]

The notion of a Baudelairean heroization of the self intensifies the theme of a virile self-mastery that is fundamental to the classical practices from which the idea of an ethics of the self is derived. In *The Use of Pleasure*, Foucault notes that the moral problematization of pleasure in the classical era turned around the notion of *enkrateia*, or self-mastery seen in terms of the domination of one's desires. This notion of self-mastery had an essentially 'virile character' which involved a struggle against the immoderate and womanly side of one's character: 'That moderation is given an essentially masculine structure has another consequence . . . immoderation derives from a passivity that relates it to femininity . . . the man of pleasures and desires, the man of nonmastery (*akrasia*) or self-indulgence (*akolasia*) was a man who could be called feminine.'[60] This mastery of the self which involves a derogation of the feminine is paralleled in the social realm through the exercise of mastery – the 'stylization of dissymetry' – over other individuals.[61]

Foucault claims, as we have seen, that it is not possible to draw uncritically on classical practices to provide a model or blueprint for a modern ethics. Despite this assertion, however, the theme of self-mastery – involving a privileging of the (implicitly masculine) self over others – appears to be transported relatively unchanged into the idea of a modern ethics of the self. Apart from the Baudelairean theme of self-mastery, Foucault also privileges the individual's relation with the self over relations with others. The idea of an ethics of the self arises out of the theme of 'government', which, at the level of individual relations, is defined as an agonistic and combative struggle between free individuals who 'try to control, to determine, to delimit the liberty of others'.[62] The importance that Foucault accords to the paradigm of struggle excludes alternative understanding of social relations as structured along the lines of normatively generated agreement or according to ties of solidarity, affection or tradition. The idea of ethics of the self remains within this agonistic framework prioritizing the relation with the self over any form of intersubjective relation.

In one of his final interviews, Foucault affirms the interviewer's question that in practices of the self all knowledge is subordinated towards the end of practical self-mastery.[63] Elsewhere, he argues that 'liberty is . . . in itself political. And then, it has a political model, in the measure where being free means not being a slave to one's self and to one's appetites, which supposes that one establishes over one's self a certain relation of domination, of mastery.'[64] The role of the other is reduced to that of passive receptacle or inert context. The interests of the other are secondary and derivative to the self: 'One must not have the care for others precede the care for self. The care for self takes moral precedence in the measure that the relationship to self takes ontological precedence.'[65]

The problem with such an undialectical conception in which relations with others are subordinate to the principle of self-mastery is that Foucault's ethics fail in their stated aim to challenge orthodox conceptions of subjectivity. As I have tried to show in more detail elsewhere, the primacy that Foucault accords the isolated subject merely replicates rather than disrupts some of the central features of a philosophy of the subject. Foucault's conception of the self remains within the fundamental dynamic of the philosophy of the subject which posits an active self acting on an objectified world and interacting with other subjects who are defined as objects or narcissistic extensions of the primary subject.[66] As Habermas has pointed out, it is possible to argue that the preoccupation with autonomy or self-mastery is simply a moment in the process of social interaction which has been artificially isolated or privileged: 'both cognitive-instrumental mastery of an objectivated nature (and society) and narcissistically overinflated autonomy (in the sense of purposively rational self-assertion) are derivative moments that have been rendered independent from the communicative structures of the lifeworld, that is, from the intersubjectivity of relationships of mutual understanding and relationships of reciprocal recognition.'[67] In its insistence on the absolute primacy of the relation with the self, Foucault's work replicates some of the more problematic aspects of a Nietzschean self-assertion or Bataille's notion of sovereign expenditure.

To the extent that Foucault fails to interrogate the implications of the centrality accorded to the themes of self-mastery and a Baudelairean heroization of the self, the transgressive force of the theory of ethics is undercut, appearing as it does to rely on an unexamined and nostalgic fantasy of masculine agency.[68] In this respect, Foucault's work replicates a manoeuvre – characteristic of much traditional moral and philosophical thought – to privilege a 'disembedded and disembodied' notion of the self, which in fact covertly represents aspects of a specific male experience.[69] Indeed, it is this gap in his thought that brings the idea of ethics of the self close to a Sartrean existentialism. Foucault disavowed any similarities between his thought and Sartre's, claiming that existentialism is predicated on an essentialist concept of the self. The idea that individuals make decisions in good or bad faith in order to establish an authentic or inauthentic relation with the self presupposes a fixed core of identity against which actions and decisions can be assessed. Foucault rejects any such notion of an essential, inner identity:

> Sartre refers the work of creation to a certain relation to oneself – the author to himself – which has the form of authenticity or of inauthenticity. I would like to say exactly the contrary: we should not have to refer the creative activity of somebody to the kind of relation he has to

himself, but should relate the kind of relation one has to oneself to a creative activity.[70]

Simone de Beauvoir has also noted that Sartre's conception of the existential self is one of an unencumbered monad, which takes no account of the constraints and oppressive forces that may over-determine the decision-making process.[71] Yet, despite his denials, a similar reliance on a notion of an unencumbered self is repli-cated in the Foucauldian ethics, which, while claiming to start from embedded practices, disregards the possible impact of the fundamentally embedding structure of gender on an aesthetics of existence.

A Foucauldian may reply to such criticisms that it is possible to jettison the notions of self-mastery and heroization in order to salvage the general idea of an ethics of the self. Against this, it can be shown that the problems arising from these themes in terms of an unexamined, gendered subtext are symptomatic of more deep-seated difficulties in the idea of an ethics of the self. The uncritical generalization of the idea of self-mastery points to a more general problem, namely that there is a lack of any ethical moment in the 'ethics' of the self beyond that of a fetishization of aesthetic practice.

The ethical moment

An ethics of the self addresses itself to a critical examination of the process in which individuals come to understand themselves within the context of culturally determined notions of identity. It examines, therefore, the process of mediation through which large-scale cultural patterns manifest themselves at the level of individual identity. This process is not one of straightforward imposition in which cultural dynamics are reflected, in a straight-forward fashion, at the level of individual identity. Nor, however, can it be characterized as a voluntarist process of self-fashioning. Foucault describes this mediated process in the following terms:

> I am interested . . . in the way in which the subject constitutes himself in an *active fashion*, by the practices of the self, these practices are neverthe-less not something that the individual invents by himself. They are patterns that he finds in his culture and which are proposed, suggested and imposed on him by his culture, his society and his social group.[72]

The ethical moment in this process arises when practices of the self are removed from the level of practical consciousness to a level of critical self-awareness or reflexivity. Forms of identity that are regarded as natural or inevitable are questioned, thereby opening up a space for the exploration of new forms of experience. Foucault calls this moment of critical reflection 'the principle of irreducibility of thought': 'there is no experience which is not a way of thinking, and which cannot be analysed from the point of view of the history of thought.'[73]

Having suggested such a complex relation of mediation, however, Foucault fails to sustain an analysis of this process. This failure arises in part because the reliance on an unexamined notion of aesthetics appears to block a thorough analysis of the power relations which overdetermine the interaction between the individuals' behaviour and the wider cultural context. Such a form of analysis is crucial in order to distinguish between practices of the self that merely replicate conventional patterns of behaviour, and those which have a radical force. For example, in a society in which the behaviour of individuals is often governed by an incitement to consumption, it may be necessary to determine the point at which the construction of one's life as a work of art ceases to be an act of conspicuous consumption – or in Bourdieu's terms a sign of 'distinction' – and becomes a gesture of resistance. The category of the aesthetic, as it stands in Foucault's work, also obscures necessary distinctions between practices of self-formation that may be easily stylized, and practices, such as those pertaining to gender and sexuality, that are deeply inscribed upon the body and the psyche and may not be dislodged simply through a process of self-stylization. By failing to contextualize the notion of an aesthetics of existence with regard to the social relations in which it is embedded, Foucault finishes by merely juxtaposing rather than relating the micro level of practices of the self against the macro level of the determining social horizon. As a result, his work often seems to imply an essentially voluntarist conception of the self.

An interesting comparison may be made between Foucault's notion of practices of the self and Michel de Certeau's work on the practices of everyday life. In *The Practice of Everyday Life*, de Certeau attempts to re-examine the everyday practices that usually remain invisible or constitute an 'obscure background' in most forms of social analysis. The re-examination of everyday practices is intended to show how, in the interstices of an increasingly rationalized and administered society, individuals make (*bricoler*) innumerable and miniscule transformations to the dominant cultural economy in order to adapt it to their own interests and rules. In other words, far from being passive dupes of a commodified, mass culture, individuals resist and evade its levelling-down effects through a routine and invisible process of resignification or what De Certeau calls 'l'art de faire' ('arts of making').

In certain respects, Foucault's ethics of the self resembles De Certeau's work on everyday practices in that both thinkers try to show how, despite the increasing penetration of rationalized techniques of administration into the lifeworld, individuals are still capable of exercising a degree of autonomy in the ordering of their daily lives. As De Certeau remarks, the preoccupation of conventional social analysis with the large-scale problematic of repression renders it unable to recognize the multiplicity of practices that are heterogeneous to a repressive paradigm.[74] Against analyses of domination which focus on institutional forms of control and socially structured inequalities, Foucault and De Certeau focus on the exercise of power at its most specific points, on the microstrategies of everyday life, in order to disclose this autonomy. This refocusing on the individual does not mean, however, a retreat to a phenomenological or subjectivist form of analysis which unproblematically privileges the individual's constitutive experience. Just as, in Foucault's view, practices of the self are always determined, but never fully imposed, by the cultural context, so, for De Certeau, practices of everyday life arise from within systems of domination but nevertheless succeed in tracing out 'ruses of other interests and desires that are neither determined nor captured by the system in which they develop'.[75]

The works of both thinkers suggest a highly mediated relation or necessary non-correspondence between the individual's actions and the wider social context. However, while De Certeau runs the risk of romanticizing existing daily practices, he goes further than Foucault in presenting a sustained account of the power relations that sustain everyday practices. For example, De Certeau situates his analysis of everyday practices within the cycles of production and consumption that structure cultural life within the capitalist system. It is through the consumption of cultural symbols and forms that everyday creativity is expressed. In a showy, productivist economy which apparently offers no choice, it is through the act of consumption that the cultural activity of the masses is expressed. Procedures of consumption maintain difference in the very space that the occupier was organizing.[76] Foucault provides very little indication of the areas of life to which an aesthetic perspective may be applied in order to release a certain emancipatory potential. In contrast, Certeau gives concrete examples of such arts of consumption: 'la perruque' where the worker's own work is disguised as work for the employer; an economy of the gift; spatial practices such as walking in the city; and, finally, reading as an act with the potential to undermine the specular economy. Furthermore, De Certeau produces a distinction between 'strategies' and 'tactics' in order to clarify everyday practices that simply reaffirm the rationalized structures of consumption and those that create a space of autonomy from these structures.[77]

In contrast to the specificity of De Certeau's analysis, Foucault's ethics of the self relies too heavily on an ambivalent and undefined notion of the 'aesthetic'. Without offering a sustained analysis of the power relations in which it is inevitably embedded, the notion of the aesthetic cannot sustain the radical force that Foucault imputes to it. Lacking such an analysis, it remains unclear how it is possible to know whether the creation of the self is a radical gesture, or whether, to use a phrase of Adorno's, it is simply another example of 'pseudo- individuality' where 'what is individual is no more than the generality's power to stamp the accidental detail so firmly that it is accepted as such.'[78] By failing to consider the aesthetic in relation to its social conditions of existence, Foucault's work replicates a conventional belief in the existence of a transcendental, pure aesthetic that necessarily transfigures its objects.[79]

Norms and the fetishization of practice

Failure to elaborate the idea of an ethics of the self in relation to a concept of power leads to a further ambiguity with regard to the normative underpinnings of Foucault's idea. By suspending the idea of an ethics of the self at a moment of aesthetic self-assertion, the ethical force of the notion is undermined. A consideration of the way in which an ethics of the self relates to its cultural context inevitably raises the issue of the validity of the actions involved. In order to assess the radical import of ethical behaviour, it is necessary to make value judgements about what constitutes a

progressive action and what merely reaffirms established patterns
of behaviour. It is necessary to distinguish between actions that
are predatory and hostile with regard to other individuals, and
those with an emancipatory force. In sum, a notion of ethical
behaviour presupposes normative judgements about legitimate
and illegitimate uses of power. It is well known that throughout
his life Foucault refused to consider the possible normative basis
of his work. This refusal arises out of a desire to avoid the imposition of alien forms of morality on groups who are able to struggle
for themselves. It is necessary for the intellectual to learn the
'indignity of speaking for others'.[80] The desire to legislate for
others ultimately replicates the mistaken Enlightenment belief
that there can be one universal rationality applicable to all. Furthermore, the prescription of a moral path of action in advance
merely closes potentially unforeseen avenues of action. The
normative becomes normalizing. The task of the intellectual is to
problematize issues rather than to tell others how to act: 'The role
of the intellectual does not consist in telling others what they must
do. What right would they have to do that? . . . It is a matter of
forming analyses in his or her own fields, of interrogating anew
the evidence and the postulates, ways of acting and thinking.'[81]

Despite Foucault's explicit refusal of any normative grounding
to his work, many commentators, most notably Habermas and
Fraser, have commented on its suppressed normative content.[82]
While Foucault is explicitly hostile to formulating a positive basis
for critique, he nevertheless implicitly draws on forms of normative judgement he claims to have forsworn. Thus, as was noted in
the previous chapter, the tone of disapprobation that Foucault
adopts when discussing modern disciplinary techniques and his
exhortations to resist the government of individualization
through an exploration of the 'body and its pleasures' derives its
force from an unacknowledged judgement about what is wrong
with the modern power-knowledge regime and from a covert
appeal to the ideals of autonomy, dignity and reciprocity.

A similar cryptonormativism operates in Foucault's work on an
ethics of the self. The idea of ethics of the self revolves around a
form of progressive individualism based on tolerance and respect
for each other's lifestyles. Foucault states, for example, that practices of the self must be governed by 'the rules of law, the techniques of management and also the ethics . . . which would allow
these games of power to be played with a *minimum of domination*'.[83] Yet, by refusing to define what forms of behaviour may

constitute a violation of another's autonomy, his theory seems to suggest an unregulated libertarianism. The question of how a 'minimum of domination' may be maintained remains unaddressed. Similarly, the relationship that the individual establishes with the self is determined in part by the relationship with others. This latter relation is characterized as an agonistic struggle between free individuals who try to influence each other's actions. It is 'the totality of practices, by which one can constitute, define, organize, instrumentalize the strategies which individuals in their liberty can have in regard to each other. It is free individuals who try to control, to determine, to delimit the liberty of others.'[84]

The difficulty here is that there is a multiplicity of ways in which individuals may influence the actions of another, some of which are more acceptable than others. The theory of government allows Foucault to distinguish between states of domination and the more open-ended power relations that operate between individuals. However, between these two extremes of domination and intersubjective relations, there is no further differentiation. Foucault groups a range of different behaviours under the term *games*, which suggests the playful ethic of certain types of postmodern theory: 'the more open the game, the more attractive and fascinating it is.'[85] Yet, as other commentators would point out, the varying power relations that underlie each practice, making it possible to distinguish manipulation from persuasion or indoctrination from reasoned argument, raise morally normative issues. To decide whether an individual is being manipulated rather than persuaded invokes issues of responsibility and moral considerations about the extent to which it is legitimate to limit or impair the choices of others. As William Connolly has pointed out, the concept of power is contestable and this is because it is a concept 'bounded by normative considerations'.[86] By working with a polarized conception of power as either domination or intersubjectivity, Foucault glosses over all intermediate cases and the moral issues necessarily raised therein. While Foucault's desire not to legislate for others is understandable, he does not distinguish sufficiently between an *a priori* legislation of acceptable and non-acceptable behaviour and the establishment of certain political aims against which behaviour can be evaluated in the name of establishing non-exploitative social relations between individuals.

This normative confusion has been attributed by some commentators to what is understood as the irreconcilable tension arising from Foucault's practical commitment to a radical politics and his intellectual investment in a theoretical relativism.[87] If the idea of an ethics of the self cannot be sustained in terms of an explicit commitment to a set of normative goals or through a thorough analysis of the power relations involved, then the basis of any ethical moment is undermined. The unifying moment of a Foucauldian ethics derives only from an insistence on an unproblematized notion of practice – a fetishization of aesthetic practice. It is the act of aesthetic self-assertion *per se*, regardless of its normative content, that seems to constitute the only basis for an ethics of the self.

The substitution of a fetishized notion of individual practice as the basis for his theory of ethics rather than a more sustained form of diagnostic and utopian social critique can be traced back to the original distinction that Foucault makes between a morality oriented towards the level of code and one oriented towards ethics. It is the latter category, defined primarily in terms of a *practical* rationality or consciousness – that is, the actual rather than the prescribed practices of individuals – that forms the basis for Foucault's definition of reflective activity: a 'patient labour', 'historical-practical test'.

The insistence on the practical nature of an ethics of the self is further intensified by Foucault's rejection of notions of ideology, signification, etc., as idealist categories. This tendency to privilege the notion of the 'material' practices of individuals over more abstract concepts is best illustrated in the discussion between Foucault and Deleuze entitled 'Intellectuals and power'. Here the problematization of the relation between theory and practice involves two manœuvres. First, the notion of theory is deprived of any specificity by being reduced to the level of practice: 'theory does not express, translate, or serve to apply practice: it is practice.'[88] Second, the dualism of theory and practice is inverted in order to privilege the latter term: 'Representation no longer exists; there's only action.'[89]

Although the discussion between Foucault and Deleuze took place more than a decade earlier, a similar insistence on an ungrounded notion of practice or action generates difficulties in the idea of an ethics of the self. This can be seen in Foucault's use of the term reflexivity. The notion of reflexivity is central to Foucault's theory of the self, providing it with its ethical dimension.[90] The autonomy of the individual can be affirmed only through the reflexive examination of the construction of oneself – a critical hermeneutics of the self which must 'put itself to the test of reality, of contemporary reality, both to grasp the points where change is possible and desirable, and to determine the precise form this change should take'.[91] Such a reference to contemporary reality involves the critical scrutiny of the self's relationship with the self and the way in which it is implicated in larger social constructions, such as 'the problem of the relationship between sanity and insanity, or sickness and health, or crime and the law; the problem of the role of sexual relations'.[92]

Yet, having stressed the importance of a process of reflexive self-monitoring, this idea is then undercut by the argument that the establishment of analytical links between the self and the social context must be rejected: 'For centuries we have been convinced that between our ethics and other social or economic or political structures, there were analytical relations . . . I think we have to get rid of this idea of an analytical or necessary link between ethics and other social or economic or political structures.'[93] The injunction to rid ourselves of the idea of an analytical link between our personal ethics and other social structures arises from Foucault's concern to escape the 'regimes of truth' imposed on the body and its pleasures by the juridico-moral codification of Christianity, psychoanalysis and science. Ethics of the self should not become a form of reverse essentialism or 'scientia sexualis', hence the insistence on its contingent, local and experimental nature: 'the historical ontology of ourselves must turn away from all projects that claim to be global or radical.'[94]

By arguing against the analytical moment in an ethics of the self, however, Foucault deprives the notion of reflexivity, around which his ethics turns, of any critical force. Without examining the links between practices of the self and the way in which they are mediated through social and symbolic structures, it is unclear how individuals can acquire any insight – apart from the most parochial and intuitive – into the implications of their actions. Foucault rhetorically poses this problem but erroneously construes the dilemma in polarized terms as a choice between a 'complete and definitive' self-knowledge and a 'limited and determined' experience of our limits.[95] The possibility that remains unadmitted is that the process of reflexivity may never be fixed and complete, but may nevertheless involve a systematic interrogation of the way in which self-representation is imbricated in wider cultural dynamics at a level of awareness that transcends a purely practical consciousness. Thus, when Foucault cites the work of the feminist movement on the relation between sexes as an example of the localized transformation about which he is talking, he fails to acknowledge that the specific achievements of the feminist movement have been based, in a large part, on making analytical links between what is regarded as the private and immutable realm of sexuality and overarching structures of patriarchal domination. By precluding the analytical moment in an ethics of the self, the notion of reflexivity is deprived of any radical, critical force and is reduced to little more than a narrow process of self-introspection.

The final irony of Foucault's reliance on a problematic notion of practice as the basis of the idea of an ethics of the self is that an essentialist moment is introduced into what is intended as a radically anti-essentialist theory. In the absence of any sustained descriptive and normative social analysis, the conception of a self-referential aesthetic activity slides into a problematic positivism, where care for the self leads directly and inexplicably to radical self-knowledge. By obviating an analytical moment in an ethics of the self, the individual can only obtain knowledge of the self from some kind of unmediated or self-evident aesthetic experience that speaks directly to the self. If the individual is unable to assess the normative implications of his/her actions through reference to overarching social dynamics, then it must be the process of aesthetic self-fashioning itself that provides the yardstick or criterion for evaluation. Far from redefining a notion of the self along anti-essentialist lines, Foucault's ethics in fact reinstals a notion of sovereign subjectivity in which there is a short-circuited link between aesthetic self-fashioning and self-knowledge. The reflexive element in this creation of a relation with the self is little more than a hermetically enclosed process of introversion.

We have seen that this essentializing gesture is not confined to Foucault's final thought. From his earliest work, he tends to imbue a certain notion of the aesthetic with an apodictic, contestatory status. This is evident in the work ranging from *Mental Illness and Psychology* through to *The Order of Things*, where a certain literary exploration of the experience of madness is understood not only to signal the limits of a post-Enlightenment rationality, but also to express a radically transgressive force. It can be seen in the curious category of the 'plebs', understood as the free-floating, vitalistic force which enters the bodies of individuals, rendering them resistant to normalizing regimes of power. It also marks aspects of Foucault's work on the body and subjugated knowledges. Finally, this essentializing gesture appears in Foucault's ethics of the self, where it is unclear what is meant by the term ethics other than an unsupported assumption of the inherently radical nature of an aesthetics of existence. A stronger notion of ethics would not dispense, as Foucault does, with an analysis of the extent to which aesthetic self-construction displaces or reinforces the normative structures on which dominant constructions of identity are based.

Conclusion

In this book, I have attempted to present a critical outline of Foucault's work through an analysis of the themes of power and the subject. It is these two themes, formulated during the period from the late 1960s to the mid-1970s, that are generally held to be paradigmatic of Foucault's entire œuvre. Archaeological analysis, which reveals that the subject is not constitutive of meaning but the effect of discursively produced enunciative positions, captures the idea of the 'death of the subject' with which Foucault is closely associated. The dissolution of the constitutive subject of thought has devastating implications for notions of rationality, and in this respect archaeology represents a formal extension of Foucault's earlier impassioned critique of the role played by Enlightenment philosophy in the derogation and exclusion of madness. The work in the mid-1970s on power makes explicit the social and political implications of the archaeological deconstruction of the subject. The notion that power is a positive characteristic of all social relations yields the idea that, rather than being anterior to these relations, the subject is in fact their effect. It is this work on the couplet of power and the subject that has had a fundamental influence on the radical rethinking of theories of identity that has taken place over the past twenty years or so.

Despite its impact on a wide range of cultural, social and political theory, I have also shown that Foucault's work on power and the subject is neither unproblematic nor completely representative of his œuvre. With regard to certain theoretical limitations, I have argued that Foucault's theory of power is hampered by a persistent dilemma, namely the tendency to lapse from a positive abstract conception to a historical vision in which power relations are conceived as negative and dominatory. This results in a reified view of the social totality and an underestimation of the complex and dynamic nature of social action in advanced captialist societies. These difficulties in the theory of power are paralleled in Foucault's work on the subject. Foucault's dissection of the subject must be understood, in part, as a reaction to the subjectivism of certain types of phenomenological and hermeneutic thought that predominated in France during the 1940s and 1950s. Furthermore, the impact of the anti-subjectivist thrust of Foucault's work on feminist, postcolonial and other radical critiques of the inherently masculinist nature of knowledge has been significant. However, whereas in feminist and postcolonial work, the critique of the subject is connected to its reformulation, in Foucault's work the critique is one-sided, in that the subject has no density beyond that of an empty space or point of convergence for various relations of force. Apart from the rather romantic presentation of the 'other' in the liminal notions of madness and transgression, an alternative substantive theory of subjectivity is on the whole eschewed. As a result, Foucault's theory is unable to explain how, despite the normalizing forces that overdetermine the process of subjectification, individuals are never subsumed entirely by these forces. The dialectic of society and individual, implied in the concepts of power and the subject, remains frozen and top-heavy, obviating theories of agency and change.

Many of the criticisms of Foucault's work discussed here are not new and I have shown that they have been made in a variety of ways by commentators who occupy divergent theoretical positions. However, I have also indicated that, despite the critical prominence accorded to the work on power and the subject, there is an important shift in the orientation of Foucault's thought in the subsequent work on governmentality and ethics of the self. On the whole, critical reception of Foucault's work has not gone beyond the theoretical impasse of his concept of individuals as docile bodies, and it is only relatively recently that the implications of his final work have begun to be explored in any detail. The idea of government is important because it alters the previous notion of disciplinary power, introducing greater differentiation between relations of force and consent, between an act of violence and the actions of free individuals. Such refinements enable Foucault to explain the complex and subtle nature of modern methods of social control: government without direct intervention. Through an array of ostensibly beneficent pastoral strategies, individuals are increasingly brought within the orbit of a totalizing power whose concealed aim is the efficient manipulation of social behaviour. In Foucault's words, individuals are supplied with a little extra life, while the state is supplied with a little extra strength. In his previous work, this process of the government of individualization is elided with a nihilistic account of the inexorable nature of a normalizing biopower. The theory of government, however, permits Foucault to explain how individuals are always resistant to complete incorporation within the normalizing process of subjectification. The idea of the government of individualization denotes, therefore, both the way in which norms are imposed on forms of individuality, and the multiplicity of ways in which individuals exceed such constraints. In sum, a more rounded view of individuals as agents capable of autonomous action replaces the cipher-like status of Foucault's earlier conception of the subject as little more than an effect of discursive power relations.

This more developed view of the self-determining subject forms the basis of the idea of an ethics of the self. Given the difficulties that Foucault regards as inherent to transcendental moral frameworks, a contemporary ethics must necessarily be formulated on an individual level. The reflexive stylization of certain techniques of self-formation provides an antidote to the forces of conformism exerted through the government of individualization. As I have shown, the presentation of the idea of a deliberate and experimental reinvention of the self as the basis for a contemporary ethics is not without its limitations. While the idea of reflexive self-construction is clearly informed by an ethical and liberatory impetus, its underlying normative assumptions remain unclear. This normative indeterminacy is circumvented in part by a reliance on a notion of aesthetics; that an ethics of the self must take the form of an aesthetics of existence, in which life is turned into a work of art. The difficulty is that, because it remains theoretically underdeveloped, especially with regard to its social and political implications, the idea of an aesthetics of existence is fetishized as some form of immediate and inherently radical experience.

Many of the theoretical difficulties with the idea of an ethics of the self must be attributed, in part, to Foucault's untimely death, and the significance of his final work should not be underestimated. As I have argued elsewhere, the development of a theory of the self necessitates a reconsideration of the implications of

Foucault's work by theorists who have rejected it previously on the grounds that the nihilist implications of its critique of the subject undermine the possibility of emancipatory political action. From this critical perspective, the notion of an aesthetics of existence has been dismissed as a variant of an apolitical post-modernism that celebrates as individual freedom an aestheticised consumerism without examining the relations of power and in-equality with which it is underlaid. Certainly, in the connection that is established between stylized activity and freedom, Fou-cault's work on an aesthetics of existence resembles certain the-ories of postmodernity, such as Michel Maffesoli's work on the ethics of aesthetics and Jean-François Lyotard's notion of lan-guage games. However, in many fundamental respects the idea of an aesthetics of existence is closer to modernist projects, such as the surrealist endeavour to poetically transform everyday life. The idea of the aestheticization of daily life is not confined, as in the postmodern theme, to a relatively uncritical celebration of existing experience. Instead it aims to transfigure and revolu-tionize the daily experience of an alienated society through the exploration of potentiality rather than actuality.

It is this emphasis on the transformation of experience in order to explore new relations with the self and others that distin-guishes Foucault's work from theories of postmodernity. Unlike the latter, an aesthetics of existence in Foucault is underlaid by a moral imperative, in that it forms part of a general political project of resistance to the 'domination of truth' through the exercise of the right of the governed to autonomous action and free speech (*parrhesia*).[1] The ambivalence of its normative content notwith-standing, it is the force of this ethical imperative underlying the notions of government and self that renews a potential conver-gence with a counter-hegemonic identity politics. The recognition among theorists involved in such projects of the arbitrary and also necessary nature of a concept of the subject for identity politics is paralleled by Foucault's insistence on the theory of an ethics of the self as both constructed and self-determining. It is this moment of self-determination that creates the space for the formulation of a political ethics.

Notes

Introduction

1 Maurice Blanchot, 'Michel Foucault as I imagine him', in Michel Foucault/Maurice Blanchot, *Foucault/Blanchot*, trans. J. Mehlman and B. Massumi, p. 93.
2 Michel Foucault, *The Archaeology of Knowledge*, p. 17. For a biographical study of Foucault's desire to escape or efface the self, see James Miller, *The Passion of Michel Foucault*.
3 Michel Foucault, 'What is Enlightenment?', in *The Foucault Reader*, ed. P. Rabinow, p. 42.
4 Ibid., p. 47.

Chapter 1 From Repression to Transgression

1 Edward Said, 'Michel Foucault 1926–1984', in *After Foucault: Humanistic Knowledge, Postmodern Challenges*, ed. J. Arac, p. 5.
2 *Maladie mentale et personalité* first appeared in 1954. A revised edition with a different second part and conclusion appeared the year following the publication of *Folie et déraison* in 1961. For bibliographical information see J. Bernauer and D. Rasmussen (eds), *The Final Foucault*; M. Clark, *Michel Foucault: An Annotated Bibliography: Tool Kit for a New Age*.
   Foucault's work on mental illness and madness is clearly situated within the intellectual debates predominant in France during the 1950s and 1960s. The principal influences on this phase of his work are those of Husserl's transcendental phenomenology, the countermovement of existential hermeneutics typified in the work of Heidegger and Maurice Merleau Ponty and structural analysis, in particular Dumézil's work on religion. For an account of the influence of Husserl and Heidegger see H. Dreyfus and P. Rabinow, *Michel Foucault: Beyond Structuralism and Hermeneutics*, esp.

pp. xiii–xxiii. For a more biographical account of early influences see C. O'Farrell, *Foucault: Historian or Philosopher* and D. Eribon, *Michel Foucault*.

3 Foucault, *Mental Illness and Psychology*, p. 8.
4 Ibid., p. 10.
5 Ibid., p. 17.
6 Ibid., p. 19.
7 Ibid., p. 41.
8 Ibid., p. 63.
9 Ibid., p. 69.
10 Ibid., pp. 79–80.
11 Ibid., p. 81.
12 Ibid., p. 84.
13 Foucault, *Folie et déraison: histoire de la Folie à l'âge classique* (1961) was reissued with a new preface and appendices in 1972 as *Histoire de la Folie à l'âge classique*; references in this chaper distinguish, between the two editions, and also cite the translated and abridged version issued in 1965 as *Madness and Civilization: A History of Insanity in the Age of Reason*.
14 Foucault, *Madness and Civilization*, p. 38.
15 Ibid., p. 46.
16 Ibid., p. 64, my parenthesis.
17 Ibid., p. 83.
18 Ibid., p. 108.
19 Foucault, *Histoire de la Folie*, p. 56. Foucault's consideration of Descartes' meditation on doubt is not included in the abridged English translation.
20 Ibid., p. 58.
21 Foucault, *Madness and Civilization*, p. 166.
22 Ibid., p. 246.
23 Ibid., pp. 257–8.
24 Ibid., p. 270.
25 Ibid., p. 278.
26 H. C. Erik Midelfort, 'Madness and civilization in early modern Europe: a reappraisal of Michel Foucault', in *After the Reformation: Essays in Honor of J. H. Hexter*, ed. B. C. Malament.
27 Ibid., p. 254.
28 Ibid., p. 256.
29 Ibid., p. 258.
30 Ibid., p. 259.
31 Colin Gordon, '*Histoire de la folie*: an unknown book by Michel Foucault', in *Rewriting the History of Madness: Studies in Foucault's 'Histoire de la folie'*, ed. A. Still and I. Velody.
32 e. g. Gayatri Spivak, 'Can the subaltern speak', in *Marxism and the Interpretation of Culture*, ed. C. Nelson and L. Grossberg. See also her *In Other Worlds: Essays in Cultural Politics*.
33 Dominick LaCapra, 'Foucault, history and madness', in *Rewriting the History of Madness*, ed. Still and Velody.
34 Foucault, *Madness and Civilization*, p. 106.

35 For an account of the antipsychiatry movement, particularly with regard to its impact on the understanding of women and mental illness, see E. Showalter, *The Female Malady: Women, Madness and Culture, 1830–1980*, pp. 220–47.

36 Foucault, *Madness and Civilization*, p. 182.

37 See Lawrence Stone, 'Madness', *New York Review of Books*, 16 Dec. 1982. Stone's exchange with Foucault has been reproduced in Peter Burke (ed.), *Critical Essays on Michel Foucault*. See also Jürgen Habermas, *The Philosophical Discourse of Modernity*, p. 291, and Gillian Rose, *Dialectic of Nihilism: Poststructuralism and Law*, pp. 171–207.

38 Gordon, '*Histoire de la folie*: an unknown book by Michel Foucault', p. 29.

39 Robert Castel, 'The two readings of *Histoire de la folie* in France', in *Rewriting the History of Madness*, ed. Still and Velody.

40 See Michel Foucault, *Power/Knowledge*, pp. 195–6.

41 Michel Foucault, *Foucault Live: Interviews 1966–84*, p. 19.

42 Foucault, *Power/Knowledge*, pp. 118–19.

43 For a consideration of the gender blindness in Foucault's work see, for example, R. Braidotti, *Patterns of Dissonance: A Study of Women in Contemporary Philosophy*; I. Diamond and L. Quinby (eds), *Feminism and Foucault: Reflections on Resistance*; P. O'Brien, 'Crime and punishment as historical problem', *Journal of Social History*, 11 (1978), pp. 508–20.

44 Showalter, *The Female Malady*, p. 3.

45 Ibid., p. 4.

46 Foucault, *Power/knowledge*, p. 185, my italics.

47 Foucault, *Madness and Civilization*, p. xi.

48 Dreyfus and Rabinow, *Michel Foucault*, p. 12.

49 Gary Gutting, *Michel Foucault's Archaeology of Scientific Reason*, p. 109.

50 Foucault, *Foucault Live*, p. 57.

51 Michel Foucault, *The Order of Things*, p. 47; also pp. 14–16.

52 Jaques Derrida, 'Cogito and the history of madness'. in *Writing and Difference*, p. 36.

53 Ibid., p. 35.

54 Ibid., p. 40.

55 Ibid.

56 Contra Foucault, Derrida holds that in Descartes's consideration of doubt, madness does not receive any privileged treatment nor is it submitted to any exclusionary logic. In his reading, madness is just a further example of doubt commensurate to the example of sensory delusion: 'All significations or ideas of sensory origin are "excluded" from the realm of truth, for the same reason as madness is excluded from it. And there is nothing astonishing about this: madness is only a particular case, and, moreover, not the most serious one, of sensory illusion which interests Descartes'. (Jacques Derrida, 'Cogito and the history of madness', p. 50).

According to Derrida, it is the case of dreams rather than madness that constitutes the 'hyperbolic exasperation of the hypothesis of madness', i.e. that provides an example of a doubt that is so radical that its troubling presence must be excluded from thought at the outset. In this reading, Descartes does not find madness a good example of doubt because it does not cover the totality of the field of sensory perception, that is to say 'the madman is not always wrong about everything; he is not wrong often enough, is never mad enough' (p. 51). In so far as the problem of know-ledge is concerned, the dreamer is far madder than the mad person because in the dream the absolute totality of ideas of sensory origin may be stripped of objective value and subject to doubt.

Related to this radicalization of sensory doubt in dreams, Descartes introduces the notion of the evil genius. If dreams represent the hyper-bolic moment in natural doubt, the notion of the evil genius is intended to be even more destabilizing in that it goes beyond sensory doubt to the intellectual origins of thought itself. The residue of truth that Descartes discerned at the heart of sensory doubt is entirely abandoned and in the fiction of the evil genius the possibility of the total derangement of thought is entertained. (p. 53) The only comfort that Descartes can find in the contemplation of such profound and radical doubt – a doubt from which ideas both of sensory and intellectual nature are not sheltered – is that the very act of philosophical communication, of language itself, must necessarily escape such madness. For Descartes, the fact that he thinks and communicates reasonably means that he cannot be mad:

> If discourse and philosophical communication (that is, language itself) are to have an intelligible meaning, that is to say, if they are to conform to their essence and vocation as discourse, they must simultaneously in fact and in principle escape madness. They must carry normality within themselves. And this is not a specifically Cartesian weakness... is not a defect or mystifica-tion linked to a determined historical structure, but rather is an essential and universal necessity from which no discourse can escape, for it belongs to the meaning of meaning. It is an essential necessity from which no discourse can escape, even the discourse which denounces a mystification or an act of force. (pp.53–54)

It is this profound silence or radical doubt exemplified in the idea of the evil genius which is the very condition of the possibility of speech, 'out-side and against which language can emerge', that confirms Foucault's assertion that madness is the absence of the work. It is not, however, as Foucault would claim, a determined and historically specific form of madness, rather it is a madness of non-meaning, against which all com-munication, thought, language can be affirmed as such.

The audacity of Descartes's assertion that I think and therefore cannot be mad does not derive, therefore, from the exclusion of the mad. In Derri-da's account, madness like dreams and sensory failure is only an example of a much less radical sensory doubt which can be overcome by discern-ing the kernels of fundamental intellectual truths that lie at their heart. The real audacity of the Cartesian ego is to pit itself against the evil genius of non-meaning, to dare to return to an original point which represents neither a determined reason nor a determined non-reason and to realize that as long as I think I cannot be mad. To reach, in other words, an impenetrable point of certainty.

The problem that arises at this point for Descartes is that once he has established that the simple existence of the cogito is in itself a guarantee against non-meaning, then the distinction between historically determined reason and historically determined madness is eroded. It is at this point, then, that Descartes seeks to reassure himself that the boundary between reason and madness has not been dissolved by identifying the Cogito with (what Derrida calls) 'reasonable reason'. The Cogito closes in on itself in order to constrain the wandering that is proper to it so that error may be circumvented. It is only with respect to this second point of closure that Derrida regards Foucault's analysis of the Cartesian exclusion of madness as having relevance: 'Foucault's interpretation seems to me to be illuminating from the moment when the Cogito must reflect and proffer itself in an organized philosophical discourse' (p. 58).

57 Braidotti, *Patterns of Dissonance*, p. 56.
58 Foucault, *Folie et déraison*, p. vii; Gordon, '*Histoire de la folie*: an unknown book by Michel Foucault', p. 35.
59 Foucault, *Madness and Civilization*, p. xii.
60 In this respect, Derrida's criticisms resonate with those made by Habermas and others of Foucault's critical standpoint in his later work. When Foucault describes, in Vol. 1 of *The History of Sexuality*, a disciplinary society which operates through the production of normalizing regimes of truth, his critique is so total that is necessarily undermines the foundations on which his own argument is based. See Jürgen Habermas, *The Philosophical Discourse of Modernity*, p. 279; Michel de Certeau, *Heterologies: Discourse on the Other*, p. 183.
61 Michel Foucault, *The History of Sexuality: An Introduction*, pp. 31–2.
62 Michel Foucault, 'My body, this paper, this fire' has been reprinted in *Oxford Literary Review*, 4:1 (Autumn 1979), pp. 9– 28.
63 Ibid., p. 27.
64 For a discussion of the influence of Heidegger on Foucault's method, see Dreyfus and Rabinow, *Michel Foucault, passim*.
65 Edward Said, *The World, the Text, and the Critic*, p. 220. See also Braidotti, *Patterns of Dissonance*, pp. 62–6.
66 See, for example, Shoshana Felman 'Madness and philosophy: or literature's reason', *Yale French Studies*, no. 52 (1975). For other commentaries on the debate, see Robert D'Amico 'Text and context: Derrida and Foucault on Descartes', in *The Structural Allegory*, ed. J. Fekete; Roy Boyne, *Foucault and Derrida: The Other Side of Reason*; Peter Flaherty, '(Con)textual contest: Derrida and Foucault on madness and the Cartesian subject', *Philosophy of the Social Sciences*, 16 (1986).
67 Said, *The World, the Text, and the Critic*, p. 12.
68 Allan Megill, 'Foucault, ambiguity and the rhetoric of historiography', in *Rewriting the History of Madness*, ed. Velody and Still.
69 See Braidotti, *Patterns of Dissonance*, p. 60.
70 Foucault, *Madness and Civilization*, p. 278.
71 Peter Stallybrass and Allon White, *The Politics and Poetics of Transgression*, p. 191.
72 Foucault, *Power/Knowledge*, p. 138.

73 For Poulantzas's critique of Foucault's theory of power, see his *State, Power, Socialism*, pp. 66–70.

74 See Foucault, *Power/Knowledge*, pp. 81–5.

75 Habermas, *The Philosophical Discourse of Modernity*, p. 281.

76 Some critics regard this shift in perspective as a direct result of the exchange with Derrida. See, for example, Boyne, *Foucault and Derrida*, p. 79, 86.

77 Georges Bataille, *Eroticism*. In interviews, Foucault frequently acknowledges the profound influence of Bataille's work on the development of his thought. See, for example, *Foucault Live*, pp. 118–19.

78 Bataille, *Eroticism*, p. 15.

79 Ibid., p. 18: 'Eroticism always entails a breaking down of established patterns, the patterns . . . of the regulated social order basic to our discountinuous mode of existence as defined and separate individuals.'

80 Ibid., p. 11.

81 Ibid., p. 65.

82 Ibid., p. 104. The essential characteristic of eroticism is a feeling of crisis of the self and of identity brought on by the sensation of plethora; this is to say the superabundance and excesses of the senses – the 'plethoric life of the body' – that overturns the mind's resistance in the erotic act. Personality dies during love-making, 'ordered, parsimonious and shuttered reality is shaken by plethoric order.'

83 Ibid., p. 86.

84 Michel Foucault, 'Preface to transgression', in *Language, Counter-memory, Practice: Selected Interviews and Essays*, ed. D. Bouchard, p. 32.

85 Ibid., pp. 29–30.

86 Ibid., p. 33.

87 Ibid., p. 32.

88 Bataille, *Eroticism*, p. 63.

89 Foucault, 'Preface to transgression', p. 34.

90 Ibid., p. 35.

91 Ibid., p. 36.

92 Ibid., p. 40.

93 Ibid., p. 42, my parenthesis.

94 Ibid., p. 51.

95 Foucault, *The Order of Things*, pp. 299–300, 382–7, and 'Language to infinity', in *Language, Counter-Memory, Practice*, ed. Bouchard, p. 65.

96 See Foucault, *The Order of Things*, pp. 208–11.

97 Foucault, 'Language to infinity', p. 65.

98 Foucault 'Preface to transgression', p. 51.

99 This phrase is taken from Stallybrass and White, *The Politics and Poetics of Transgression*.

100 Michel Foucault, 'The father's "no"', in *Language, Counter-memory, Practice*, ed. Bouchard, pp. 84–5.

101 Charles Taylor, *Sources of the Self: The Making of Modern Identity*, p. 465.

102 Stallybrass and White, *The Politics and Poetics of Transgression*, p. 200.

103 Foucault, *Mental Illness and Psychology*, p. 84.

Chapter 2   The Subject of Knowledge

1 Foucault, *The Order of Things: An Archaeology of the Human Sciences*, p. xxiv; also *Foucault Live*, p. 1.
2 Foucault, *The Order of Things*, p. xxiv.
3 Foucault, *The Archaeology of Knowledge*, p. 12.
4 Michel Foucault, *Naissance de la clinique: une archéologie du regard medical*, 1963, translated as *The Birth of the Clinic: An Archaeology of Medical Perception*.
5 Ibid., p. 195.
6 Ibid.
7 Ibid., p. 39.
8 Ibid., p. 136.
9 Ibid., p. 172.
10 Ibid., p. 137.
11 De Certeau, *Heterologies*, p. 174.
12 Foucault, *The Order of Things*, p. xi.
13 Ibid., p. xxi.
14 Foucault, *Foucault Live*, p. 2.
15 Foucault, *The Order of Things*, p. ix.
16 Ibid., p. x.
17 For a discussion of Gaston Bachelard's influence on Foucault, see Gutting, *Michel Foucault's Archaeology of Scientific Reason*, pp. 9–32.
18 For a comparison of the thought of Foucault and Kuhn, see Ian Hacking, 'Michel Foucault's immature science'. *Nous*, 13 (1979), pp. 39–57.
19 Foucault, *The Order of Things*, p. xiv.
20 For Foucault's discussion of the 'document', see *The Archaeology of Knowledge*, pp. 6–7.
21 Foucault, *Foucault Live*, p. 21.
22 Ibid., p. 23.
23 See Ibid., pp. 20–3. For a fuller account of the regulatory role played by the concept of the author in the social distribution of discourse, see Foucault, 'What is an author?' in *The Foucault Reader*, ed. Rabinow.
24 Foucault, *The Order of Things*, p. xxiii.
25 Ibid., p. 387.
26 Ibid., p. 27.
27 Ibid., p. 12.
28 Ibid., pp. 36–7.
29 Ibid., p. 49.
30 Ibid., p. 72.
31 Ibid., p. 57.
32 Ibid., pp. 57–8.
33 Ibid., p. 152.
34 Ibid., p. 209.
35 Ibid.
36 Ibid., p. 211.
37 Ibid., p. 237.

38 Ibid., pp. 235-9.

39 Ibid., p. 251.

40 Foucault's claims that it is the work of David Ricardo and not Karl Marx that initiated a fundamental break with the classical analysis of wealth has aroused some controversy. See Foucault *Power/Knowledge*, p. 76, and *Remarks on Marx*, pp. 103-7.

41 Foucault, *The Order of Things*, p. 258.

42 Ibid., p. 277.

43 Ibid., p. 281.

44 For a fuller discussion of 'man and his doubles' see Dreyfus and Rabinow, *Michel Foucault*, pp. 26-43.

45 Foucault, *The Order of Things*, p. 300.

46 Ibid.

47 G. S. Rousseau, 'Whose Enlightenment? Not man's: the case of Michel Foucault', *Eighteenth Century Studies*, no. 6 (1972-3), p. 238.

48 George Huppert, 'Divinatio et eruditio: thoughts on Foucault', *History and Theory*, no. 13 (1974), pp. 191-207. For similar historical critiques, see also J. Greene, 'Les mots et les choses', *Social Science Information*, no. 6 (1967), pp. 131-8.

49 Foucault, *The Archaeology of Knowledge*, p. 12.

50 Foucault, *Foucault Live*, p. 16. There is a much quoted passage from one of his interviews where Foucault describes himself as flabbergasted to discover that in the Petit Larousse he is defined as 'a philosopher who founds his theory of history in discontinuity'; *Power/Knowledge*, p. 111.

51 Foucault, *Foucault Live*, p. 47.

52 For a discussion of Foucault's annexation of the long-term history of the *Annales* school to a study of the 'event', see James Bernauer, *Michel Foucault's Force of Flight: Toward an Ethics for Thought*, pp. 100-3.

53 Foucault, *The Archaeology of Knowledge*, pp. 6-7; also *Foucault Live*, pp. 47-8.

54 See Jean-Paul Sartre, 'Jean-Paul Sartre répond', *L'Arc*, no. 30 (Oct. 1966), pp. 87-96 (p. 87). See also Foucault, *Foucault Live*, pp. 15, 59.

55 Foucault, *Foucault Live*, p. 18.

56 For an account of the relations between intellectuals and the Parti Communiste Français during the 1960s see Ted Benton's study of Althusser, *The Rise and Fall of Structural Marxism: Althusser and his Influence*. There is some debate about the relation of Foucault's work to Marxist thought. See Mark Poster, *Foucault, Marxism and History: Mode of Production versus Mode of Information*; O'Farrell, *Foucault*, pp. 99-101.

57 Foucault, *Foucault Live*, pp. 18-19.

58 Michel Foucault, *Discipline and Punish: The Birth of the Prison*, p. 27.

59 On this see Peter Dews, *Logics of Distintegration: Post-structuralist Thought and the Claims of Critical Theory*, pp. 166-7, 188-9.

60 Foucault, *Foucault Live*, p. 16.

61 Ibid., p. 18.

62 Foucault, *The Order of Things*, pp. 217-18; see also p. xiii.

63 Ernesto Laclau, *Politics and the Study of Ideology*, p. 64.

64 See Raymond Williams, *Marxism and Literature*, pp. 121-7.

65 Foucault, *Foucault Live*, p. 26.

66   Foucault, *The Archaeology of Knowledge*, p. 16.
67   Ibid., p. 130.
68   Ibid., p. 128.
69   Ibid., p. 127.
70   Foucault, *Foucault Live*, p. 2.
71   In this chapter I will not be dealing with the problematic nature of Foucault's definition of a statement. The notion of the statement has attracted widespread criticism, for example, see Axel Honneth, *The Critique of Power: Reflective Stages in a Critical Social Theory*, pp. 105–48; Beverly Brown and Mark Cousins, 'The linguistic fault: the case of Michel Foucault's archaeology', *Economy and Society*, 9:3 (Aug. 1980), pp. 251–78.
72   Foucault, *The Archaeology of Knowledge*, p. 33.
73   Ibid., pp. 35–6.
74   Ibid., p. 72.
75   For a fuller account of Foucault's definition of a discursive formation, see Gutting, *Michel Foucault's Archaeology of Scientific Reason*, pp. 227–60; also Dreyfus and Rabinow, *Michel Foucault*, pp. 44–78.
76   Foucault, *The Archaeology of Knowledge*, p. 51.
77   Ibid., p. 55.
78   Ibid., pp. 48–9. For a more detailed discussion of the non-linguistic nature of discourse see Jeffrey Minson, *Genealogies of Morals: Nietzsche, Foucault, Donzelot and the Eccentricity of Ethics*, pp. 116–24.
79   Foucault, *The Order of Things*, p. xiv.
80   See John Thompson, *Ideology and Modern Culture: Critical Social Theory in the Era of Mass Communication*, p. 137.
81   Foucault, *The Archaeology of Knowledge*, p. 168.
82   Ibid., pp. 53–4.
83   Dreyfus and Rabinow, *Michel Foucault*, p. 66.
84   Ernesto Laclau and Chantal Mouffe, *Hegemony and Socialist Strategy: Toward a Radical Democratic Politics*, p. 108.
85   Ibid., p. 107.
86   Foucault, *The Archaeology of Knowledge*, p. 42.
87   Ibid.
88   Ibid., pp. 45–6, my parenthesis.
89   Foucault, *Foucault Live*, p. 2.
90   Michèle Barrett, *The Politics of Truth: From Marx to Foucault*, pp. 125–56.
91   Barrett's argument that Foucault's thinking on the relations between the discursive and the non-discursive is 'profoundly different from the conventions of Marxism' is further problematized by the fact that in *The Archaeology of Knowledge* Foucault still seems to adhere to a relatively conventional notion of ideology, see pp. 184–6. Also Gutting, *Michel Foucault's Archaeology of Scientific Reason*, pp. 258–60 and Dominique Lecourt, *Marxism and Epistemology: Bachelard, Canguihelm and Foucault*, pp. 198ff.
92   On the antinomic nature of structuralist thought, see Paul Ricoeur, 'Structure, word, event', in *The Conflict of Interpretations: Essays in Hermeneutics*.
93   Foucault, *The Archaeology of Knowledge*, p. 119.
94   Dreyfus and Rabinow, *Michel Foucault*, p. 83.
95   For an example of such a struggle, see Nancy Fraser on the 'discourse of need' in *Unruly Practices: Power, Discourse and Gender in Contemporary Social Theory*.

96 Foucault, *The Archaeology of Knowledge*, p. 120, my italics.
97 Laclau and Mouffe, *Hegemony and Socialist Strategy*, pp. 115–16.
98 Foucault, *The Archaeology of Knowledge*, p. 95.
99 Brown and Cousins, 'The linguistic fault', p. 272.
100 Ricoeur, 'Structure, word, event'.
101 Ibid., pp. 84–5.
102 Foucault, 'What is an author?', p. 120.
103 See, for example, Nancy Harstock, 'Feminism, science and the anti-Enlightenment critiques', in *Feminism/Postmodernism*, ed. L. Nicholson (London: Routledge, 1990), p. 163.
104 Spivak, *In Other Worlds*, p. 205. See also Spivak, 'Can the subaltern speak'; Homi Bhabha, 'Interrogating identity', in his edited collection *Identity*. On the politics of location: Elspeth Probyn 'Travels in the postmodern: making sense of the local', in *Feminism/Postmodernism*, ed. Nicholson; Adrienne Rich, 'Notes towards a politics of location', in her *Blood, Bread and Poetry: Selected Prose 1979–85*.
105 Stuart Hall, 'Minimal selves', in *Identity*, ed. Bhabha, p. 45.
106 Gillian Rose, *Dialectic of Nihilism*, p. 182.
107 Foucault, *The Order of Things*, p. xxiv.
108 Laclau and Mouffe, *Hegemony and Socialist Strategy*, p. 139.
109 Foucault, *The Order of Things*, p. 384.
110 Ibid., p. 383.
111 Foucault, Ibid., p. 386.
112 Foucault, Ibid., p. xi.
113 Michel De Certeau, *Heterologies*, p. 183.
114 Foucault, *The Order of Things*, p. xiii, and *The Archaeology of Knowledge*, pp. 190–2.
115 Michel Pecheux, 'Discourse: structure or event?' in *Marxism and the Interpretation of Culture*, ed. C. Nelson and L. Grossberg, p. 646.
116 The process of the stabilization of discourse involves the insertion of statements into a discursive space governed by logical propositions (true or false) and disjunctive interrogations (i.e., is this state of affairs a or not a?) whose essential function is to forbid the play of interpretation. Thus Pecheux gives the example of the statement 'such and such a person is very military in civilian life', which is prohibited at the level of logical stabilization although, at the interpretative level, it makes sense.
117 Pecheux, 'Discourse: structure or event?, pp. 637–8.
118 Ibid., p. 639.
119 Ibid., p. 647.
120 Ibid., p. 644–5.

Chapter 3   From Discipline to Government

1 Foucault, *Power/Knowledge*, p. 133.
2 Michel Foucault, *L'ordre du discours*, inaugural lecture of 1970, translated as 'The order of discourse', in *Untying the Text: A Poststructuralist Reader*, ed. R. Young.

3   Foucault, 'The order of discource', p. 55.
4   Ibid., p. 59.
5   Ibid., p. 60.
6   Ibid., p. 66.
7   Ibid., p. 68.
8   Michel Foucault, 'Nietzsche, genealogy, history', in *The Foucault Reader*, ed. Rabinow, p. 89.
9   Ibid., p. 85.
10 Ibid., pp. 94–5.
11 Ibid., p. 78.
12 Ibid., p. 79.
13 Foucault, 'The order of discourse', p. 69.
14 Foucault, 'Nietzsche genealogy, history', p. 85.
15 Ibid., pp. 87–8.
16 Ibid., p. 83.
17 Foucault, *Power/Knowledge*, p. 98.
18 Ibid., p. 97.
19 Ibid., pp. 88–9.
20 Ibid., p. 102.
21 Foucault, *Discipline and Punish*, p. 78.
22 Ibid., p. 81.
23 Ibid., pp. 220–1.
24 Ibid., pp. 25–6.
25 Ibid., p. 228.
26 Ibid., pp. 141–9.
27 Ibid., pp. 206–7.
28 Ibid., p. 216.
29 Ibid., pp. 20–1.
30 Foucault, *The History of Sexuality: An Introduction*, p. 10.
31 Ibid., p. 18.
32 Ibid., p. 36.
33 Ibid., pp. 47–8.
34 Ibid., p. 69.
35 Ibid., p. 63.
36 Ibid., pp. 61–2.
37 Ibid., pp. 129–30.
38 Ibid., p. 60.
39 Ibid., pp. 88–91.
40 Ibid., p. 49.
41 Ibid., pp. 98–101.
42 Ibid., p. 103.
43 Ibid., pp. 104–5.
44 Ibid., p. 144.
45 Anthony Giddens, *The Constitution of Society: Outline of the Theory of Structuration*, pp. 153–5.
46 Ibid., p. 155; see also Erving Goffman, *Asylums*.
47 Dews, *Logics of Disintegration*, p. 188. See also Centre for Contemporary Cultural Studies, *Unpopular Education: Schooling and Social Democracy in England since 1944*, pp. 15–16.

48 Foucault, *Power/Knowledge*, p. 142.
49 Foucault, *The History of Sexuality: An Introduction*, pp. 33, 101.
50 Ibid., p. 101.
51 Foucault, *Discipline and Punish*, p. 138.
52 Foucault, *The History of Sexuality: An Introduction*, pp. 59–60.
53 For an example of such practices see Michel De Certeau, *The Practice of Everyday Life*; also Linda Gordon, *Heroes of their Own Lives: The Politics and History of Family Violence: Boston 1880–1960*.
54 De Certeau, *The Practice of Everyday Life*, p. 48.
55 Foucault, *Discipline and Punish*, pp. 29–30.
56 See Rose, *Dialectic of Nihilism*, ch. 9.
57 Christopher Norris, *The Truth about Postmodernism*, p. 33.
58 Foucault, *The History of Sexuality: An Introduction*, p. 131.
59 See Isaac D. Balbus, 'Disciplining women: Michel Foucault and the power of feminist discourse', in *Feminism as Critique: Essays on the Politics of Gender in Late Capitalist Societies*, ed. S. Benhabib and D. Cornell; Habermas, *The Philosophical Discourse of Modernity*, p. 292; Lois McNay, *Foucault and Feminism: Power, Gender and the Self*, pp. 39–42.
60 Honneth, *The Critique of Power*, p. 189.
61 Poulantzas, *State, Power, Socialism*, pp. 66–9.
62 Foucault, *Power/Knowledge*, p. 131.
63 Habermas, *The Philosophical Discourse of Modernity*, p. 287.
64 Michel Foucault, 'Sexual choice, sexual act: Foucault and homosexuality', in Foucault, *Politics, Philosophy, Culture: Interviews and Other Writings, 1977–1984*, ed. L. Kritzman, p. 294.
65 Habermas, *Philosophical Discourse of Modernity*, p. 291.
66 See Rose, *Dialectic of Nihilism*, pp. 171–207.
67 Habermas, *The Philosophical Discourse of Modernity*, p. 291.
68 Foucault, *Power/Knowledge*, p. 118.
69 Foucault, *The Archaeology of Knowledge*, p. 185.
70 Foucault, *Power/Knowledge*, p. 118.
71 Ibid.
72 Foucault, *Discipline and Punish*, p. 27.
73 Foucault, *The History of Sexuality: An Introduction*, p. 100.
74 Foucault, *Power/Knowledge*, pp. 195–6. For a concrete illustration of the apparatus, see Foucault's introduction to the English translation *Herculine Barbin: Being the Recently Discovered Memoirs of a Nineteenth Century French Hermaphrodite*; trans. R. McDougall, pp. vii–xvii. Also Michel Foucault, 'Tales of murder', in *I, Pierre Rivière, Having Slaughtered my Mother, my Sister and my Brother: A Case of Parricide in the Nineteenth Century*, ed. Michel Foucault.
75 Foucault, *The History of Sexuality: An Introduction*, pp. 94–5.
76 Ibid., p. 117.
77 Pierre Bourdieu expresses the difference between his notion of symbolic power and the Foucauldian notion of discipline in the following way: 'Discipline . . . points towards something external. Discipline is enforced by a military strength; you must obey. In a sense it is easy to revolt against discipline because you are conscious of it. In fact, I think that in terms of

symbolic domination, resistance is more difficult, since it is something you absorb like air, something you don't feel pressured by; it is everywhere and nowhere, and to escape from that is very difficult.' Pierre Bourdieu and Terry Eagleton (in conversation), 'Doxa and common life', *New Left Review*, 191 (Jan/Feb 1992), pp. 111–21 (p. 115).

78 Michel Foucault and Gilles Deleuze, 'Intellectuals and power', in *Language, Counter-memory, Practice*, ed. Bouchard, p. 203.
79 Ibid., p. 206.
80 On the fetishization of a notion of desire, see Terry Eagleton, 'The politics of subjectivity', in *Identity*, ed. Bhabha, p. 47.
81 Spivak, 'Can the subaltern speak', p. 280.
82 Foucault and Deleuze, 'Intellectuals and power', p. 212.
83 Habermas, *The Philosophical Discourse of Modernity*, p. 283.
84 Foucault, 'Nietzsche, genealogy, history', p. 85.
85 Foucault, *Power/Knowledge*, p. 90.
86 See Ibid., pp. 187–8, and *Discipline and Punish*, p. 304.
87 Honneth, *The Critique of Power*, p. 174.
88 Ibid., p. 175.
89 Michel Foucault, 'Governmentality' in *The Foucault Effect: Studies in Governmentality*, ed. G. Burchell, C. Gordon and P. Miller.
90 Ibid., p. 87.
91 Ibid., p. 96.
92 Ibid., p. 91.
93 Ibid., p. 92.
94 Ibid., p. 93.
95 Ibid., p. 95.
96 Ibid.
97 Ibid.
98 Ibid., p. 97.
99 Foucault, *The History of Sexuality: An Introduction*, p. 139.
100 Foucault, 'Governmentality', p. 100.
101 Ibid., p. 101.
102 Foucault, *Power/Knowledge*, p. 122; see also, pp. 94–5, 121–2, 140–1, 158, 188.
103 Foucault, *Remarks on Marx*, p. 164.
104 Foucault, 'Governmentality', p. 103.
105 Ibid.
106 The Tanner Lectures on Human Values (10 and 16 Oct. 1979), reproduced as 'Politics and reason', in Foucault, *Politics, Philosophy, Culture*.
107 Ibid., pp. 77–8.
108 Ibid., p. 79.
109 Ibid., p. 81.
110 See Foucault, *The History of Sexuality: An Introduction*, pp. 18–20.
111 Foucault, 'Politics and reason', p. 60.
112 Ibid., p. 62.
113 Ibid., p. 68.
114 Ibid., p. 69.
115 Ibid., p. 70.

116 Michel Foucault, 'The subject and power', in Dreyfus and Rabinow, *Michel Foucault*, p. 215.
117 Foucault, 'Politics and reason', p. 82.
118 Foucault, 'The subject and power', p. 212.
119 Foucault, *The History of Sexuality: An Introduction*, pp. 58–9.
120 Ibid., pp. 59–70.
121 Foucault, 'The subject and power', p. 208.
122 Foucault, *Power/Knowledge*, p. 186.
123 Foucault, 'The subject and power', p. 214.
124 Ibid., p. 212, my parenthesis.
125 Ibid., p. 224.
126 Ibid., p. 216.
127 Foucault, *Power/Knowledge*, p. 114.
128 Foucault, 'Subject and power', pp. 217–18.
129 Ibid.
130 Michel Foucault, 'The ethic of care for the self as a practice of freedom', in *The Final Foucault*, ed. Bernauer and Rasmussen, p. 18; also Michel Foucault, 'Politics and ethics: an interview', in *The Foucault Reader*, ed. Rabinow, p. 378.
131 Foucault, 'Politics and ethics', p. 379.
132 Foucault, 'The subject and power', p. 218.
133 Ibid.
134 Ibid., p. 219; see also Foucault, 'Politics and ethics', p. 380.
135 Foucault, 'The subject and power', p. 219.
136 Ibid., p. 220.
137 Ibid.
138 Ibid.
139 Ibid.
140 Colin Gordon, 'The soul of the citizen: Max Weber and Michel Foucault on rationality and government', in *Max Weber, Rationality and Modernity*, ed. Whimster and Lash, p. 296.
141 Foucault, 'The subject and power', p. 221; see also Foucault, 'The ethic of care', p. 19.
142 For example, see Habermas, *The Philosphical Discourse of Modernity*, p. 284, and Nancy Fraser, *Unruly Practices*, p. 29.
143 We shall see in the final chapter, however, that there remains some confusion with regard to the normative basis of Foucault's use of these concepts.
144 Foucault, *Power/Knowledge*, p. 93.
145 Foucault, 'The subject and power', p. 221.
146 Ibid., pp. 211–12.
147 Michel Foucault, 'Social security', in Foucault, *Politics, Philosophy, Culture*, p. 162.
148 Ibid., p. 161, my italics.
149 Ibid.
150 Ibid., pp. 160–1.
151 Foucault, 'The subject and power', p. 223.
152 Michel Foucault, 'Space, knowledge and power', in *The Foucault Reader*, ed. Rabinow, p. 241.

153 Ibid., p. 242.
154 Ibid., p. 245.
155 Foucault, 'The ethic of care', pp. 3–4.
156 Foucault, *Power/Knowledge*, p. 98.
157 Michel Foucault, 'An aesthetics of existence', in Foucault, *Politics, Philosophy, Culture*, p. 50.
158 Gilles Deleuze, *Foucault*, p. 100.
159 Foucault, 'Sexual choice, sexual act', p. 294.

Chapter 4   Aesthetics as Ethics

1 Michel Foucault, 'Sexuality and solitude', in *On Signs: A Semiotic Reader*, ed. M. Blonsky, p. 367.
 2 Michel Foucault, *The Use of Pleasure*, pp. 15–17.
 3 Ibid., pp. 19–20.
 4 Ibid., p. 20.
 5 Ibid., p. 23, my italics.
 6 Ibid., p. 25.
 7 Ibid., pp. 10–11.
 8 The following description of *The Use of Pleasure* and *Care of the Self* draws heavily on pp. 54–9 of my *Foucault and Feminism*.
 9 Foucault, *The Use of Pleasure*, p. 47.
10 Ibid., p. 151.
11 Ibid., p. 170.
12 Ibid., p. 203.
13 Ibid., p. 221.
14 Ibid., p. 225.
15 Ibid., p. 245.
16 Michel Foucault, *The Care of the Self*, p. 85.
17 Ibid., pp. 166–7.
18 Ibid., p. 192.
19 Ibid., pp. 228–32.
20 Ibid., p. 68.
21 Foucault, *Use of Pleasure*, pp. 29–30.
22 Foucault, 'An aesthetics of existence', p. 49.
23 Michel Foucault, 'On the genealogy of ethics: an overview of work in progress', in *The Foucault Reader*, ed. Rabinow, p. 343.
24 Foucault, 'An aesthetics of existence', p. 49.
25 Foucault, 'The subject and power', p. 212.
26 Ibid., p. 216.
27 Michel Foucault, 'The art of telling the truth', in Foucault, *Politics, Philosophy, Culture*, p. 88.
28 Jürgen Habermas, *The New Conservatism: Cultural Criticism and the Historians' Debate*, p. 177.
29 Foucault, 'The subject and power', p. 210.
30 Foucault, 'What is Enlightenment?', in *The Foucault Reader*, ed. Rabinow, p. 44.

31 Michel Foucault, 'Structuralism and poststructuralism: an interview with Michel Foucault', *Telos*, 55 (1983), pp. 195–211 (p. 202).

32 Foucault, 'What is Enlightenment?' p. 38.

33 Ibid., pp. 49–50.

34 Ibid., p. 43.

35 John Rajchman, 'Ethics after Foucault', *Social Text*, 13 (1985), pp. 165–83 (pp. 166–7).

36 Foucault, 'Preface to transgression', in *Language, Counter-memory, Practice*, ed. Bouchard, p. 33.

37 Foucault, 'What is Enlightenment', p. 45.

38 Ibid., p. 42.

39 Michel Foucault, 'On the genealogy of ethics: An overview of work in progress', in *The Foucault Reader*, ed. Rabinow, p. 351.

40 Rainer Rochlitz, 'The aesthetics of existence: post-conventional morality and the theory of power in Michel Foucault', in *Michel Foucault Philosopher*, ed. T. Armstrong, p. 255. See also Richard Wolin, 'Foucault's aesthetic decisionism', *Telos*, 67 (1986), pp. 71–86.

41 Terry Eagleton, *The Ideology of the Aesthetic*, p. 395.

42 Foucault, 'On the genealogy of ethics', p. 350.

43 Michèle Barrett argues that the dismissal of aesthetics as an irredeemably bourgeois category leaves radical criticism in a weak position because it cannot fully engage with popular conceptions of art; see Barrett, 'The place of aesthetics in Marxist criticism', in *Marxism and the Interpretation of Culture*, in ed. C Nelson and L. Grossberg.

44 Williams, *Marxism and Literature*, p. 151. See also Charles Taylor, *Sources of the Self*, pp. 461–2.

45 Gaston Bachelard quoted in Richard Kearney, *Poetics of Imagining: From Husserl to Lyotard*, p. 7.

46 Taylor, *Sources of the Self*, p. 14; Henri Lefebvre, 'Toward a leftist cultural politics: remarks occasioned by the centenary of Marx's death', in *Marxism and the Interpretation of Culture*, ed. Nelson and Grossberg.

47 Lefebvre, 'Toward a leftist cultural politics', p. 79.

48 Ibid., p. 80.

49 Georg Simmel, 'The problem of style', *Theory, Culture and Society*, 8 (1991), pp. 63–71 (p. 69).

50 Foucault, 'What is Enlightenment?' p. 41.

51 Ibid., p. 42.

52 See Griselda Pollock, 'Modernity and the spaces of femininity', in her *Vision and Difference: Femininity, Feminism and the Histories of Art*.

53 Foucault addresses one aspect of this intensification of gender relations with his notion of the hysterization of the bodies of women in *The History of Sexuality: An Introduction*, p. 104.

54 Griselda Pollock, 'Feminism and modernism', in *Framing Feminism: Art and the Women's Movement 1970–1985*, ed. Rosizka Parker and Griselda Pollock, p. 87.

55 For example, Sandra Lee Bartky, 'Foucault, femininity and the modernization of patriarchal power', in *Feminism and Foucault*, ed. Diamond and Quinby; Braidotti, *Patterns of Dissonance*, pp. 92–7; Naomi Schor, 'Dreaming

dissymmetry: Barthes, 'Foucault and sexual differences', in *Men in Feminism*, ed. A. Jardine and P. Smith.

56 Meaghan Morris, 'The pirate's fiancée: feminists and philosophers, or maybe tonight it'll happen', in *Feminism and Foucault*, ed. Diamond and Quinby, p. 26.
57 Pierre Bourdieu, *The Logic of Practice*, p. 29.
58 See Anthony Giddens, *Modernity and Self Identity: Self and Society in the Late Modern Age*, p. 216.
59 See Pollock, 'Feminism and Modernism', p. 86.
60 Foucault, *The Use of Pleasure*, pp. 84–5.
61 Ibid., pp. 151–65.
62 Foucault, 'The ethic of care for the self', p. 20.
63 Foucault, 'On the genealogy of ethics', pp. 360–1.
64 Foucault, 'The ethic of care for the self', p. 6.
65 Ibid., p. 7.
66 See McNay, *Foucault and Feminism*, ch. 5, esp. pp. 165–77.
67 Habermas, *Philosophical Discourse of Modernity*, p. 315.
68 Foucault's indifference to the problematic implications of proposing a Baudelairean notion of the heroization of the self as a model for a contemporary ethics has been commented on by Rainer Rochlitz. He regards it as a theoretical complacency connected to the unchallenged position that Foucault occupied in the Collège de France; Rochlitz, 'The aesthetics of existence', p. 257.
69 Seyla Benhabib, *Situating the Self: Gender, Community and Postmodernism in Contemporary Ethics*, p. 152.
70 Foucault, 'On the genealogy of ethics', p. 351.
71 Moira Gatens, *Feminism and Philosophy: Perspectives on Difference and Equality*, p. 50.
72 Foucault, 'The ethic of care for the self', p. 11; see also 'Preface to *The History of Sexuality*, vol. 2' in *The Foucault Reader*, ed. Rabinow, p. 335.
73 Foucault, 'Preface to *The History of Sexuality*, vol. 2', p. 335.
74 De Certeau, *The Practice of Everyday Life*, pp. 41–2.
75 Ibid., p. xviii.
76 Ibid., pp. 30–2.
77 Ibid., pp. 38–41.
78 Theodor Adorno and Max Horkheimer, *Dialectic of Enlightenment*, p. 154.
79 See Pierre Bourdieu, 'The historical genesis of a pure aesthetic', in Bourdieu, *The Field of Cultural Production*.
80 Foucault and Deleuze, 'Intellectuals and power', in *Language, Countermemory, Practice*, ed. Bouchard p. 209.
81 Foucault, *Remarks on Marx*, pp. 11–12.
82 See Habermas, *The Philosophical Discourse of Modernity*, pp. 282–86; Nancy Fraser, 'Foucault's body-language: a post-humanist political rhetoric', *Salmagundi*, 61, pp. 55–70 (also in Fraser, *Unruly Practices*).
83 Foucault, 'The ethics of care for the self', p. 18, my italics.
84 Ibid., pp. 19–20
85 Ibid., p. 20.
86 William E. Connolly, *The Forms of Political Discourse*, ch. 3.

87 For example, see Derek D. Nikolinakos, 'Foucault's ethical quandry', *Telos*, no. 83 (Spring 1990).
88 Foucault and Deleuze, 'Intellectuals and power', p. 208.
89 Ibid., pp. 206–7.
90 Foucault makes frequent reference to the notion of reflexivity, see 'Structuralism and poststructuralism: an interview with Michel Foucault', pp. 195–211.
91 Foucault, 'What is Enlightenment?', p. 46.
92 Ibid., p. 49.
93 Foucault, 'On the genealogy of ethics', p. 350.
94 Foucault, 'What is Enlightenment?', p. 46.
95 Ibid., p. 47.

Conclusion

1 Foucault, *Foucault Live*, p. 314.

Bibliography

WORKS BY FOUCAULT

Only works referred to in this study are included here. Works by Foucault are ordered chronologically in their sections, books according to date of first publication and articles and interviews according to either date of first publication or date of the collected volume in which they appear. Other works are arranged alphabetically by author. For a more complete bibliography of Foucault's writings see Michael Clark, *Michel Foucault: An Annotated Bibliography: Tool Kit for a New Age* (New York: Garland, 1983) and J. Bernauer and D. Rasmussen (eds), *The Final Foucault* (Cambridge, Mass.: MIT Press, 1988).

Books in the original French

Maladie mentale et personalité (Paris: Presses Universitaires de France, 1954). Revised, with a different second part and conclusion, as *Maladie mentale et psychologie* (Paris: Presses Universitaires de France, 1962).
Folie et déraison: histoire de la folie à l'âge classique (Paris: Plon, 1961). Reprinted with new preface and appendices as *Histoire de la folie à l'âge classique* (Paris: Gallimard, 1972).
Naissance de la clinique: une archéologie du regard médical (Paris: Presses Universitaires de France, 1963).
Les Mots et les choses: une archéologie des sciences humaines (Paris Gallimard, 1966).
L'Archéologie du savoir (Paris: Gallimard, 1969).
L'Ordre du discours: leçon inaugurale au Collège de France prononcée le 2 décembre 1970 (Paris: Gallimard, 1971).
Moi, Pierre Rivière, ayant égorgé ma mère, ma sœur, mon frère: un cas de parricide au XIXe siècle, ed. Foucault (Paris: Gallimard, 1973).
Surveiller et punir: naissance de la prison (Paris: Gallimard, 1975).
Histoire de la sexualité, vol. 1: *La Volonté de savoir* (Paris: Gallimard, 1976).

Herculine Barbin dite Alexina B. ed. Foucault (Paris: Gallimard, 1978).
Histoire de la sexualité, vol. 2: *L'Usage des plaisirs* (Paris: Gallimard, 1984).
Histoire de la sexualité, vol. 3: *Le Souci de soi* (Paris: Gallimard, 1984).

English translations of books

Madness and Civilization: A History of Insanity in the Age of Reason, trans. of abridged version of *Folie et déraison* (1961) by R. Howard (London: Tavistock, 1965).
Mental Illness and Psychology, trans. of *Maladie mentale et psychologie* (1962) by A. M. Sheridan-Smith (New York: Harper and Row, 1976).
The Birth of the Clinic: An Archaeology of Medical Perception, trans. of *Naissance de la clinique* (1963) by A. M. Sheridan-Smith (London: Tavistock, 1973).
The Order of Things: An Archaeology of the Human Sciences, anon. trans. of *Les Mots et les choses* (1966) (London: Tavistock, 1970).
The Archaeology of Knowledge, trans. of *L'Archéologie du savoir* (1969) by A. M. Sheridan-Smith (London: Tavistock, 1972).
'The order of discourse', trans. of *L'Ordre du discours* (1971) by R. Young, in *Untying the Text: A Poststructuralist Reader*, ed. R. Young (London: Routledge, 1981).
I, Pierre Rivière, Having Slaughtered my Mother, my Sister and my Brother: A Case of Parricide in the Nineteenth Century, ed. Foucault, trans. of *Moi, Pierre Rivière, ayant égorgé ma mère ma sœur, mon frère* (1973) by F. Jellinek (Harmondsworth: Penguin, 1975).
Discipline and Punish: The Birth of the Prison, trans. of *Surveiller et punir* (1975) by A. M. Sheridan-Smith (Harmondsworth: Penguin, 1977).
The History of Sexuality: An Introduction, trans. of *Histoire de la sexualité*, vol. 1: *La Volonté de savoir* (1976) by R. Hurley (Harmondsworth: Penguin, 1978).
Herculine Barbin: Being the Recently Discovered Memoirs of a Nineteenth-Century French Hermaphrodite, edited and with a note by Foucault, trans. of *Herculine Barbin dite Alexina B.* (1978) by R. McDougall (New York: Pantheon, 1980).
The Use of Pleasure, trans. of *Histoire de la sexualité*, vol. 2: *L'Usage des plaisirs* (1984) by R. Hurley (Harmondsworth: Penguin, 1985).
The Care of the Self, trans. of *Histoire de la sexualité*, vol. 3: *Le Souci de soi* (1984) by R. Hurley (Harmondsworth: Penguin, 1986).

Articles and interviews

Language, Counter-memory, Practice: Selected Interviews and Essays, ed. D. F. Bouchard (New York: Cornell University Press, 1977). Includes: 'Preface to transgression'; 'Language to infinity', 'The father's "no"', 'Intellectuals and power' (with Gilles Deleuze).
'Politics and the study of discourse', *Ideology and Consciousness*, 3 (1978), pp. 7–26.

'My body, this paper, this fire', *Oxford Literary Review*, 4:1 (Autumn 1979), pp. 9–28.

Power/Knowledge: Selected Interviews and Other Writings, 1972–77, ed. C. Gordon (Brighton: Harvester, 1980).

'The subject and power', H. Dreyfus and P. Rabinow, *Michel Foucault: Beyond Structuralism and Hermeneutics* (London: Harvester Wheatsheaf, 1982).

'Structuralism and poststructuralism: an interview with Michel Foucault', *Telos*, 55 (1983), pp. 195–211.

The Foucault Reader, ed. P. Rabinow (Harmondsworth: Penguin, 1984). Includes: 'What is an author?'; 'Nietzsche, genealogy, history'; 'What is Enlightenment?'; 'Politics and ethics: an interview'; 'Space, knowledge and power'; 'On the genealogy of ethics: an overview of work in progress'; 'Polemics, politics and problematisations: an interview with Michel Foucault'; 'Preface to *The History of Sexuality*, vol. 2'.

'Sexuality and solitude', in *On Signs: A Semiotic Reader*, ed. M. Blonsky (Oxford: Blackwell, 1985).

'The ethic of the care for the self as a practice of freedom', in *The Final Foucault*, ed. J. Bernauer and D. Rasmussen (Cambridge Mass.: MIT Press, 1988).

Politics, Philosophy, Culture: Interviews and Other Writings, 1977–1984, ed. L. Kritzman (London: Routledge, 1988). Includes: 'Social security'; 'Politics and reason' (Tanner Lectures on Human values, 10 and 16 Oct. 1979); 'An aesthetics of existence'; 'Sexual choice, sexual act: Foucault and homosexuality'; 'The return of morality'; 'The art of telling the truth'.

Foucault Live: Interviews 1966–84 (New York: Semiotext(e), 1989).

'Governmentality', in *The Foucault Effect: Studies in Governmentality*, ed. G. Burchell, C. Gordon and P. Miller (London: Harvester Wheatsheaf, 1991).

Remarks on Marx (New York: Semiotext(e), 1991).

WORKS ON FOUCAULT

Arac, J.(ed.), *After Foucault: Humanistic Knowledge, Postmodern Challenges* (London: Rutgers University Press, 1988).

Armstrong, T. (ed), *Michel Foucault Philosopher* (Hemel Hempstead: Harvester Wheatsheaf, 1992).

Balbus, I., 'Disciplining women: Michel Foucault and the power of feminist discourse', in *Feminism as Critique: Essays on the Politics of Gender in Late Capitalist Societies*, ed. S. Benhabib and D. Cornell (Cambridge: Polity Press, 1986).

Bartky, S., 'Foucault, femininity and the modernization of patriarchal power', in *Feminism and Foucault: Reflections on Resistance*, ed. I. Diamond and L. Quinby (Boston: Northeastern University Press, 1988).

Bernauer, J., *Michel Foucault's Force of Flight: Towards an Ethics for Thought* (London: Humanities, 1990).

Bernauer, J. and Rasmussen, D. (eds), *The Final Foucault* (Cambridge, Mass.: MIT Press, 1988).

Blanchot, M., 'Michel Foucault as I imagine him', in Michel Foucault/Maurice Blanchot,*Foucault/Blanchot*, trans. J. Mehlman and B. Massumi (New York: Zone Books,1990).

Boyne, R., *Foucault and Derrida: The Other Side of Reason* (London: Unwin Hyman, 1990).

Brown, B. and Cousins, M., 'The linguistic fault: the case of Michel Foucault's archaeology', *Economy and Society*, 9:3 (Aug. 1980), pp. 251–78.

Burke, P., (ed.), *Critical Essays on Michel Foucault*, Critical Thought Series 2 (Cambridge: Scolar Press, 1992).

Castel, R., 'The two readings of *Histoire de la folie* in France', in *Rewriting the History of Madness: Studies in Foucault's 'Histoire de la folie'*, ed. A. Still and I. Velody (London: Routledge 1992).

Clark, M., *Michel Foucault: An Annotated Bibliography: Tool Kit for a New Age* (New York: Garland, 1983).

D'Amico, R., 'Text and context: Derrida and Foucault on Descartes', in *The Structural Allegory*, ed. J. Fekete (Manchester: Manchester University Press, 1984).

Deleuze, G., *Foucault*, trans. S. Hand (Minneapolis: University of Minnesota Press, 1988).

Derrida, J., 'Cogito and the history of madness', in *Writing and Difference* (London: Routledge and Kegan Paul, 1978).

Diamond, I. and Quinby, L. (eds), *Feminism and Foucault: Reflections on Resistance* (Boston: Northeastern University Press, 1988).

Dreyfus, H. and Rabinow, P., *Michel Foucault: Beyond Structuralism and Hermeneutics* (Chicago: Chicago University Press, 1982).

Eribon, D., *Michel Foucault* (London: Faber, 1991).

Felman, S., 'Madness and philosophy *or* literature's reason', *Yale French Studies*, no. 52, (1975), pp. 206–28.

Flaherty, P., '(Con))textual contest: Derrida and Foucault on madness and the Cartesian subject', *Philosophy of the Social Sciences*, 16 (1986), pp. 157–75.

Fraser, N., 'Foucault's body-language: a post-humanist political rhetoric', *Salmagundi* 61 (1983), pp. 55–70.

Gordon, C., 'The soul of the citizen: Max Weber and Michel Foucault on rationality and government', in *Max Weber, Rationality and Modernity*, ed. S. Whimster and S. Lash (London: Allen and Unwin, 1986).

—— 'Histoire de la folie: an unknown book by Michel Foucault', in *Rewriting the History of Madness: Studies in Foucault's 'Histoire de la folie'*, ed. A. Still and I. Velody (London: Routledge, 1992).

Greene, J., 'Les mots et les choses', *Social Science Information*, no. 6 (1967), pp. 131–8.

Guttting, G., *Michel Foucault's Archaeology of Scientific Reason* (Cambridge: Cambridge University Press, 1989).

Hacking, I., 'Michel Foucault's immature science', *Nous*, 13 (1979), pp. 39–57.

Huppert, G., 'Divinatio et eruditio: thoughts on Foucault', *History and Theory*, no. 13 (1974), pp. 191–207.

LaCapra, D., 'Foucault, history and madness', in *Rewriting the History of Madness: Studies in Foucault's 'Histoire de la folie'*, ed. A. Still and I. Velody (London: Routledge, 1992).

McNay, L., *Foucault and Feminism: Power, Gender and the Self* (Cambridge: Polity Press, 1992).

Megill, A., 'Foucault, ambiguity and the rhetoric of historiography', in *Rewriting the History of Madness: Studies in Foucault's 'Histoire de la folie'*, ed. A. Still and I. Velody (London: Routledge, 1992).

Midelfort, H. C. Erik, 'Madness and civilization in early modern Europe: a reappraisal of Michel Foucault', in *After the Reformation: Essays in Honor of J. H. Hexter*, ed. B. C. Malament (Philadelphia: University of Pennsylvania Press, 1980).

Miller, J., *The Passion of Michel Foucault* (London: Harper Collins, 1993).

Nikolinakos, D., 'Foucault's ethical quandry', *Telos*, no. 83 ((Spring 1990), pp. 123–40.

O'Brien, P., 'Crime and punishment as historical problems', *Journal of Social History*, 11 (1978), pp. 508–20.

O'Farrell, C., *Foucault: Historian or Philosopher?* (London: Macmillan, 1989).

Poster, M., *Foucault, Marxism and History: Mode of Production versus Mode of Information* (Cambridge: Polity Press, 1984).

Rajchman, J., 'Ethics after Foucault', *Social Text*, 13 (1985), pp. 165–83.

Rochlitz, R., 'The aesthetics of existence: post-conventional morality and the theory of power', in *Michel Foucault Philosopher*, ed. T. Armstrong (Hemel Hempstead: Harvester Wheatsheaf, 1992).

Rousseau, G. S., 'Whose enlightenment? Not man's: the case of Michel Foucault', *Eighteenth Century Studies*, no. 6 (1972–3), pp. 238–56.

Said, E., 'Criticism between culture and system', in Said, *The World, the Text, and the Critic* (London: Vintage, 1983).

—— 'Michel Foucault 1926–1984', in *After Foucault: Humanistic Knowledge, Postmodern Challenges*, ed. J. Arac (London: Rutgers University Press, 1988).

Sartre, J.-P., 'Jean-Paul Sartre répond', *L'Arc*, no. 30 (Oct. 1966), pp. 87–96.

Still, A. and Velody, I. (eds), *Rewriting the History of Madness: Studies in Foucault's 'Histoire de la Folie'* (London: Routledge, 1992).

Stone, L., 'Madness', *New York Review of Books*, 16 Dec. 1982.

Wolin, R., 'Foucault's aesthetic decisionism', *Telos*, 67 (1986), pp. 71–86.

OTHER WORKS CITED

Adorno, T. and Horkheimer, M., *Dialectic of Enlightenment* (New York: Herder and Herder, 1972).

Bataille, G., *Eroticism* (London: Marion Boyars, 1962).

Barrett, M., 'The place of aesthetics in Marxist criticism', in *Marxism and the Interpretation of Culture*, ed. C. Nelson and L Grossberg (London: Macmillan, 1988).

—— *The Politics of Truth: From Marx to Foucault* (Cambridge: Polity Press, 1992).

Benhabib, S., *Situating the Self: Gender, Community and Postmodernism in Contemporary Ethics* (Cambridge: Polity Press, 1992).

Benhabib, S., and Cornell, D. (eds), *Feminism as Critique: Essays on the Politics of Gender in Late Capitalist Societies* (Cambridge: Polity Press, 1986).

Benton, T., *The Rise and Fall of Structural Marxism: Althusser and his Influence* (London: Macmillan, 1984).

Bhabha, H., 'Interrogating identity', in *Identity*, ed. H. Bhabha (London: ICA, 1987).

—— (ed.), *Identity* (London: ICA, 1987).

Bourdieu, P., *The logic of Practice* (Cambridge: Polity Press, 1990).

—— 'The historical genesis of a pure aesthetic', in *The Field of Cultural Production* (Cambridge: Polity Press, 1993).

Bourdieu, P. and Eagleton, T. (in conversation), 'Doxa and common life', *New Left Review*, 191 (Jan.–Feb. 1992), pp. 111–21.

Braidotti, R., *Patterns of Dissonance: A Study of Women in Contemporary Philosophy* (Cambridge: Polity Press, 1991).

Centre for Contemporary Cultural Studies, *Unpopular Education: Schooling and Social Democracy in England since 1944* (London: Hutchinson, 1981).

Connolly, W. E., *The Forms of Political Discourse* (London: D.C. Heath, 1974).

De Certeau, M., *The Practice of Everyday Life* (Berkeley: University of California Press, 1984).

—— *Heterologies: Discourse on the Other* (Manchester: Manchester University Press, 1986).

Dews, P., *Logics of Disintegration: Post-structuralist Thought and the Claims of Critical Theory* (London: Verso, 1987).

Eagleton, T., 'The politics of subjectivity', in *Identity*, ed. H. Bhabha (London: ICA, 1987).

—— *The Ideology of the Aesthetic* (Oxford: Blackwell, 1990).

Fekete, J. (ed.), *The Structural Allegory* (Manchester: Manchester University Press, 1984).

Fraser, N., *Unruly Practices: Power, Discourse and Gender in Contemporary Social Theory* (Cambridge: Polity Press, 1989).

Gatens, M., *Feminism and Philosophy: Perspectives on Difference and Equality* (Cambridge: Polity Press, 1991).

Giddens, A., *The Constitution of Society: Outline of the Theory of Structuration* (Cambridge: Polity Press, 1984).

—— *Modernity and Self Identity: Self and Society in the Late Modern Age* (Cambridge: Polity Press, 1990).

Goffman, E., *Asylums* (Harmondsworth: Penguin, 1961).

Gordon, L., *Heroes of their Own Lives: The Politics and History of Family Violence: Boston 1880–1960* (London: Virago, 1989).

Habermas, J., *The Philosophical Discourse of Modernity* (Cambridge: Polity Press, 1987).

—— *The New Conservatism: Cultural Criticism and the Historians' Debate* (Cambridge: Polity Press, 1989).

Hall, S., 'Minimal selves', in *Identity*, ed. H. Bhabha (London: ICA, 1987).

Harstock, N., 'Feminism, science and the anti-Enlightenment critiques', in *Feminism/Postmodernism* ed. L. Nicholson (London: Routledge, 1990).

Honneth, A., *The Critique of Power: Reflective Stages in Critical Social Theory* (London: MIT Press, 1991).

Kearney, R., *Poetics of Imagining: From Husserl to Lyotard* (London: Harper Collins, 1991).

Laclau, E., *Politics and the Study of Ideology* (London: Verso, 1977).

Laclau, E. and Mouffe, C., *Hegemony and Socialist Strategy: Toward a Radical Democratic Politics* (London: Verso, 1985).

Lecourt, D., *Marxism and Epistemology: Bachelard, Canguihelm and Foucault* (London: NLB, 1975).

Lefebvre, H., 'Toward a leftist cultural politics: remarks occasioned by the centenary of Marx's death', in *Marxism and the Interpretation of Culture*, ed. C. Nelson and L. Grossberg (London: Macmillan, 1988).

Minson, J., *Genealogies of Morals: Nietzsche, Foucault, Donzelot and the Eccentricity of Ethics* (Basingstoke: Macmillan, 1985).

Morris, M., 'The pirate's fiancée: feminists and philosophers, or maybe tonight it'll happen', in *Feminism and Foucault: Reflections on Resistance*, ed. I. Diamond and L. Quinby (Boston: Northeastern University Press, 1988).

Nelson, C. and Grossberg, L. (eds), *Marxism and the Interpretation of Culture* (London: Macmillan, 1988).

Nicholson, L. (ed.), *Feminism/Postmodernism* (London: Routledge, 1990).

Norris, C., *The Truth about Postmodernism* (Oxford: Blackwell, 1993).

Pecheux, M., 'Discourse: structure or event?', in *Marxism and the Interpretation of Culture*, ed. C. Nelson and L. Grossberg (London: Macmillan, 1988).

Pollock, G., 'Feminism and modernism', in *Framing Feminism: Art and the Women's Movement 1970–1985*, ed. R. Parker and G. Pollock (London: Pandora/Routledge, 1987).

—— 'Modernity and the spaces of femininity', in Pollock, *Vision and Difference: Femininity, Feminism and the Histories of Art* (London: Routledge, 1988).

Poulantzas, N., *State, Power, Socialism* (London: NLB, 1978).

Probyn, E., 'Travels in the postmodern: making sense of the local', in *Feminism/Postmodernism*, ed. L. Nicholson (London: Routledge, 1990).

Rich, A., 'Notes towards a politics of location', in Rich, *Blood, Bread and Poetry: Selected Prose 1979–85* (New York: W. W. Norton, 1986).

Ricoeur, P., 'Structure, word, event', in Ricœur, *The Conflict of Interpretations: Essays in Hermeneutics* (Evanston: Northwestern University Press, 1974).

Rose, G., *Dialectic of Nihilism: Poststructuralism and Law* (Oxford: Blackwell, 1984).

Said, E., *The World, the Text, and the Critic* (London: Vintage, 1983).

Schor, N., 'Dreaming dissymmetry: Barthes, Foucault and sexual differences', in *Men in Feminism*, ed. A. Jardine and P. Smith (London: Methuen, 1987).

Showalter, E., *The Female Malady: Women, Madness and Culture, 1830–1980* (London: Virago, 1985).

Simmel, G., 'The problem of style', *Theory, Culture and Society, 8 (1991), pp. 63–71*.

Spivak, G., *In Other Worlds: Essays in Cultural Politics* (London: Methuen, 1987).

—— 'Can the subaltern speak?' in *Marxism and the Interpretation of Culture*, ed. C. Nelson and L. Grossberg (London: Macmillan, 1988).

Stallybrass, P. and White, A., *The Politics and Poetics of Transgression* (London: Methuen, 1986).

Taylor, C., *Sources of the Self: The Making of Modern Identity* (Cambridge: Cambridge University Press, 1986).

Thompson, J., *Ideology and Modern Culture: Critical Social Theory in the Era of Mass Communication* (Cambridge: Polity Press, 1990).

Williams, R., *Marxism and Literature* (Oxford: Oxford University Press, 1977).

Young, R. (ed.), *Untying the Text: A Poststructuralist Reader* (London: Routledge, 1981).

Index